HELGA BECKER

FROM THREAD AND WIRE

Other Schiffer Books on Related Subjects:

Designing Jewelry: Brooches, Bracelets, Necklaces & Accessories,
Maurice P. Galli, Dominique Rivière, and Fanfan Li,
ISBN 978-0-88740-631-7

Braided Wire Jewelry with Loretta Henry, Loretta Henry,
ISBN 978-0-88740-867-0

Paper Jewelry: 55 Projects for Reusing Paper, Barbara Baumann,
Photography by Flurina Hodel, ISBN 978-0-7643-4852-5

Copyright © 2015 by Schiffer Publishing, Ltd.

Originally published as *Aus Faden und Draht* by Haupt Verlag AG, Bern, Switzerland, Copyright © 2013 Haupt Bern. Translated from the German by Jonee Tiedemann.

Library of Congress Control Number: 2015950608

All rights reserved. No part of this work may be reproduced or used in any form or by any means—graphic, electronic, or mechanical, including photocopying or information storage and retrieval systems—without written permission from the publisher.

The scanning, uploading, and distribution of this book or any part there of via the Internet or via any other means without the permission of the publisher is illegal and punishable by law. Please purchase only authorized editions and do not participate in or encourage the electronic piracy of copyrighted materials.

"Schiffer," "Schiffer Publishing, Ltd. & Design," and the "Design of pen and inkwell" are registered trademarks of Schiffer Publishing, Ltd.

Design: Stefanie Grams, www.undfreun.de
Type set in Adabi
ISBN: 978-0-7643-4976-8

Printed in China

Published by Schiffer Publishing, Ltd.
4880 Lower Valley Road | Atglen, PA 19310
Phone: (610) 593-1777; Fax: (610) 593-2002
E-mail: Info@schifferbooks.com
Web: www.schifferbooks.com

For our complete selection of fine books on this and related subjects, please visit our website at www.schifferbooks.com. You may also write for a free catalog.

This book may be purchased from the publisher. Please try your bookstore first.

We are always looking for people to write books on new and related subjects. If you have an idea for a book, please contact us at proposals@schifferbooks.com.

Schiffer Publishing's titles are available at special discounts for bulk purchases for sales promotions or premiums. Special editions, including personalized covers, corporate imprints, and excerpts, can be created in large quantities for special needs. For more information, contact the publisher.

HELGA BECKER

FROM THREAD AND WIRE

60 JEWELRY PROJECTS USING KNITTING AND CROCHETING

HELGA BECKER
PHOTOGRAPHS BY HELGA AND RICHARD BECKER

4880 Lower Valley Road · Atglen, PA 19310

ABOUT THE AUTHOR

Helga Becker specializes in artisan craftwork, architecture, and building techniques. She is the author of several books on topics including wood turning and jewelry making, and she also writes frequently for international craft journals.

CONTENTS

7 Preface

9 HOW TO WORK WITH THIS BOOK

11 CHAPTER 1: MATERIALS, TOOLS, AND TECHNIQUES

17 Technique 1 – Crocheting

25 Technique 2 – Knitting with the Wooden Knitting Loom

31 Technique 3 – Knitting with the Metal Knitting Loom

43 Technique 4 – Even More Possibilities

49 CHAPTER 2: JOYOUS FASHION JEWELRY

Projects 1–17

85 CHAPTER 3: ELEGANT FASHION JEWELRY

Projects 18–39

131 CHAPTER 4: SILVER JEWELRY

Projects 40–60

174 Glossary

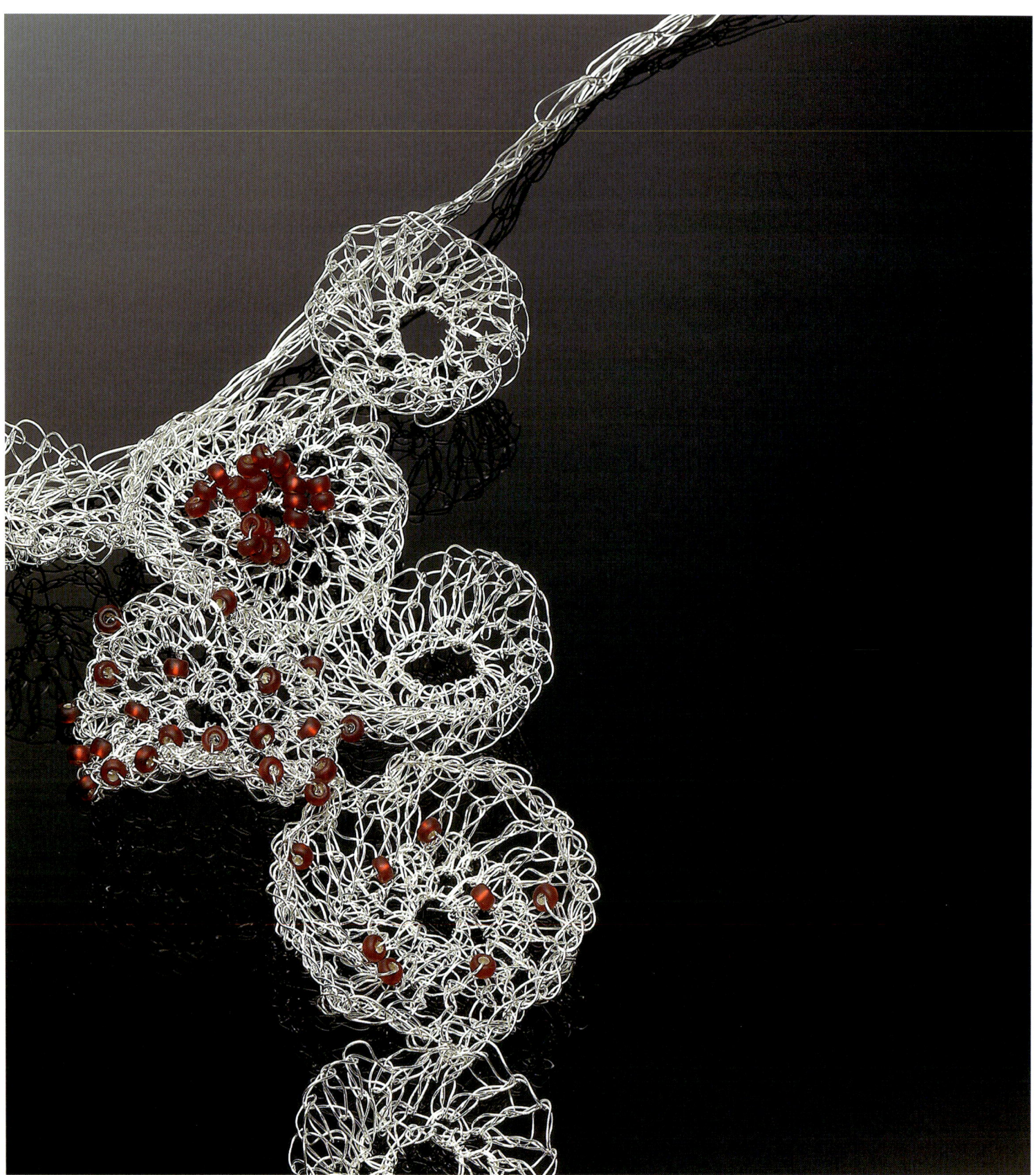

"JEWELRY IS NOT MEANT TO CAUSE JEALOUSY—BUT WONDER."

Coco Chanel

Coco Chanel, the French fashion and style icon of the twentieth century, made "fashion jewelry" fashionable. The word was created in the 1920s, when Chanel started to design faux jewelry matching her fashion collections. She was the first one in the industry to use jewelry's aesthetic effect as a design element.

Coco Chanel's approach is the inspiration for the approach this book takes toward jewelry. I want to show that well-known materials like yarn, wool, string, or wire, when used together with other elements, result in extraordinary pieces of jewelry that can be perfectly matched to your existing (or planned) wardrobe.

You can experiment with colors or with tone-on-tone effects, utilize scraps, discover new materials, and collect "ingredients" while taking walks. The projects here include small gifts which can be made in no time, as well as delicate "webs" that require more patience and time. You'll find marvelously playful pieces of jewelry; classic pieces; bracelets; rings. And the best part about every object is the process of creation: everything is CROCHETED OR KNITTED!

Even children can learn the techniques and soon be turning out delightful jewelry and friendship bracelets or necklaces. The fun starts while collecting sticks and stones, or when shaping beads from Fimo modeling resin.

Jewelry fans (boys and girls, men and women) who have become infected with my crocheting-knitting virus will be raiding the scrap boxes of mothers and grandmothers, or looking through basements, garages, and garage sales for appropriate and interesting materials to use.

For those who like things on the classy side, I show precious one-of-a-kind pieces made from silver. Solid silver wire turns these pieces of jewelry into eyecatchers. The simple method for creating them is a knitting technique that has been used for 2,000 years, and which has been newly redeveloped by a jewelry museum.

You'll be surprised at how many ideas you can develop on your own while you re-create my suggested projects here! And your audience will be astounded as well: at the variety of the materials used, the distinct and different looks, and the fact that simple knitting or crocheting techniques can result in such gems.

So don't be surprised when the eyes of your onlookers reflect not only wonder, but a little bit of jealousy too...

Enjoy the book, and these projects!

Helga Becker

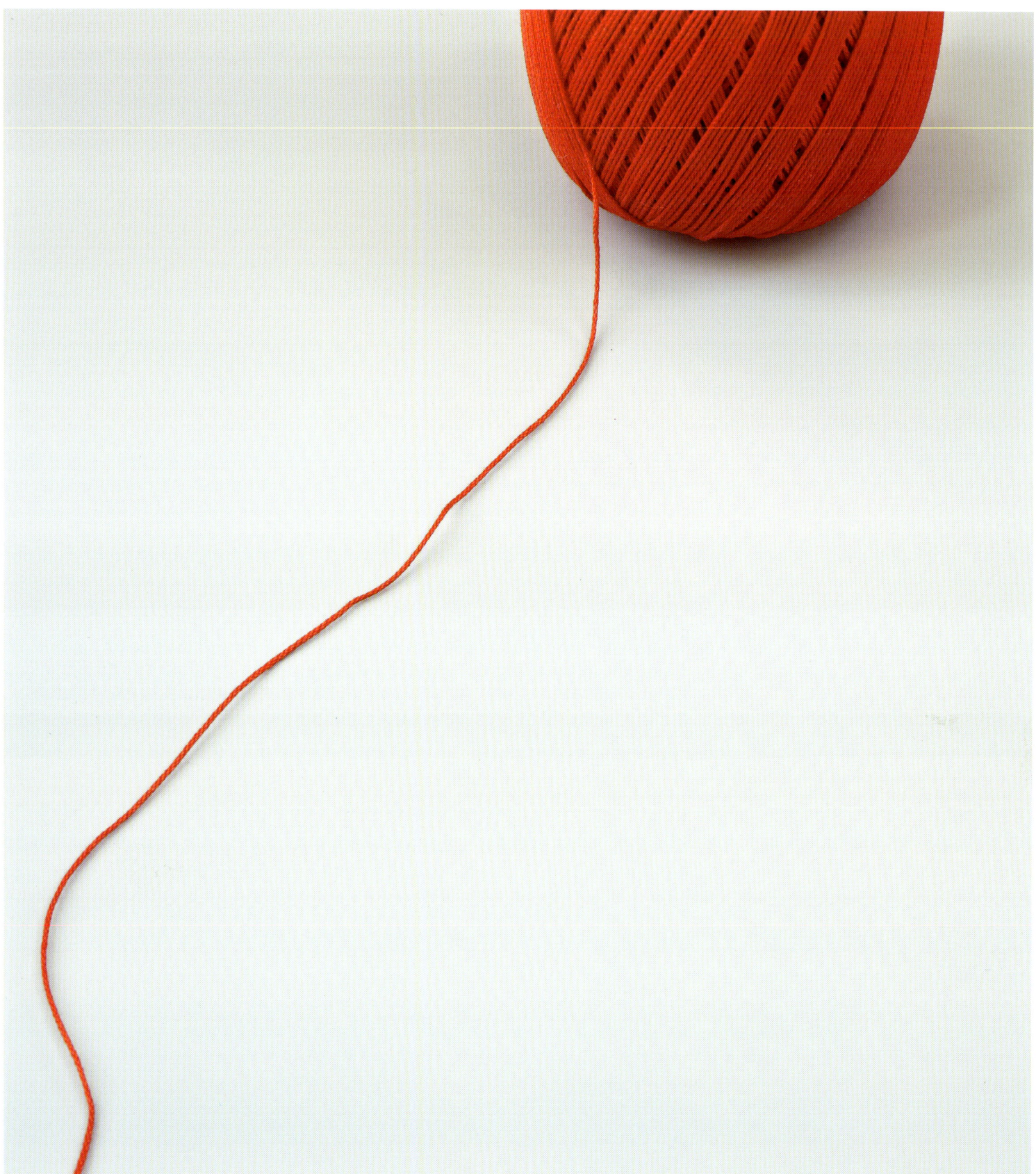

HOW TO WORK WITH THIS BOOK

Various techniques and levels of difficulty are presented with 60 projects of jewelry pieces. The book is divided into four chapters:

CHAPTER 1 – presents tools, materials, and techniques.
CHAPTER 2 – shows the creation of jewelry pieces from thread. The brightly colored objects are created using chain stitches and a knitting loom.
CHAPTER 3 – presents jewelry pieces made from pure lacquered copper wire. We work with chain stitches, and both wood and metal knitting looms.
CHAPTER 4 – shows how noble jewelry pieces are made from solid silver wire of different gauges. Here as well, the chain stitch and wood and metal knitting looms are used.

All the projects feature a graphic icon: the number of **KNITTING LOOMS** shown indicates the project's difficulty. Projects marked with **1 KNITTING LOOM** are easiest. **2 KNITTING LOOMS** mark projects of medium difficulty. Difficult projects are indicated by **3 KNITTING LOOMS.**

The chapter **MATERIALS, TOOLS, AND TECHNIQUES** introduces basic materials such as yarn, wire, beads, clasps or catches, and more, as well as tools and additional accessories.

Throughout the book, under the headings **TIP** and **IMPORTANT** you will find my suggestions for additional creations, technical insights, precautions, the best uses of tools and accessories, shortcuts, and more.

The first chapter shows the basic techniques in detail, so I have not included them with the individual projects. The instructions for each project refer you to the corresponding technique to be applied. However, detailed instructions are provided for the preparatory work steps or any steps which go beyond the normal process in creating the piece.

I suggest that you start with the simplest technique, the chain stitch, and first make the projects in chapters 2 to 4 that are marked as the easiest (1 knitting loom symbol). Then you can begin working with the two other techniques and the projects where those are applied.

Alternatively you can learn the three techniques and practice using the tools and accessories. Once you have mastered all of the techniques (or, if you already know them) you can make the projects in any order. However, it is generally a good idea to start out with simple (cheap) materials and only then switch to the more valuable silver wire.

The projects in chapter 4 not only use silver wire but sheet silver as well. It is cut, forged, shaped, soldered, blackened, or annealed. The explanations for these processes go beyond the scope of this book, and for more detailed guidance you can refer to metalsmithing books. Generally the processing of silver can be performed by laypeople, but alternatives are included.

If you are unsure about being able to make these parts, or if it seems like the effort is too great (although only a limited amount of very economical equipment is required!) you can buy pre-manufactured elements and accessories. And your trustworthy local jeweler will be happy to make the right pieces for you.

Along with practicing the knitting and crocheting techniques here, you should also spend some time doing your own experiments. You'll see that you can develop many additional ideas from one project. If you are thinking about making small production runs of a piece it is helpful to keep a notebook where you write down the materials used, tools (e.g., looms), wire gauges, final finishes, etc. Without this data it is difficult to recreate the process for additional pieces. This notebook can also be used to collect inspiring samples of materials, or photos and small drawings of your ideas. With time you will create a treasure box for many new creations.

At the end of the book you will find a **GLOSSARY** with the explanation of the technical terms.

MATERIALS, TOOLS, AND TECHNIQUES

"FASHION IS NOT ONLY A MATTER OF CLOTHING. FASHION HAS TO DO WITH IDEAS, WITH HOW WE LIVE."

Coco Chanel

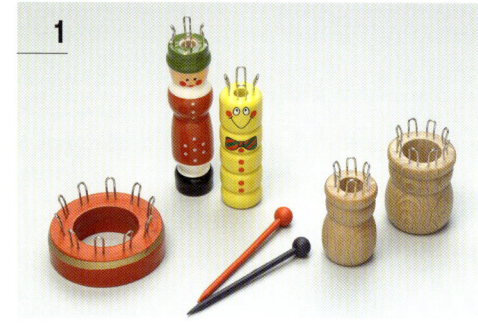

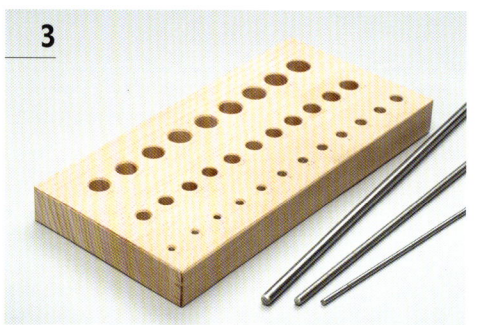

MATERIALS, TOOLS, AND TECHNIQUES

The knitting and crocheting techniques presented here feature three main advantages: you can manufacture outstanding jewelry pieces in little time and your selection of individual necklaces, earrings, bracelets, and rings which perfectly complement your outfits will increase enormously.

Furthermore, the material is readily available in many variations, and can be used immediately without needing to be prepared in some way beforehand (the way wood, papier maché, clay, etc. do).

And third, only a few small tools are needed. This, in turn, means that you need only little space and—this is the best part for me—you can sit on the sofa and knit or crochet while watching TV or listening to the radio. Or, in the waiting room at the doctor's office. Or, on the train or subway, in the yard, at the hotel, at the beach. Practically anywhere. Perhaps at this point I should warn you of the potential for addiction...

1 The **WOODEN KNITTING LOOM** is available in several versions at arts and crafts retailers. Usually it is made of wood, but it is also available made from metal or plexiglass. But I personally like the good old wooden knitting loom. The wood feels nice and it lies well in the hand because of its turned profile. The metal rods at the "head" of the loom are well-suited for knitting with thread (yarn, string, etc.) and with wire. Knitting is done with a small hook made from wood or plastic.

2 The **METAL KNITTING LOOM** is primarily used for knitting wire. The wire gauges are usually 30 to 26, or more rarely, 24 or 22. The metal knitting looms feature metal pegs soldered to the top edge. Round, oval, rhombus-shaped, or square metal knitting looms are available. However, these special versions are only available via specialty retailers, from a jeweler, or by making them at home. Metal hooks are used for knitting, with their size matching the gauge of the wire.

3 In order to stretch the knitted metal wire and/or to get a more even knitted pattern you use a **DRAW PLATE**. It is made from a piece of hardwood and features drilled holes of various diameters. Metal rods fitting the diameters are used for drawing the items through.

4 Because the projects can be made from thread (fiber, like yarn or string) or from wire (metal), there is an endless variety of materials. You can search for your thread or wire online, at specialty retailers, at mom-and-pop stores, in your basement, or in the garage.

Also think about materials you don't immediately associate with jewelry, such as packing twine or floral wire. You will surprised at the things you discover!

5 For the projects here that use the metal knitting loom, only wire is used. It is available in a multitude of colors, structures, and metals. Wavy bullion wire and silver-plated or lacquered copper wires are available at arts and crafts retailers. Barked wire is used by flower shops, and thin steel wire from the hardware store is appropriate for certain projects. Solid silver wire can usually only be purchased at specialty retailers. I use genuine 0.935 silver alloy only.

6 In order to turn the knitted chains and tubes into actual pieces of jewelry you will also need fasteners, jump rings, earring hooks, and so on. For jewelry pieces made from silver wire you should use only those made from genuine silver, not only because it looks more valuable, but also because genuine silver jewelry can be cleaned in special solutions, and these solutions are not always appropriate for other metals or alloys.

MATERIALS, TOOLS, AND TECHNIQUES

The choice of the "thread and wire" to be used for knitted and crocheted jewelry is up to your own personal taste and the look you want for the piece. The projects incorporate very different materials: stone, pearls, wood, sheet silver, plastic, felt, and many others. I want to show the variety and the possibilities in order to stimulate your imagination for your own projects.

7 Stones and semi-precious stones are wonderful objects and can be embedded into knitted necklaces or bands. You could collect colored stones when taking walks or when hiking. I already have a rather impressive collection spanning porphyry to pebbles. I keep them organized according to color and size.

Semi-precious stones can be found at various markets or at retailers. They not only offer cut and uncut stones but also drilled ones.

They can be embedded into the webs and bands or hung from them.

8 Pearls of all shapes and sizes are also great for making jewelry, including glass, lava, or coral beads, silver spheres, or even homemade Fimo beads, genuine freshwater pearls, or plastic ones. Whenever I see strands for sale at a good price, I grab a few for my collection of materials.

9 Arts and crafts shops feature a large selection of glass beads, rocailles, farfalle, faceted glass beads, and more. They are offered in many sizes and colors, with or without silver plating, single- or multi-colored, matte, shiny, transparent...

10 Wood in jewelry also allows for nice effects. Colored or natural beads can be found at retailers. A (hobby) woodturner, if you know of one nearby, might provide small profile pieces such as furniture buttons, or you can order objects based on your own designs. Look for scrap pieces of wood with a nice grain. While you're outdoors walking you might want to look for pieces of bark or driftwood.

11 Colored materials are particularly well-suited for children's jewelry: homemade Fimo beads or those made from glass or plastic, heart shaped ones, or those with printed letters to allow for making up names; fluffy pompons or small figures work too.

12 And then there are all kinds of things that accumulate in any household over the years: gifts and curios from vacations, or gifts from family and friends. Many elements of these can be recycled, and will acquire an entirely different look when combined with knitted and crocheted pieces. Also, there are many materials available at arts and crafts retailers which were not intended to be used for jewelrymaking in particular. The idea is to become inspired, to dare, to play, to develop ideas.

13 And there is another thing you shouldn't overlook: your leftover knitting and crocheting efforts, like scrap pieces of bracelets that turned out too long, or other knitted tubes that you chose not to finish. These can be used as pendants, or you can make small objects like rings and earrings from them. Knitted scraps from wire can be cut open and stretched over small wooden frames. This can result in decorative brooches and pendants. These scraps are also great to use to create interesting embossing patterns. This is particularly easy with Fimo or other air-drying modeling clays. Embossing sheet silver is a little more involved (project 48). It requires an appropriate metal roller. Perhaps you can check with a goldsmith or jeweler about whether he or she can do the job for you.

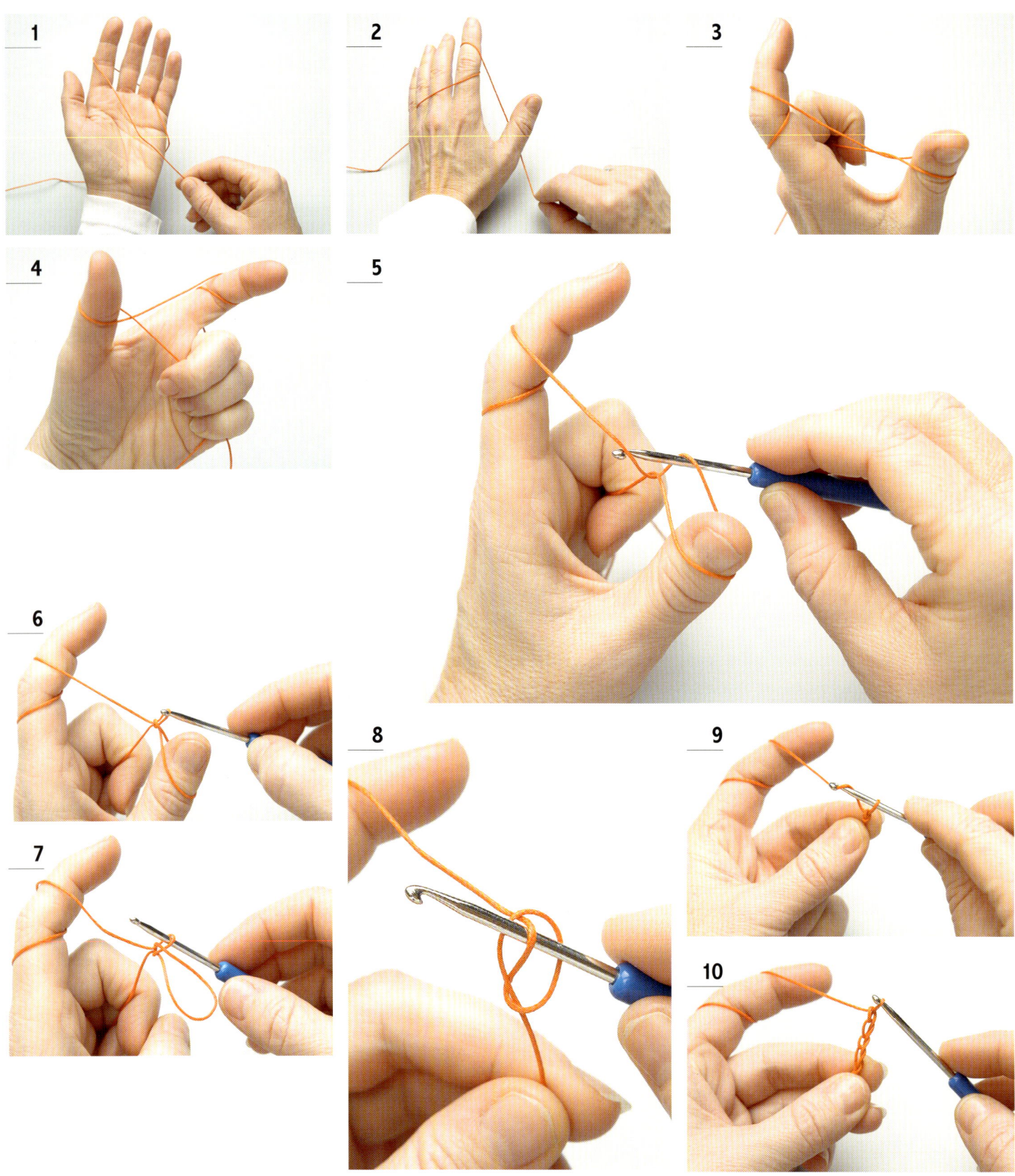

TECHNIQUE 1 CROCHETING

CHAIN STITCH THREAD

1 To be able to start making a chain stitch thread you first need to make a starting stitch. Hold your left hand with the palm upward. Use the right hand to guide the thread (yarn, string) from the palm of the hand between the little finger and the ring finger. Pull it along the back of the fingers and then toward the palm of the hand again, along the index finger.

2 Now the thread is wound once around the index finger and run toward the thumb.

3 The thumb is also wrapped once and the thread is stretched between the index finger and thumb and run toward the other fingers.

4 The thread is held with the middle, ring, and little finger. Spread the thumb and index finger so that the thread is tensioned between the two fingers.

5 Run the crochet hook from below through the loop which was created around the thumb, and catch the thread that is stretched between the index finger and thumb from behind with the hook of the needle.

6 The caught thread is pulled through the loop with the crochet hook.

7 Now pull out the thumb from the loop, downward.

8 Grab the end of the thread with the thumb and middle finger and pull downward. Meanwhile the crochet hook secures the small new loop so that it can't slip through the large loop. The large loop shrinks into a knot when pulling downward. The starting stitch is now on the crochet hook.

9 Now grab the thread directly at the knot with the thumb and middle finger of the left hand. The crochet hook is run from the front with the right hand under the stretched section of the thread and once again over the thread. The thread is thus held for a new loop and run through the existing stitch.

10 Repeat the process, and try to make the loops of even size. The photo shows that almost all of the stitches are oriented the same way. This allows for making a chain stitch thread of any length desired.

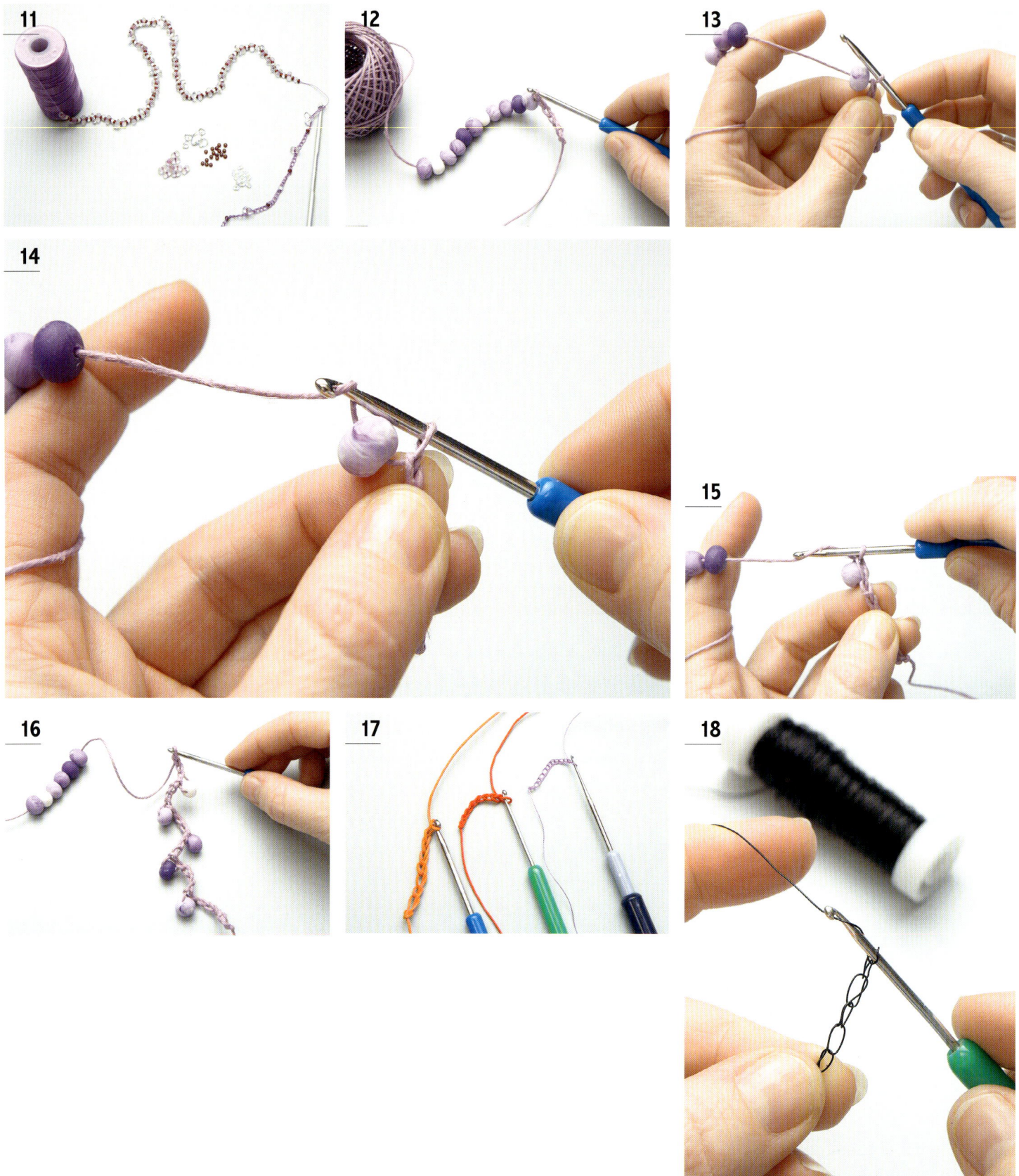

TECHNIQUE 1   CROCHETING

CROCHETING BEADS

11   Beads, stones, found objects, or other items must be threaded on **BEFORE** you start the crocheting or knitting. Use needles for soft materials like yarn, thread, or string. Make sure the holes of the beads, stones, etc. are large enough for the thread and needle. If they are too small you can dip the end of the thread into thin glue and allow it to harden, to get a relatively firm tip which might be sufficient to thread the beads without a needle.

With wire it usually works out fine to thread without any needle or other aid.

It is best to think about the arrangement of the beads beforehand. Then thread the beads in that order. The projects in this book describe the order of the beads. However, that sequence is just a suggestion, and you can change it according to your taste and the materials available to you.

12   After threading the beads you start by making a chain stitch thread, as shown in steps 1 to 10.

13   To add a bead by crocheting, place it close to the crochet hook and the last stitch.

TIP:
Always thread enough beads. In case of doubt, better too many than too few. If the threaded beads are not sufficient for your piece of jewelry you can unwind the wool or yarn and thread the beads from the other end.
Make sure the order of the beads is correct.

14   Grab the thread behind the bead by pushing the crochet hook below the thread and pull the thread through the stitch which was crocheted last. Now the bead is affixed to the chain stitch thread.

When you are more experienced you can "store" a few beads on your index finger and add them when they need to be crocheted in.

15   After the bead you add a few "normal" chain stitches. It works best to use the same consistent number of stitches between the beads. This allows you to get into a nice rhythm with even distances between beads.

16   In the case of thick cotton yarn or packing string as shown here the stiffness of the material results in a zigzag line. For necklaces or bracelets this characteristic is best taken advantage of when uniting several strands.

17   Generally the thickness of the crochet hook should match the gauge of the material being used: thick thread = large crochet hook, thin thread = small crochet hook. But, as is often the case, there are exceptions: if you use a needle that is too large for thin yarn, large stitches are the result, providing an airy and light look. You might want to try out the variations.

18   When crocheting with wire the individual stitches are slightly skewed because the wire is somewhat stiff and the stitches don't join each other as easily as with soft yarn. The entire chain stitch thread or band is stiffer, which results in a nice effect for the finished object. Don't become frustrated when the stitches don't turn out evenly at first. With more experience you'll make more regular and even stitches. Also, as a bonus, incorporating beads will distract attention from minor irregularities in the weave.

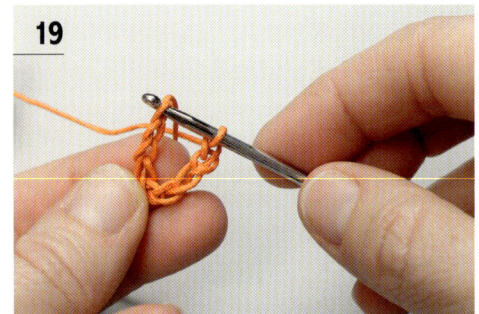

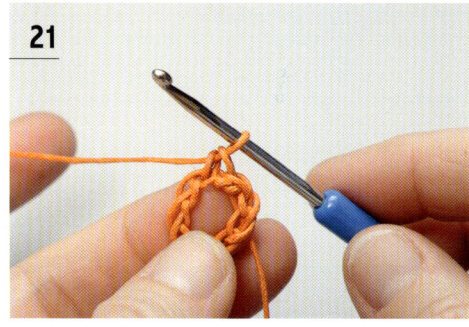

TECHNIQUE 1 CROCHETING

CROCHETED ROSETTES

For the rosettes in project 52 and project 59, chain stitch threads are made into rings. Before making these rosettes from wire, practice the technique with wool or cotton yarn because they will allow you to see the individual stitches more clearly.

19 Start out with one chain stitch thread consisting of eight stitches. Now insert the needle at the first stitch of the chain stitch thread and pull the thread through this first stitch and the eighth stitch, which is still on the crochet hook. This way you close the chain stitch thread into a ring.

20 Now insert the crochet hook into the second stitch of the chain stitch. Grab the thread with the crochet hook and pull it through the stitch. Now you have two stitches on the crochet hook.

21 Hook the thread again and pull it through the two stitches onto the crochet hook. The first ring is now done. Insert the hook at the third stitch of the chain stitch thread and make another single crochet as described.

22 Now repeat the process at the third (!) stitch of the chain stitch thread.

23 So you are making two single stitches into the third chain stitch. The fourth stitch gets one single crochet, the fifth and seventh get two single crochets again, the sixth and the eighth only one single stitch.

24 The result of this switch between one and two single crochets is that the rosette doesn't warp but remains flat.

25 Close this second row by inserting the crochet hook through the top two threads of the first single crochet, pulling the thread through the single crochet and through the stitch still lying on the crochet hook.

Start the third row with a chain stitch.

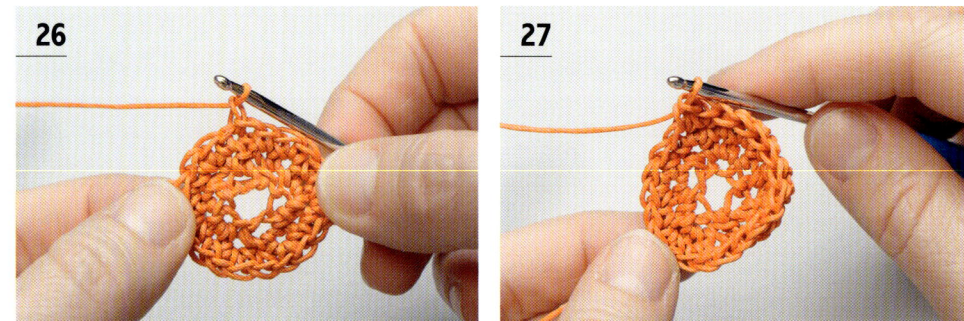

TECHNIQUE 1   CROCHETING

SINGLE STITCHES OR CROCHETS

26 Depending on the desired size of the rosette you can once again crochet one and two single stitches alternatingly (in the case of larger diameters). The rosette in this case will remain flat.

27 Or, you can make only one single stitch into the stitch below (in the case of smaller diameters). This causes the edge to bend slightly upward.

28 To emphasize the edge's bend you can, at the fourth row, add only one single crochet every other stitch to the stitch below. Then the edge will pull together even more. The size of the rosette depends on the number of stitches...

29 ...and on the type of stitches. If, instead of the single crochets, you stitch double crochets (see the following description) the row will be higher and the crochet pattern will be looser.

STITCHING DOUBLE CROCHETS

30 Double crochets are basically tall single crochets. In order for them to be the right height, wrap the thread once around the crochet hook (this results in an "auxiliary stitch") and only then insert the hook into the desired stitch. Then you grab the thread with the crochet hook and pull it back through the stitch. Now you have three stitches lying on the crochet hook.

31 Grab the thread again and pull it through the first two stitches.

32 Grab the thread once more and pull it through the last two stitches.

> **TIP:**
> Try different variations or mix different rosettes for a piece like project 59. If you want to make other rosettes that match your first, remember to take notes on how you line up the stitches next to and on top of each other.

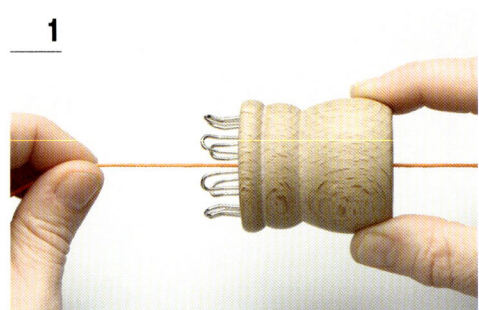

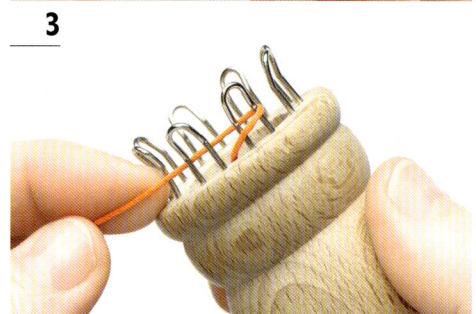
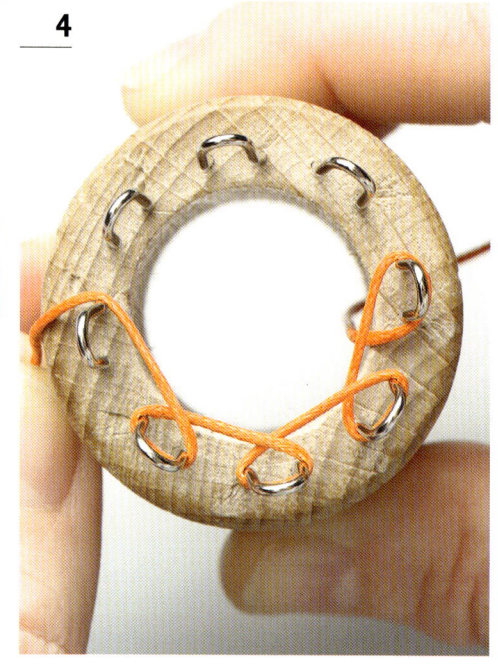
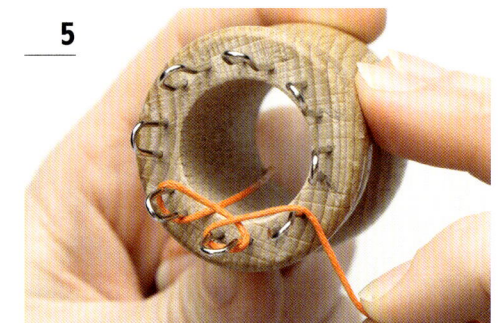

TECHNIQUE 2   KNITTING WITH THE WOODEN KNITTING LOOM

The small tool that is used for this knitting technique has ancient roots, and is also sometimes called a "knitting jenny," probably due to the fact that the curved and turned profiles were often made for children, and sometimes painted to resemble the figure of a woman.

Knitting looms are available in several sizes and diameters, with wooden, plastic, or plexiglass handles and with different numbers of pegs (or loops) around which the thread is run. Usually knitting looms have an even number of pegs. You can find knitting looms with 4, 6, 8, or 10 pegs. You can knit single or double with them. You can't knit offset since that requires an uneven number of pegs; for that you have to make the appropriate loom yourself. Instructions on how to knit double and offset are found under **TECHNIQUE 3**.

I'll refer to all of the looms with metal pegs as "wooden looms" within the project descriptions to differentiate them from the real "metal looms" (**TECHNIQUE 3**).

IMPORTANT: Wooden looms can be used to knit yarn (thread, string, etc.) as well as thin wire. Metal looms are only used for working with wire (see page 13).

SIMPLE KNITTING

1 Pull the end of the thread from the top through the body of the loom. If you are using a narrow loom and thin thread, you might want to use a crochet hook for assistance.

2 Hold the end of the thread and the loom with your right hand. Use the left hand to guide the thread forward around the first metal peg and, behind the peg, toward the next peg which lies left of it.

3 The thread is run behind this second peg and forward, between the second and third peg. Run it around the second peg just like the first one. Meanwhile, turn the loom counterclockwise, step by step. Wrap the thread or wire around the following pegs.

4 This perspective allows you to see how the thread is wrapped around the pegs.

5 Left-handed people work the other way around and hence thread the yarn toward the right side.

6 Once all of the pegs have been wrapped, make a second layer in the same way. Now two threads lie on top of each other on each peg.

7 Once the last peg has been wrapped for the second time the thread is run to the left and outside over the body or handle of the loom and held with the thumb of the left hand. The photo clearly shows how the thread runs out of the body or handle upward, and how it is placed around the peg.

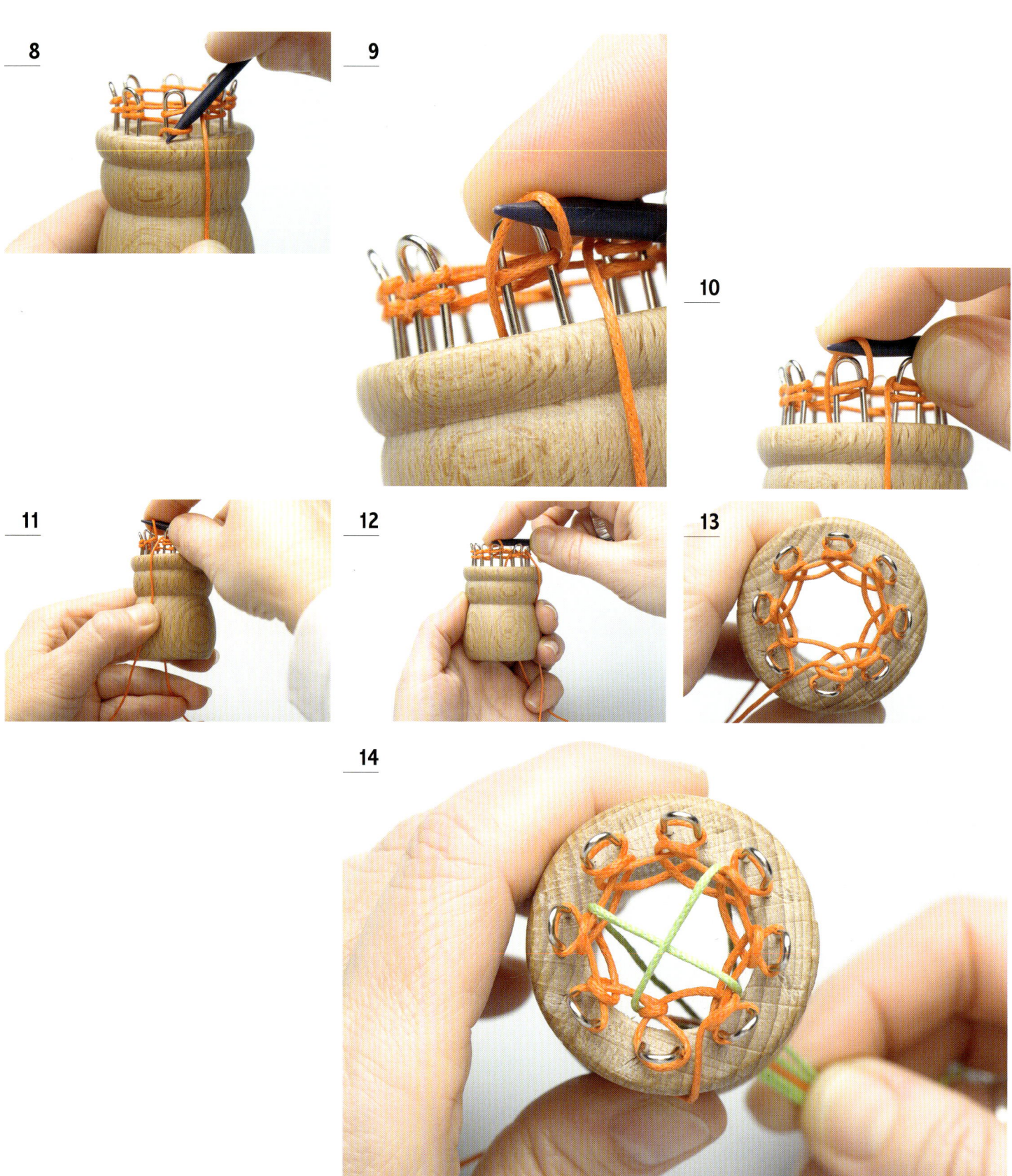

TECHNIQUE 2 KNITTING WITH THE WOODEN KNITTING LOOM

8 Now grab the lower loop at the first peg with the hook (in this case a plastic tool, usually sold together with the knitting loom).

IMPORTANT: It is important that you start at the first loop you wound because this is where the end of the thread lies and only here the loop can be widened.

9 Widen the loop with the tool and pull upward. So the loop over it does not slip over the tip of the peg, put your index finger onto the peg.

> **TIP:**
> It is important that the first loop be large enough but that it is not widened too much. This measure determines whether the mesh is rather loose or rather firm. In the beginning you'll need some practice in order to find the right size.

10 The loop is now dropped behind the peg. If it turned out to be too large it can be pulled tighter by pulling on the end of the thread. There is now only one loop on the peg (the one from the second winding).

11 Hold the end of the thread tightly during the first steps in particular. This prevents the first loop from being widened without control and the last loop from slipping off the peg.

12 Now the lower loop is lifted over the top one at the second peg and dropped behind the peg. This second and all further loops can usually be widened just like the first one. So it is important to find the right tension with the very first loop (see the tip at step 9).

13 Knit as described around all of the pegs. Seen from the top, there is a regular and even pattern. There is only one loop around each peg.

14 In order for the knitted tube to be slipped through the loom, auxiliary stitches (of yarn or wire) must be inserted after the first knitted round. The auxiliary threads must be long enough to be able to be held at the bottom of the loom. Make sure that the auxiliary threads are placed into each section, and stretched between the pegs that lie opposite each other.

After the first knitted round the thread is run around the pegs once again as shown in photos 2 to 4 and the second round is knitted. Until you get the desired length of the knitted tube the threading and the knitting rounds alternate. The end of the thread no longer has to be held.

> **TIP:**
> After each round, pull the knitted tube downward with the auxiliary wires. This causes the loops at the pegs to also be pulled downward and you have sufficient room for a new round of winding.

When you finish the knitted tube (cast off) you cut off the knitting thread from the rest of the ball. Leave about 8 inches of thread. Use a crochet hook to pull the entire end of the thread through each stitch on the pegs. Now the stitches are "hanging" on the thread and can be lifted off the pegs. If you pull at the end of the thread, the stitches pull together and the knitted tube closes.

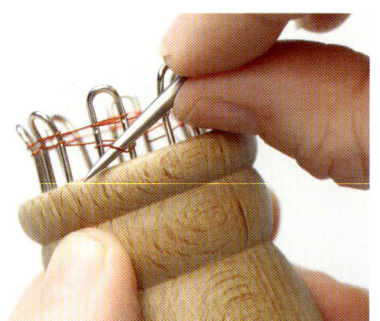
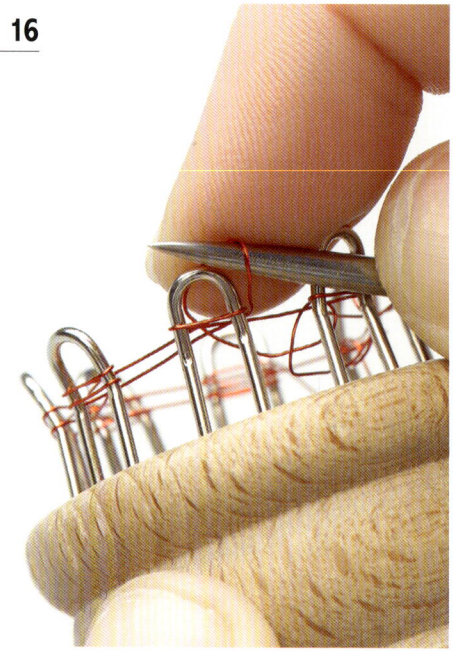
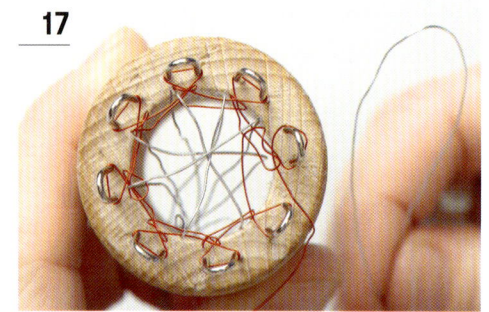
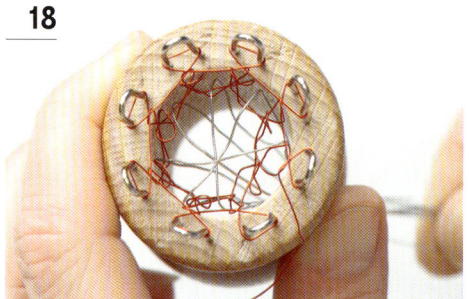
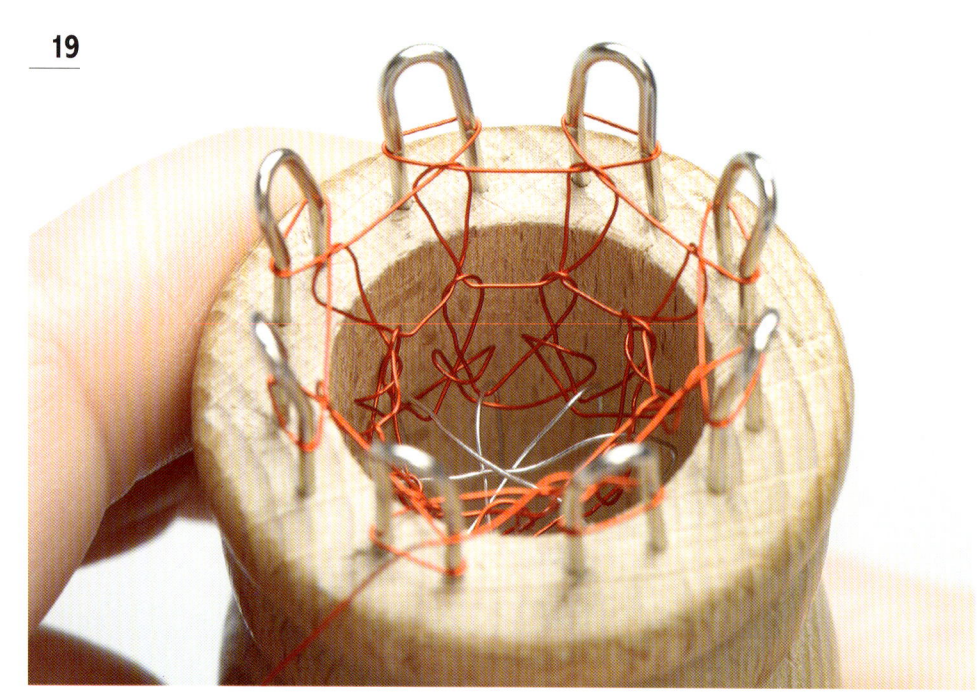

TECHNIQUE 2   KNITTING WITH THE WOODEN KNITTING LOOM

15 The process of working with wire is no different from the technique used for thread, yarn, or string. Thin wire, however, is somewhat more difficult to handle and can tear with too much tension. Wind the pegs of the wooden loom as shown in photos 1 to 7. Instead of a plastic tool you should use a metal tool because the wire offers more resistance to the tool than string or yarn do.

16 With thin wire the two loops lie close to each other on the peg. So be careful that you catch the lower loop when knitting. Carefully lift it over the top one. The wire might resist a little. Here as well, put your index finger onto the peg so that the top loop cannot slip over the top of the peg.

The knitting pattern seen here is somewhat uneven.

17 This is due, among other things, to the fact that the wire can't be wound as smoothly around the pegs as a textile thread can be wound. Add wire auxiliary threads after the first round. With a relatively large loom diameter the wires should be appropriately pre-bent. The number of wires depends on the number of pegs. In the case of an 8-peg loom you need four auxiliary wires, with a 6-peg loom you need three, and so on.

18 By using auxiliary wires the mesh can be pulled downward evenly through the loom. Now for the second round the wire lies more smoothly at the pegs.

19 With each additional knitting round the tube slides deeper into the loom and forms a more or less regular web.

> **TIP:**
> When working wire with a wooden loom the mesh will be very loose and airy. Be careful not to pull too tightly on the auxiliary wires or the diameter of the tube shrinks drastically and more than you want it to. Once the tube has been pulled too close you cannot really widen it again. You might, however, take advantage in some of your projects of the fact that the tube increases in length while its diameter shrinks (see project 32).

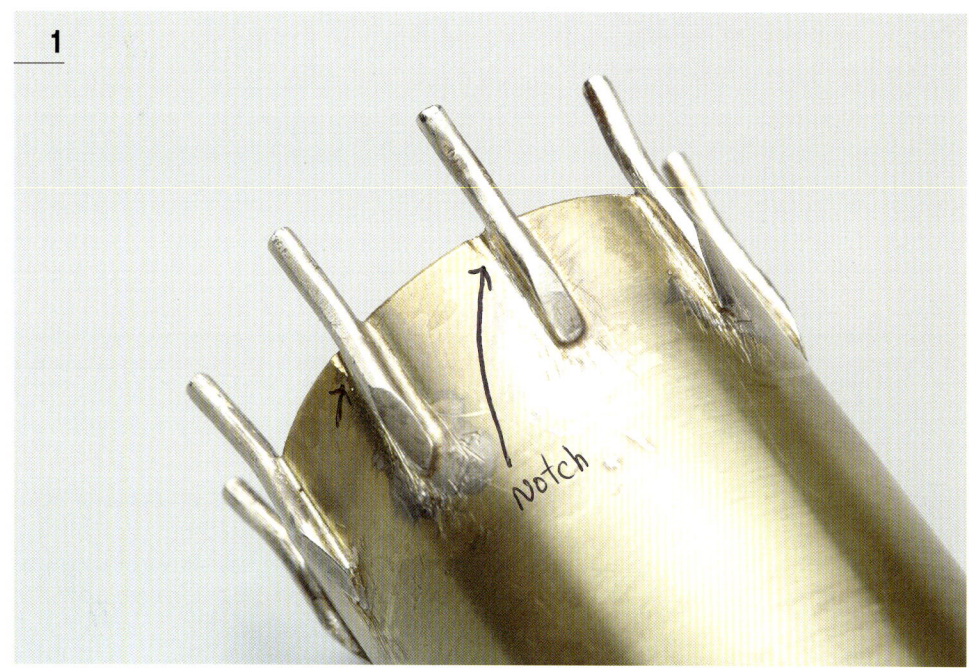

1

2

3

4

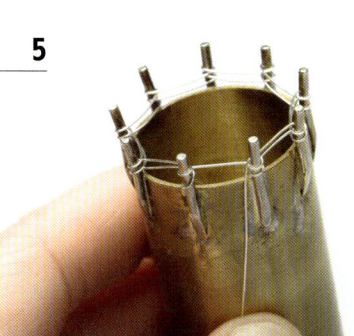

5

TECHNIQUE 3 KNITTING WITH THE METAL KNITTING LOOM

Metal knitting looms are usually made from copper or brass tubes with soldered pegs. You can purchase them in various diameters in regular or custom-made sizes and shapes.

1

TIP:
If you can solder, you can make knitting looms yourself. Some things to keep in mind: looms with the same diameters can be fitted with different numbers of pegs. However, if pegs are added the diameter of the pegs might have to be decreased. The important thing is to ensure the pegs are spaced evenly so that the mesh will be even. The weave will become more light and airy when you lower the number of pegs while keeping the same diameter of the loom. The pegs should stick out about ¼ inch over the edge and should have a diameter of 1.2 to 1.8 mm, depending on the diameter of the tube.

IMPORTANT: On the left side of each peg, a small notch must be made using a small file. Otherwise it will be very difficult to catch the wire with the tool later.

With metal looms that have an even number of pegs you can knit single or double. In order to knit offset you need an uneven number of pegs. You can also leave out certain pegs for certain shapes or techniques (**TECHNIQUE 4**).

IMPORTANT: Knitting looms with an even number of pegs are required for bracelets, rings, or flat necklaces so that the upper and lower side are of the same width.

As the pegs are very thin, yarn or string is not really suitable. The best material is 30-gauge to 22-gauge wire. For small looms you use mainly thin wire; with larger loom diameters the wire should be thicker. Wire that is thinner than 30 gauge tends to break. But with experience you can take on the challenge. With wire of 24 or 32 gauge the amount of force needed to wrap and knit the wire is significant. Furthermore, the finished objects are relatively stiff and heavy. For my projects we will use 30-, 28-, and 26-gauge wire.

SIMPLE KNITTING

2 Craft wire is usually sold in small spools or rolls. Silver wire is sold on large spools. It helps to place the spool on a support to facilitate working with it. I bought a support stand that was originally intended to hold sculptures. It is sufficiently heavy and perfect for holding the silver spool. You can make one like this yourself, too.

3 Just as with the wooden knitting looms, the end of the wire is run through the loom and held with one hand. With the other hand you wind the wire counterclockwise around the peg and run it to the next one (to the left for right-handed people, to the right for left-handed people).

4 Wrap all of the pegs this way. Even loops should result between the pegs. Always keep tension on the wire but don't pull it too tight.

5 Now wrap the second row. Two loops should lie on all of the pegs. The wire is run to the left side of the last peg toward the outside and held.

6

7

8 **9**

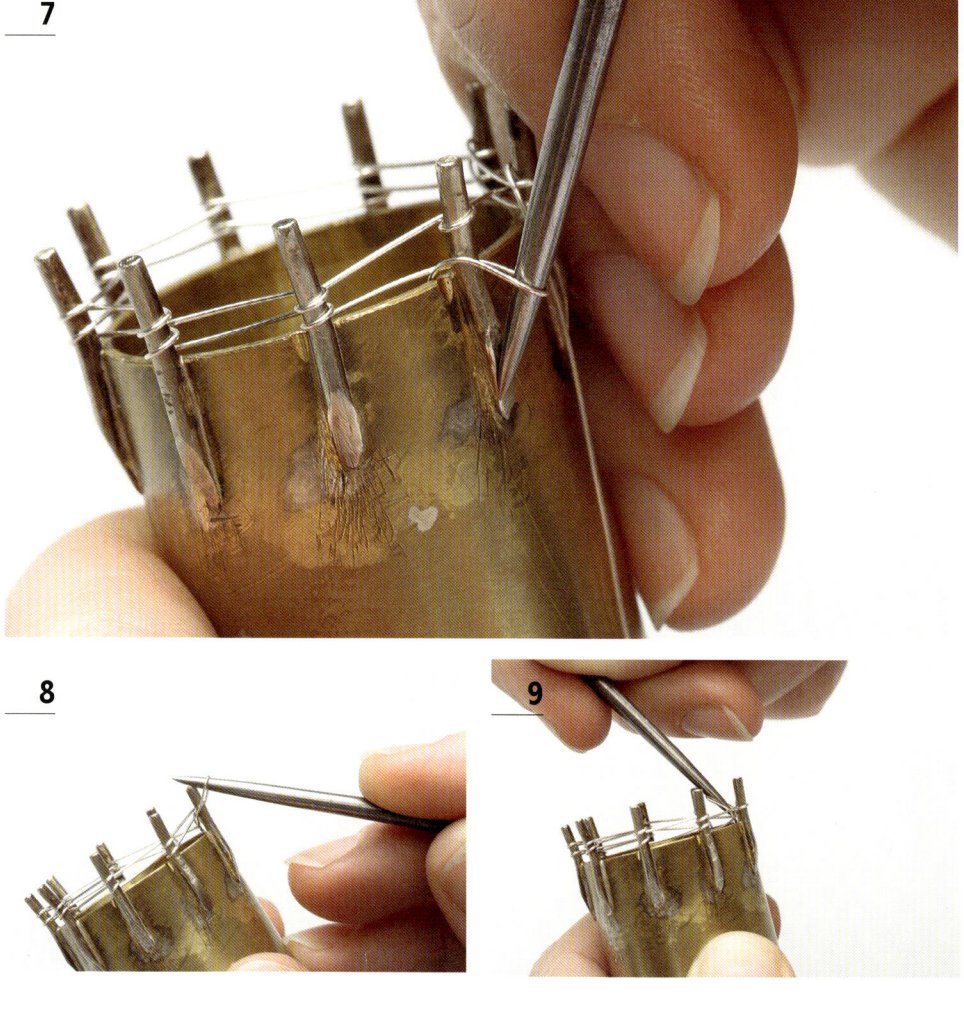

TECHNIQUE 3   KNITTING WITH THE METAL KNITTING LOOM

6 Start knitting at the first peg that you have wound. You can recognize it due to the end of the wire which sticks up. With the tool (soft plastic needles won't work here!) you reach vertically from the top into the lower loop. To do this you must set the tip of the tool on the left side of the peg and run it downward over the small notch on the loom.

IMPORTANT: When the tool slips off or can't be easily inserted into the loop, use a magnifying glass to check for the cause. If you miss the wire several times it can be damaged to the point that it will break with only a little pressure. Sometimes the point of pressure is more toward the rear. Once you have seen it magnified it's easier to place the tool correctly. You can also use a darning needle; the thinner tip is easier to place. Once the loop is slightly widened you can switch over to the tool again.

7 Once you have correctly placed the tool the loop can be widened by setting the tip of the tool at the tube and pulling the top of the tool toward you. With this minor leverage you can **CAREFULLY** widen the loop.

IMPORTANT: If the loop can't be widened you should check whether you might have started at the wrong peg. The first knitted stitch is always where the end of the wire is located because this is the only place where enough wire can be pulled through to form a stitch. If you encounter a situation where you can't widen a stitch while knitting you might have jumped a peg. It may also be due to the fact that the second loop has slipped under the first one while threading. Use a magnifying glass and carefully put the loops into their correct order. Don't pull too hard!

8 After widening the loop you have to set the tool again and enter the loop from below. The tool is then placed onto the peg and "levered." If you can't do this without pulling hard you first have to widen the loop a bit.

9 The stitch is dropped behind the peg. Bend the tool backward quite a bit. The stitch is now bent backward and can't slip forward over the peg when the next stitch is pulled tight. Knit all of the pegs this way and wrap the next round as described previously.

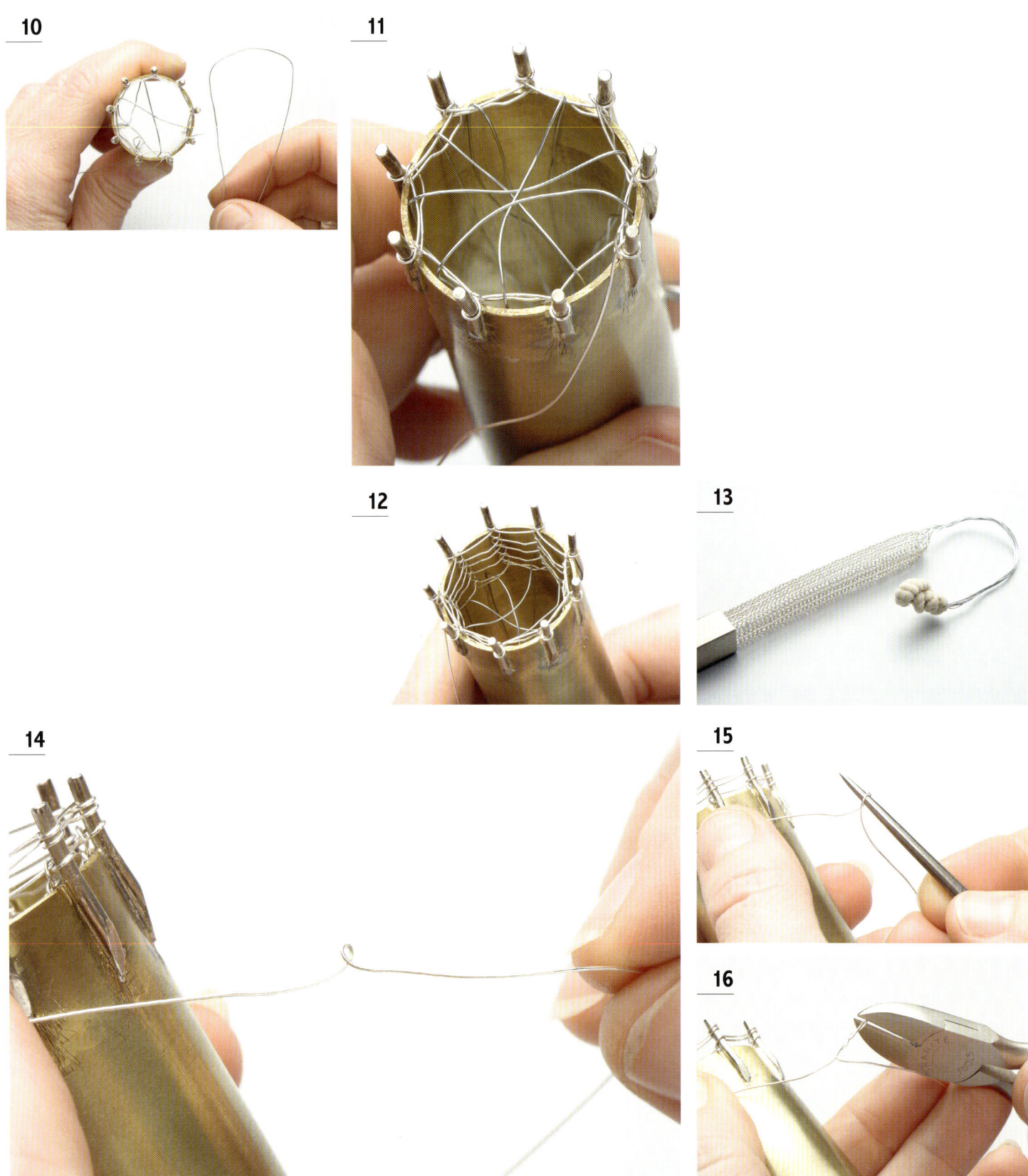

TECHNIQUE 3   KNITTING WITH THE METAL KNITTING LOOM

10 Once one or two rounds have been knitted, the auxiliary wires which allow for pulling the mesh tube through the loom must be added. The auxiliary wires need to be long enough so they can be comfortably picked up at the lower end of the loom. With large-diameter looms it is helpful to first bend the wires as needed.

11 Make sure that the auxiliary wires are placed into each section, and stretched between the pegs that lie opposite each other. With an uneven number of pegs the last winding only comprises a section.

12 After each knitted round the tube is pulled downward with the auxiliary wires. The photo shows the mesh of the wires lying on the inside of the loom.

13

> **TIP:**
> For the auxiliary wires to not become entangled with your clothing while turning the loom back and forth (particularly in the case of knitted clothing!) it helps to twist the wires, to fold over the last ¾ inch, and to wrap a rubber band around the ends of the wires. This allows you to grab the wires when pulling the tube.

14 Occasionally it may happen that while unwinding the wire a small loop is formed. You definitely should loosen this loop and not knit it into the web. Always make sure that the wire can be unwound easily. You may have to turn the loom around its axis a few times after each round of knitting to avoid this twisting of the wire.

15 To loosen the loop, push the tip of the tool (or, if the loop is already very small, a darning needle) into it, and keep pushing the needle. Due to the increasing diameter of the needle the loop widens and the wire can be flattened by hand.

16 Occasionally the wire breaks (more so with beginners). Stronger silver wire might be fixed by soldering if you know how to do it. For beginners it's more convenient to twist the ends of the wire. You should backstitch a few stitches, that is, undo a few of them. This way the broken wire can be lengthened. The two ends of the wire are tightly twisted together. The end should lie inside and as close to a peg as possible so that the spot will be hardly noticeable. The twisted piece of wire might be slightly shortened.

17

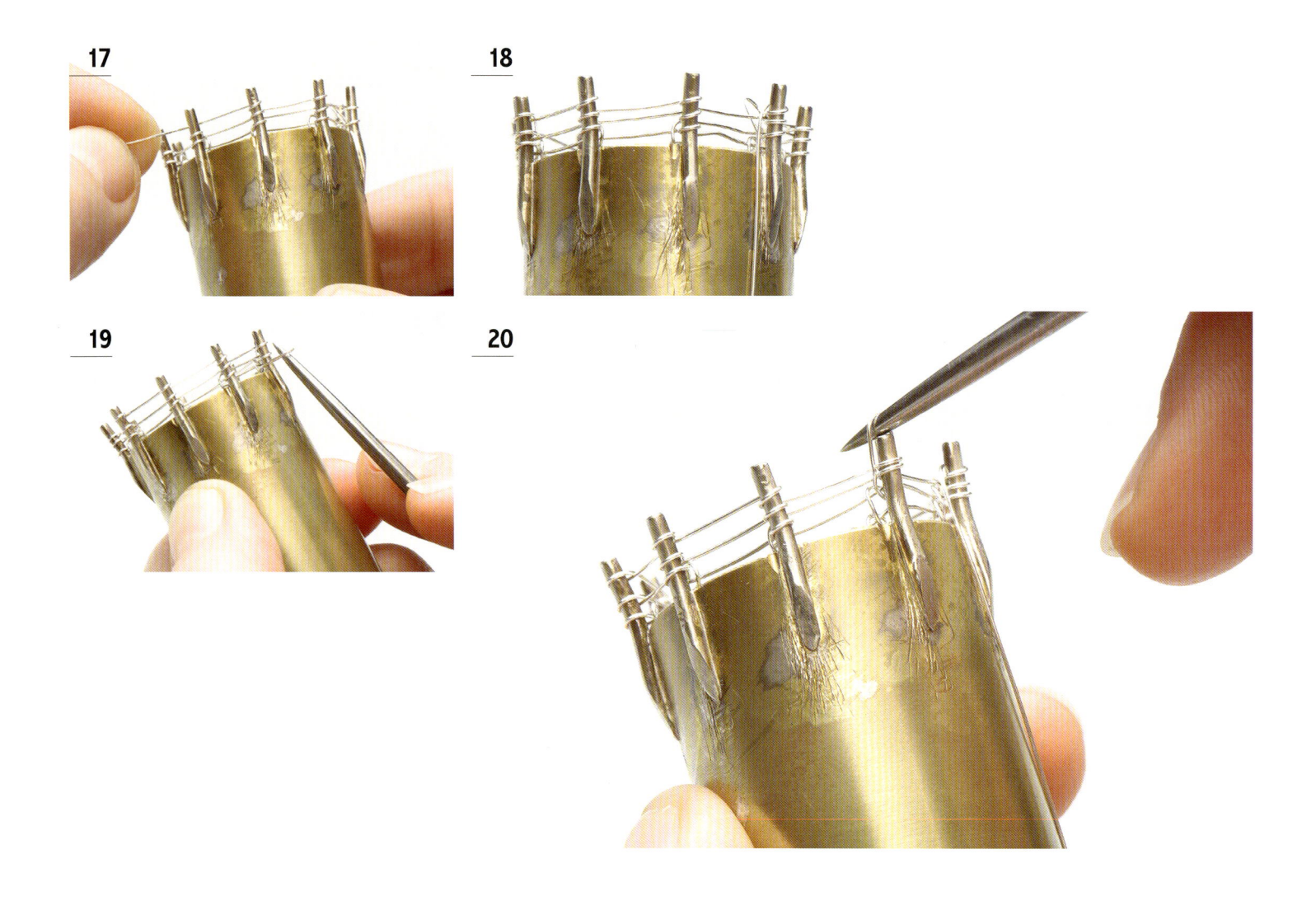

18

19

20

TECHNIQUE 3   KNITTING WITH THE METAL KNITTING LOOM

DOUBLE KNITTING

17 When double knitting you wind three, not two, rounds when you start out. It is important that the pegs of the loom are long enough, since otherwise the top loops might slip over the pegs.

18 Once all the pegs have been wound three times, the wire is placed to the left of the last peg on the outside and held.

19 The round starts again at the peg where the wire exits the loom upward. Set the tool **AT THE LOWER LOOP** as can be seen in photo 5. The loop is widened and picked up from below with the tool.

20 With the tool the lower loop is levered over **BOTH** loops and dropped behind the peg. This process is repeated with all of the pegs. After this round, two rows of loops remain on the pegs.

Now a third row is wound and the loops of the lowest row are lifted over the other two. This way you switch the winding and the rounds until you get the desired length of the knitted tube. If you want to end the tube, leave out the winding of the third row and knit the two remaining rows just as with simple knitting. At the end there is only one row of loops left. This is cast off as described in **TECHNIQUE 1.**

21 22 23

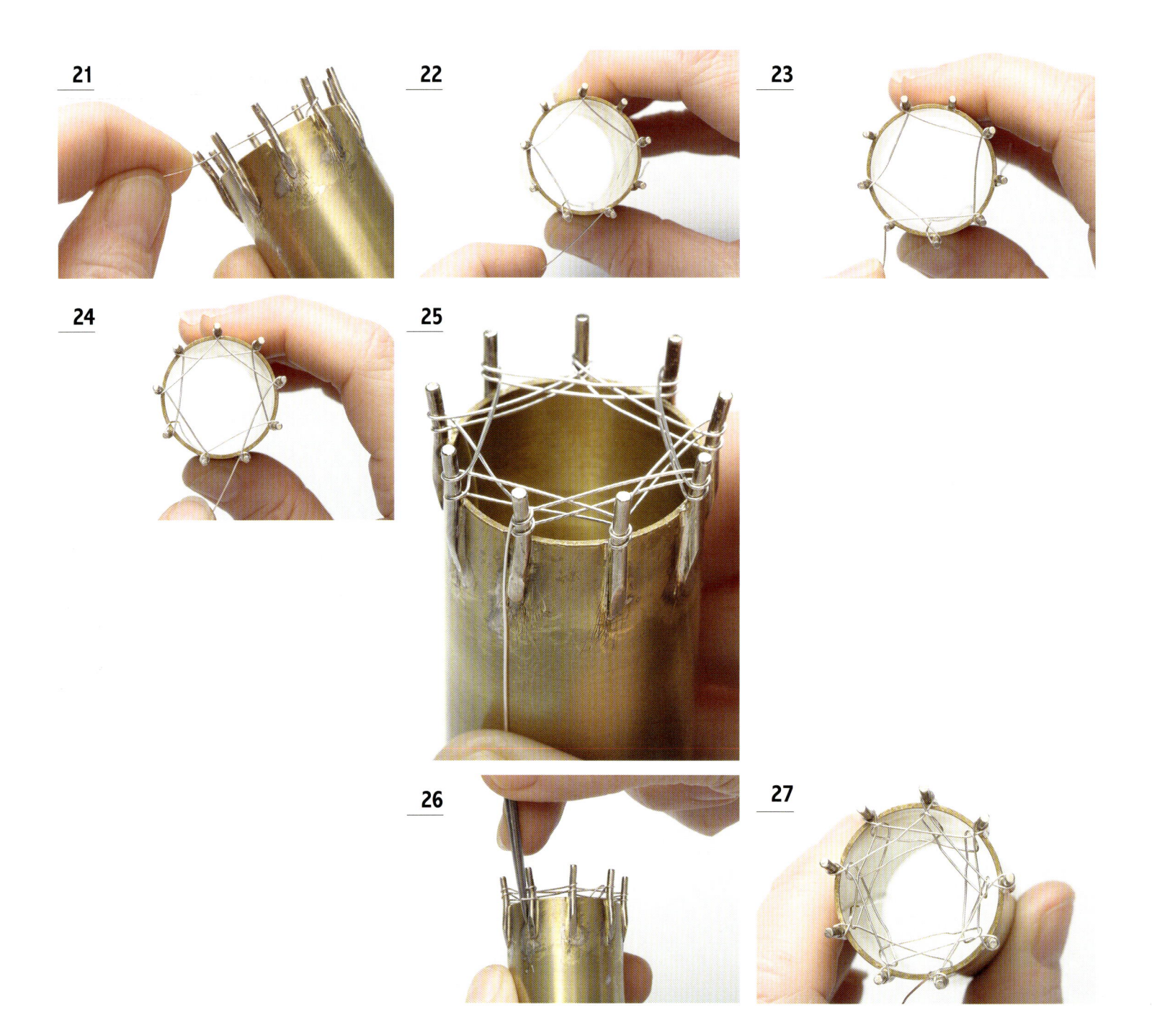

24 25

26 27

TECHNIQUE 3 KNITTING WITH THE METAL KNITTING LOOM

OFFSET KNITTING

You can only knit offset with a loom that features an **UNEVEN NUMBER OF PEGS**. In our case the loom has nine pegs.

21 For offset knitting, start out as you did for simple knitting by winding the first peg. The second peg is left out and only the third one is wound. The fourth peg is skipped again, but you wind the fifth. Then leave out the sixth and eighth, and wind around the seventh and ninth.

22 Now two wound pegs, the first and the ninth, lie next to each other.

23 The first peg is skipped and all of the "empty" pegs are wound, that is, every second (the second, fourth, sixth, eighth) peg. The first round of winding ends at the eighth peg. The second round of winding starts again at the first peg.

24 Now all of the pegs have been wound once and the starting wire lies at the first peg, the end of the wire at the eighth peg.

25 Now wrap the second round as described earlier. The wires cross each other on two rows between pegs. The thread is run outward at the eighth peg and held.

26 Knitting is done from the first peg onward because this is where the thread comes out of the loom.

IMPORTANT: When knitting, every second peg is treated, that is, offset. Once you have reached the eighth peg when knitting you wind another round.

27 The first round is cast off and the crossing wires sink into the loom. Now the auxiliary wires are also inserted as shown in photos 10 and 11.

> **TIP:**
> When you start out you can easily lose your rhythm when winding and skipping. While knitting, too, you may run into times when you don't know which peg's turn it is. A little tip: if the loop can't be easily widened you are probably at the wrong peg. Check immediately which pegs have been set without pulling from the wire. With some practice you'll get into the right pattern quickly.

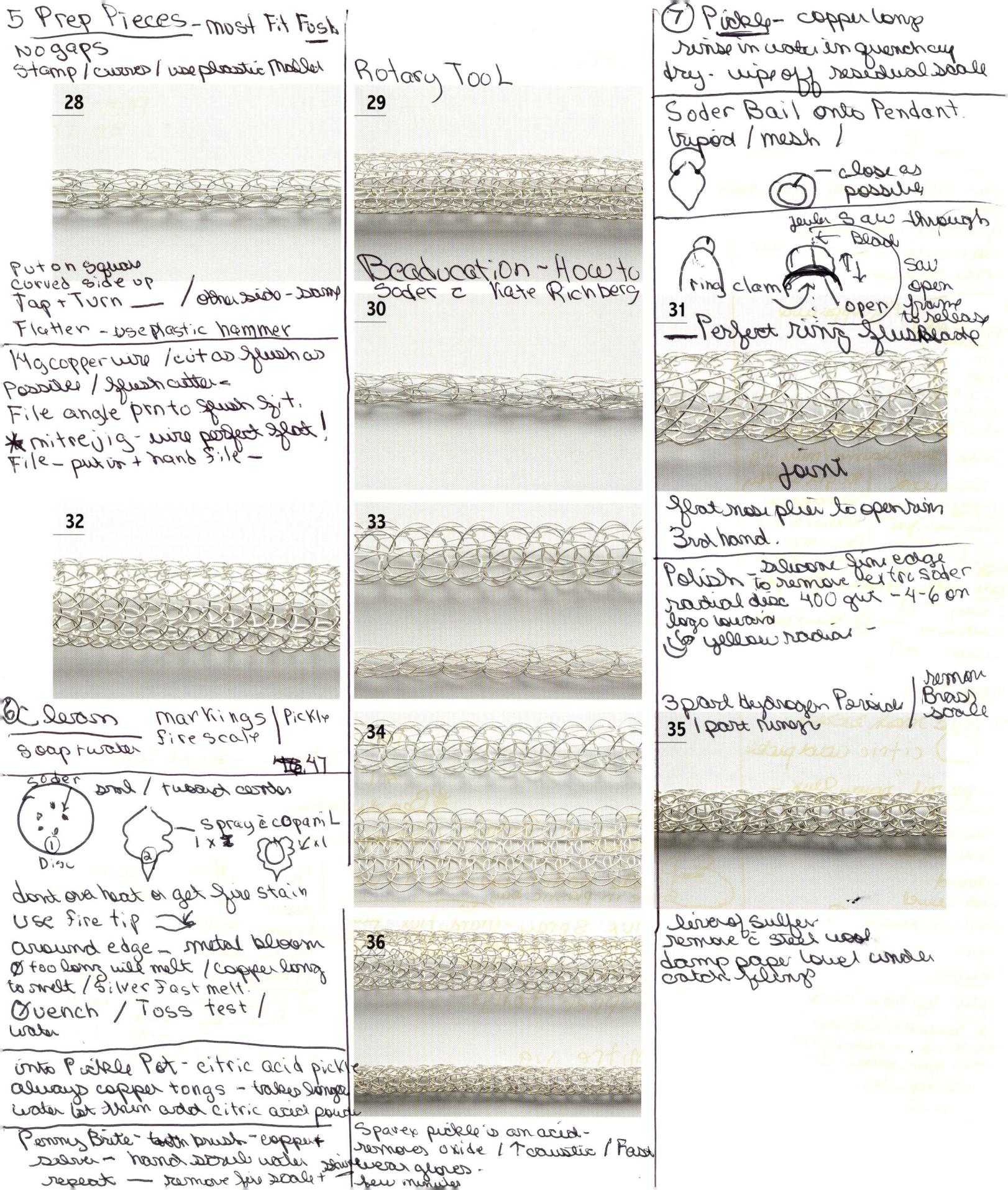

5 Prep Pieces - must Fit Flush
no gaps
stamp / curves / use plastic mallet

28

Put on square
curved side up
Tap + Turn / other side - damp
Flatter - use plastic hammer

14g copper wire / cut as flush as
possible / flush cutter -
File angle prior to squish fit.
* mitre jig - wire perfect & flat!
File - put in + hand file -

32

BC Lemon   markings / Pickle
                 fire scale
soap + water   pg 47

soder smal / tweezer center
⊙ Disc   ② spray c coparil
              1 x 1   ⊙ x 1

don't overheat or get fire stain
use fire tip ↙
around edge - metal bloom
if too long will melt / copper long
to melt / silver fast melt.
⊙ Quench / Toss test /
water

into Pickle Pot - citric acid pickle
always copper tongs - takes longer
water hot then add citric acid pour

Penny Brite - tooth brush - copper +
silver - hand scrub water
repeat - remove fire scale +

Rotary Tool

29

Beaducation - How to
Soder c Kate Richbourg

30

33

34

36

Sparex pickle is an acid -
removes oxide / ↑ caustic / Rash
wear gloves.
few minutes

⑦ Pickle - copper tongs
rinse in water in quench cup
dry - wipe off residual scale

Soder Bail onto Pendant.
tripod / mesh /

- close as possible

                    Jewler Saw through
                    Bead
ring clamp   saw
                    open
31 Perfect ring flush blade
                    open frame
                    to release

joint

flat nose plier to open ring
3rd hand.

Polish - silicone fine edge
to remove extra soder
radial disc 400 grit - 4-6 on
logo towards
yellow radial

3 part hydrogen peroxide / remove
35 1 part kumji   brass
                              scale

liver of sulfur
remove c steel wool
damp paper towel under
catch fillings

TECHNIQUE 3 KNITTING WITH THE METAL KNITTING LOOM

KNITTING PATTERNS

Here you can see the different knitting technique variations (simple, double, and offset), used with different sizes of looms and different wire gauges to show how they influence the pattern.

28 wire, 30 gauge
metal loom, dia. 1 3/16 in., 9 pegs
simple knitting, calibrated
(TECHNIQUE 4)

29 wire, 30 gauge
metal loom, dia. 1 3/16 in., 9 pegs
double knitting, calibrated

30 wire, 30 gauge
metal loom, dia. 1 3/16 in., 9 pegs
offset knitting, drawn by hand

31 wire, 26 gauge
metal loom, dia. 1 3/8 in., 11 pegs
offset knitting, not yet drawn or calibrated

32 wire, 26 gauge
metal loom, dia. 1 3/8 in., 11 pegs
simple knitting with draw plate, no metal insert

33 wire, 26 gauge (top)
wire, 30 gauge (bottom)
wood loom, 8 pegs
simple knitting, slightly pulled by hand

34 wire, 26 gauge
wood loom, 8 pegs
simple knitting, slightly pulled by hand
left round for necklace (top)
pressed flat for bracelet (below)

35 wire, 26 gauge
metal loom, dia. 9/16 in., 9 pegs
simple knitting and calibration, with metal insert

36 top
wire, 26 gauge
metal loom, dia. 1 3/8 in., 11 pegs
simple knitting with draw plate, no metal insert

below
wire, 26 gauge
metal loom, dia. 9/16 in., 9 pegs
simple knitting and calibration, with metal insert

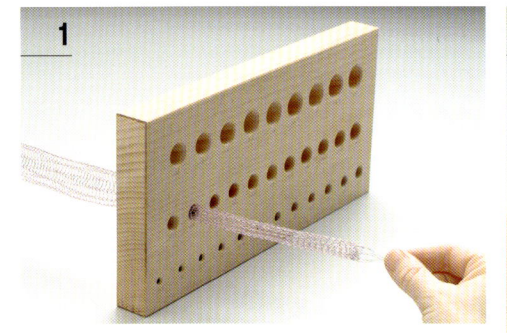

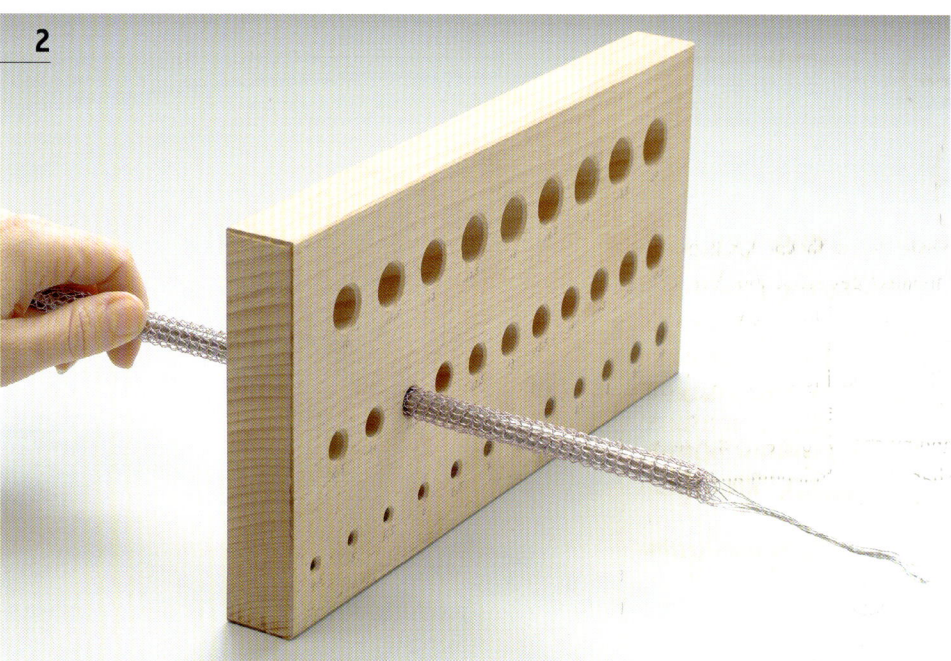

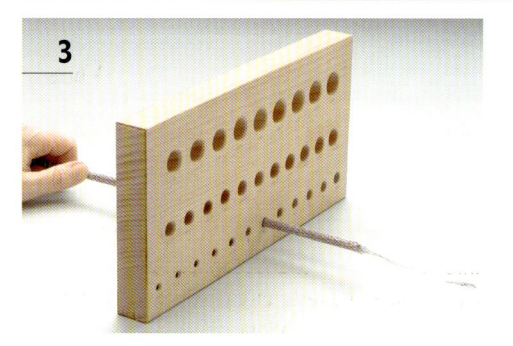

1

2

3

TECHNIQUE 4   EVEN MORE POSSIBILITIES

PULLING AND CALIBRATING

These finishing processes can only be performed with threads made of knitted wire.

PULLING

While knitting, tubes are pulled through the looms with auxiliary wires. This pulling results in the tubes becoming somewhat longer, particularly with wooden knitting looms, because the mesh pattern is looser and the individual stitches have more "give."

Although pulling always reduces the circumference of the tube, with some experience and by choosing the appropriate looms the change in both length and diameter can be worked into the planning.

By pulling, the mesh pattern also becomes more regular, which is useful particularly for beginners.

Apart from the automatic pulling while knitting, a knitted tube can also be pulled "on purpose." There are two possibilities:

1. Pull the thread while it is done but still on the loom.

Hold the loom in one hand and the auxiliary wires of the thread in the other hand and carefully pull the thread apart (don't jerk it!). You might have to apply some force.

2. Remove the knitted tube from the loom after casting off and insert auxiliary wires at the cast-off end. These are clamped into a vise. Grab the auxiliary wires at the other side with the hand or with pliers and pull the thread apart. Now you have to once again pull carefully and evenly. The flexibility of the material is limited!

With silver threads you can anneal in between two or more pulling operations. The thread is heated with a gas flame. The material loses some of its tension and might be pulled even further.

CALIBRATING

The calibration process results in a knitted tube with the same diameter over its entire length, and the mesh appears more regular than if the tube were only stretched and pulled.

A draw plate, a hardwood board with holes of different diameters, is used for calibration. The drilled holes must be beveled at the edges and well-sanded inside so the threads are not damaged when they are pulled through.

1   While calibrating, the thread is pulled through the draw plate via the auxiliary wires. In the case of a loose mesh pattern, for example one that you worked with a rather large wooden knitting loom, the tube can be reduced down to a relatively small diameter. This reduction should be done in several steps so that the mesh can take on the new shape little by little.

> **TIP:**
> The draw plate should be affixed to the work table with a clamp so it offers enough resistance during the pulling operation. For practical reasons we did not feature the fixation of the draw plate when taking the photographs.

2   The mesh will be even more regular if a metal rod is inserted into the tube as a core and both are pushed through the draw plate. The metal insert prevents individual stitches from moving inward due to the pressure.

The stitches of the thread become longer and more regular.

3   If the diameter of the knitted tube is to be reduced when calibrating with the metal insert, the metal rod must be switched to one with a smaller diameter before each calibration process. Then the tube with the insert is pulled through a smaller hole of the draw plate. The diameter of the thread is reduced while it becomes longer at the same time.

> **TIP:**
> Carefully and slowly pull the thread through the draw plate so the thread won't tear. The hole to use depends on the gauge of the wire and the density of the mesh. With some experience you'll recognize when the limit of the knitted material has been reached.

4

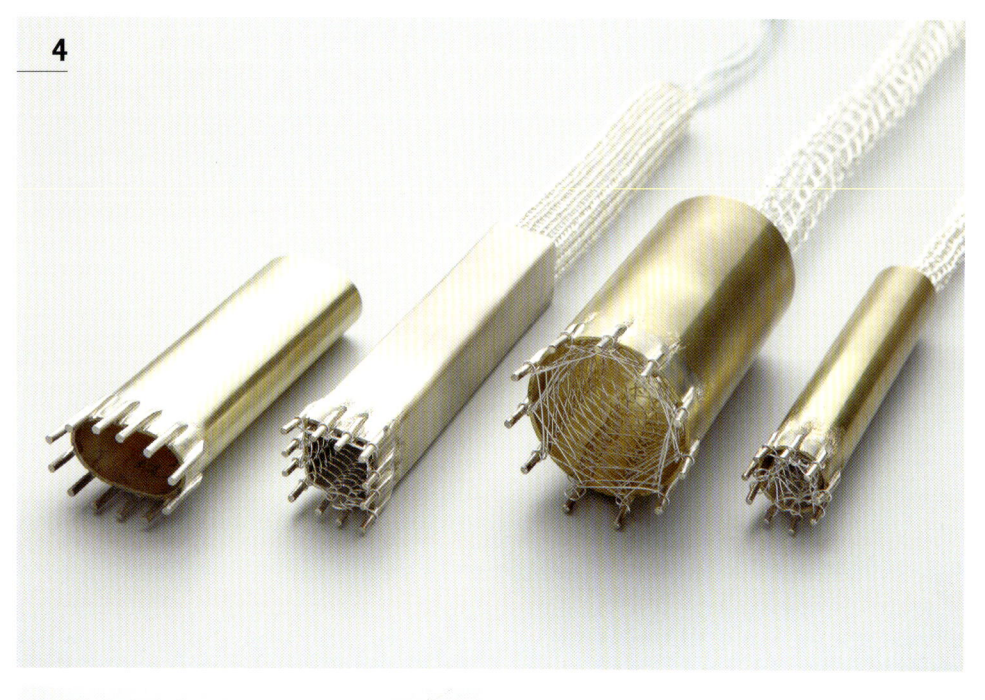

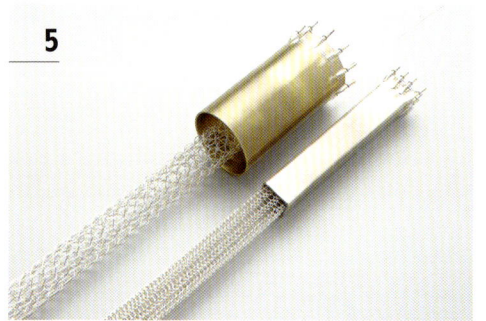

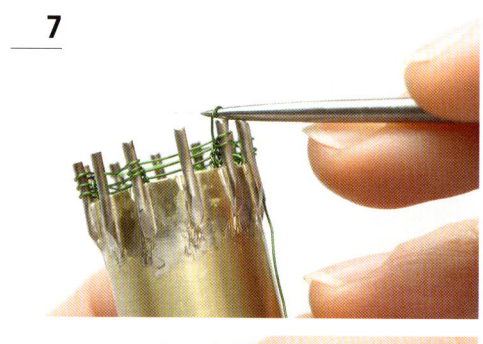

5

7

6

8

TECHNIQUE 4   EVEN MORE POSSIBILITIES

CUSTOM SHAPES

4 To obtain different shapes for your knitted tubes, different shapes of looms can be used.

At the far left you see an oval knitting loom. It was made from a round piece of copper tubing that was pressed into an oval. After that the pegs were soldered to it. Next to it lies a square loom. It is appropriate for making rings or bracelets (depending on the size) because the knitted tube is pressed flat for these jewelry pieces. The loom must have an even number of pegs.

The two round looms show how the number of pegs has an influence on the look of the knitted mesh: with large diameters and few pegs the mesh is light and airy, while with small diameters and/or many pegs it becomes dense.

5 While the diameter of the tube with airy and light mesh decreases just by pulling while knitting, the diameter or the shape of a dense mesh is left almost entirely intact.

VARIATIONS

The possibilities of your looms can be increased when you don't use all of the pegs. You can work in beads, or create new geometric shapes.

WORKING IN BEADS

6 In this example of a knitting loom with a diameter of 0.59 inches and nine pegs, two of the pegs were purposely skipped to make room for the beads. A straight section of wire is created where the three beads are placed.

ALL OF THE BEADS have to be threaded onto the wire **BEFORE** you can start winding and knitting. The selected beads must then be placed during the corresponding round of winding.

In our example, first the pegs one to seven are wound twice and knitted. The eighth and ninth peg remain empty. Behind them the wire between the seventh and the first peg is stretched.

Before the second round of winding the three beads are placed onto the wire directly next to the seventh peg, and then the round of winding is started at the first peg. The beads are thus placed between pegs seven and one.

The following round of knitting starts at the first peg and ends at the seventh.

Next comes one additional round of winding and knitting without beads. Then the beads are worked in again as described. So there is always an "empty" row of wire on the mesh tube between the rows of beads. This way the beads have sufficient space at the top and bottom.

CHANGING GEOMETRIC SHAPE

7 The loom in this example has twelve pegs. But only every other peg is wound and knitted, so only six stitches are done.

IMPORTANT: Don't confuse this technique with offset knitting. The difference is that in offset knitting only every other peg is initially wound and knitted. But due to the uneven number of pegs all of the pegs are worked. When skipping pegs as described here the skipped pegs are not worked at all.

8 The skipping of every other peg results in a nice hexagonal shape. This is particularly nice when using thicker wire (e.g., with a diameter of 0.4 mm).

By skipping certain pegs you can make triangular or pentagonal knitted tubes.

> **TIP:**
> The longer sections of wire resulting from skipping can also be fitted with beads.

9

10

11

12

13

14

TECHNIQUE 4 EVEN MORE POSSIBILITIES

KNITTING IN, KNITTING AROUND, INSERTING, SEWING ON

9 As shown with **TECHNIQUE 1 AND 4** beads can be inserted into pieces by crocheting or knitting. Generally, enough beads must be threaded when you start the project. The beads on the thread are pushed toward the last stitch worked, and then crocheted or knitted in.

10 Beads or other items such as these bells can be affixed to the piece of jewelry after the fact too. Use transparent nylon thread.

11 Inserted—or, as in this case, knitted-in—objects are very attractive. It is surprising how flexible the knitted material really is. You can also insert asymmetric objects, such as this amethyst.

12 At this scale, and being asymmetric, an object can only be worked in during the knitting process. The loom has to be large enough for the stone to fit through it.

IMPORTANT: Before knitting, check the diameter of the loom, keeping in mind that the thread will become more narrow while knitting. Or pick an appropriate stone while you knit. After knitting, the mesh cannot be stretched enough to insert a large and asymmetric object.

13 With large spheres, too, it's better to knit them into the mesh right away. Except when the finished knitted tube has an inner diameter approximately the same as the sphere's. As the tube narrows when knitting in the bead, before it and after it, it can no longer slip, but you also can no longer move it. So you should envision the future position of the sphere in the piece in advance, in detail, and insert it at the right place when knitting.

14 Small spheres can also be inserted into the tube once the piece has been finished. The diameter of the spheres should be about that of the inside of the tube. Use a rod or a metal tube (a calibrating rod works well) to insert the spheres where they should go. To keep the spheres from shifting position, the tube is tightened to both sides of the sphere. This results in a smaller diameter and the sphere becoming "caught."

TIP:
The tube becomes somewhat longer when pulled, so keep this increase in size in mind when you are planning.

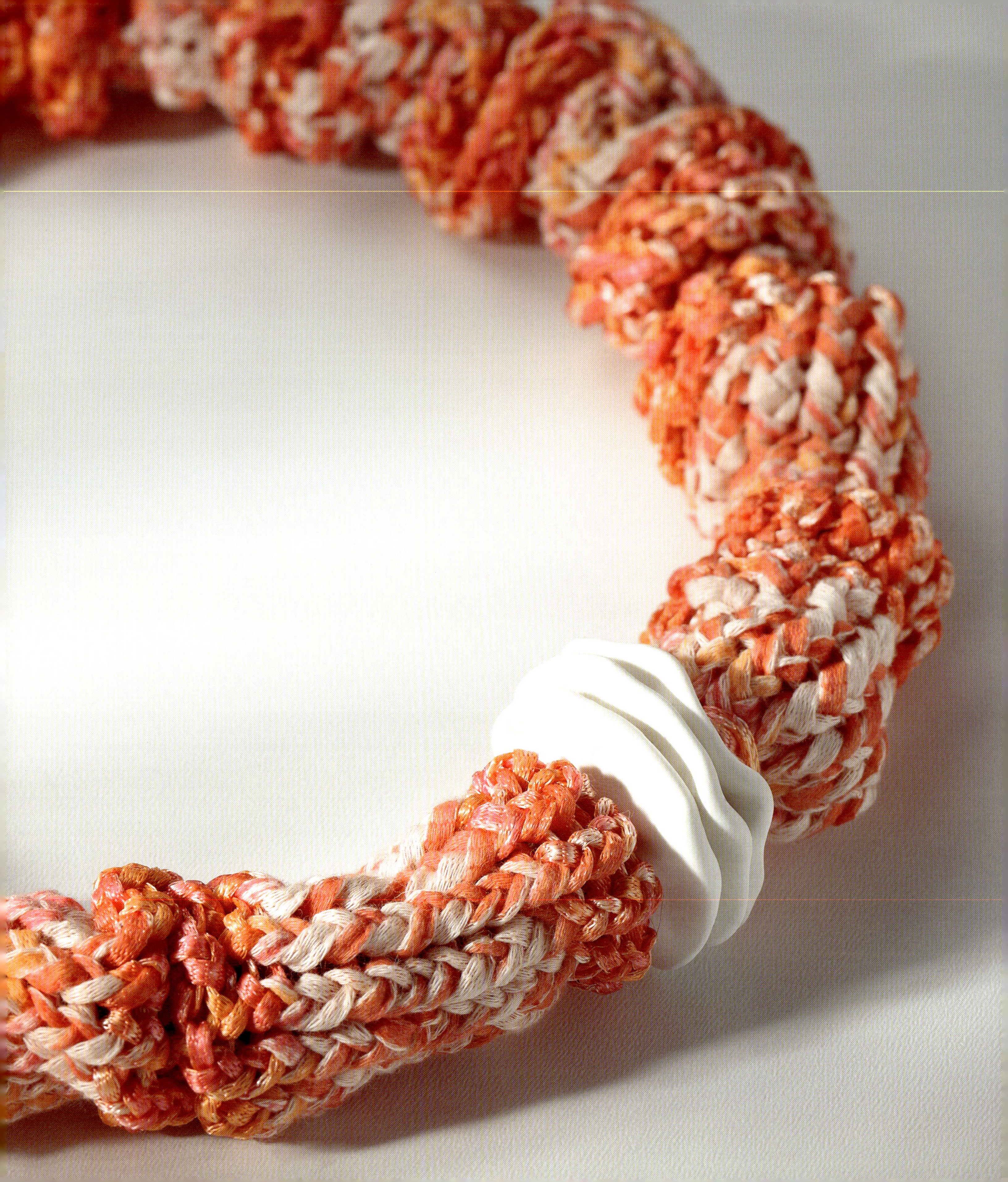

JOYOUS FASHION JEWELRY

"JEWELRY IS NOT MEANT TO MAKE YOU LOOK WEALTHY, BUT TO GRACE YOU. FOR THIS REASON I HAVE ALWAYS LIKED TO WEAR FAUX JEWELRY."

Coco Chanel

1 WOOLLUMINOUS

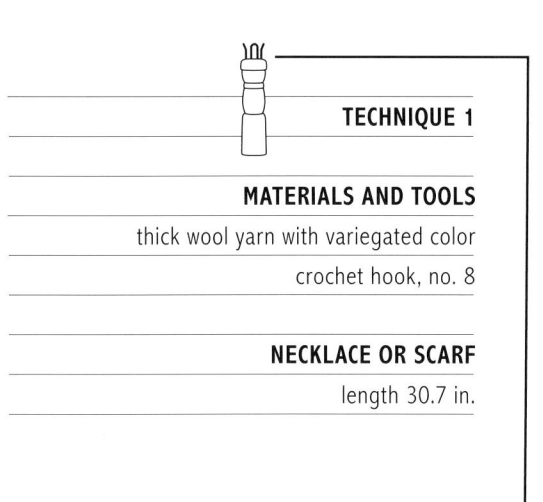

TECHNIQUE 1

MATERIALS AND TOOLS

thick wool yarn with variegated color

crochet hook, no. 8

NECKLACE OR SCARF

length 30.7 in.

This unconventional necklace, which can also be worn as a scarf, is done only with chain stitches. It's a great project for becoming familiar with this technique.

The wool features a nice variegated color gradient, from light to medium to dark grays then to black. Crochet chain stitches with a no. 8 hook until the entire ball has been used up or the amount you imagined has been reached (**TECHNIQUE 1**). For my project I used 100 grams of yarn.

Create a long chain stitch thread of about 30.7 inches of loops; the loops shouldn't be too even so the necklace won't be dull. The individual loops fall more nicely if they are "all over the place."

The last 12 to 16 inches of the chain stitch thread are threaded tightly around all of the loops and the two ends of the thread are secured. The winding creates a kind of knot which holds the loops together. The necklace can be worn so that the knot lies at the back of the neck or at the front.

Due to its volume and its coloring this necklace is an eye-catcher, whether worn over a turtleneck, with a T-shirt, or with a sleeveless top.

TIP:
If you use slightly thinner yarn in bright colors (50 g) this project is also great for kids.

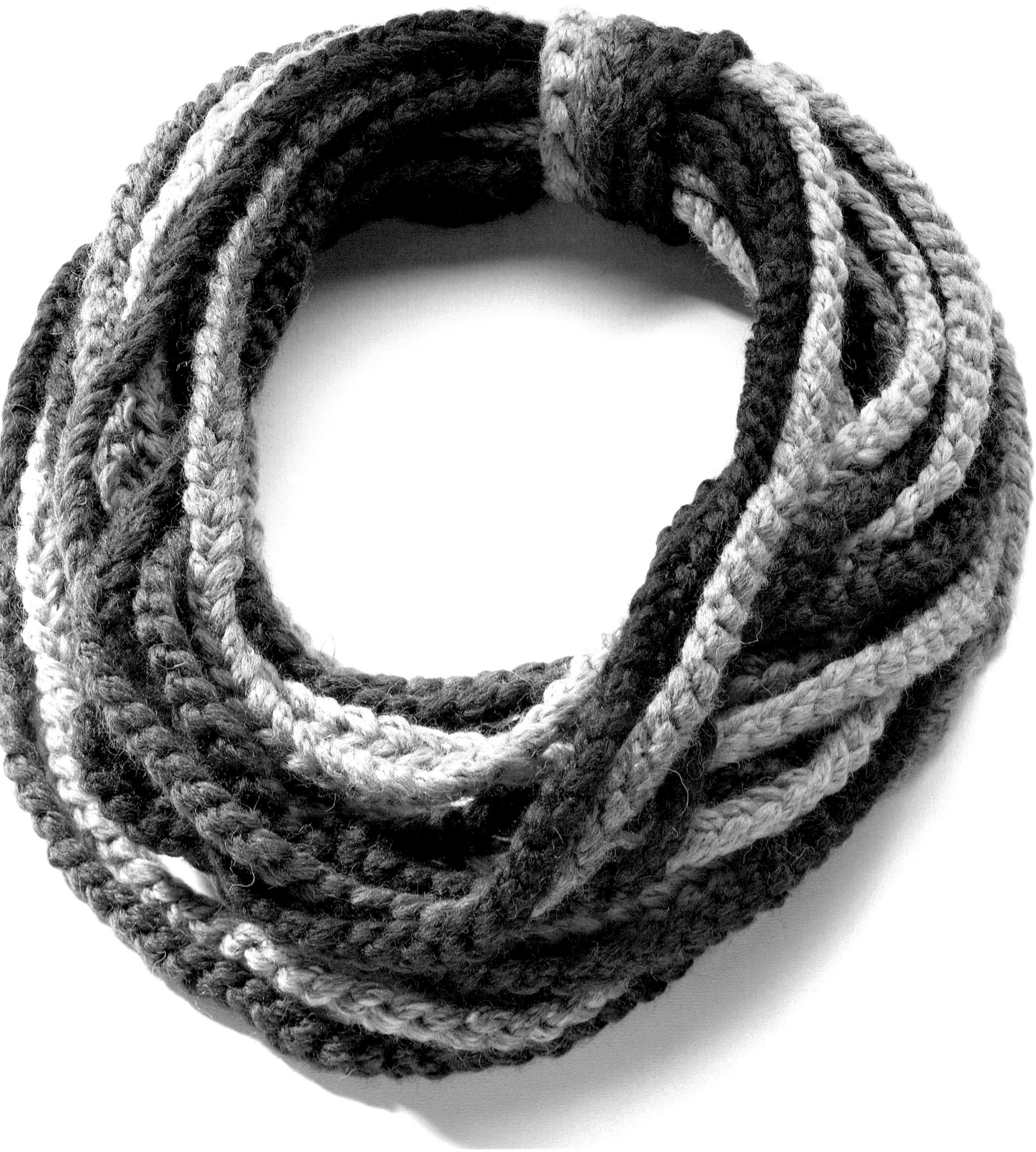

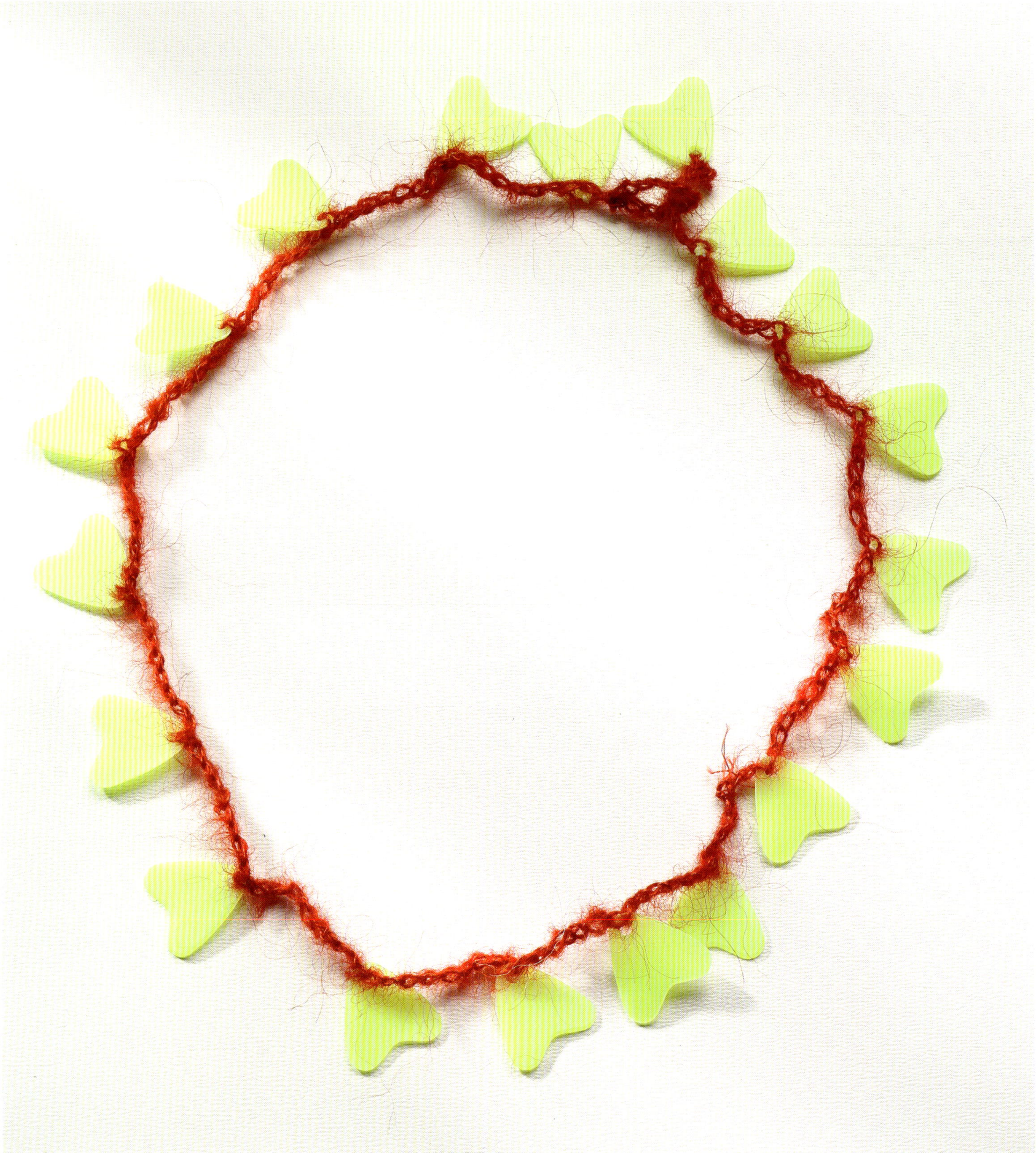

2 MOHAIR YELLOW

This and the following six projects are also suitable for kids.

First, the 19 fishing lure pieces, heart-shaped here, must be threaded for the delicate mohair necklace. Then a chain stitch thread is crocheted (**TECHNIQUE 1**).

Start with three chain stitches and work a small lure piece into the fourth stitch. Then crochet seven chain stitches and work a lure piece into the eighth one. Repeat this process until 19 lure pieces have been added.

After the last lure piece a small loop for the clasp must be made. Crochet twelve chain stitches. Then insert the crochet hook into the fourth stitch after the last lure piece, pull the thread through this loop with the crochet hook without grabbing a new thread, as well as through the last chain stitch (it still lies on the hook). This creates a small loop and the last stitch lies on the crochet hook.

Finally the thread is cut off from the ball and the last stitch is widened until the thread has entirely slipped through. Now the thread is secured and the chain stitch thread can't open up anymore.

The thread is secured by sewing both ends of the chain stitch thread in an inconspicuous way.

The first lure piece that you worked into the necklace can now be hooked into the loop in order to close the necklace.

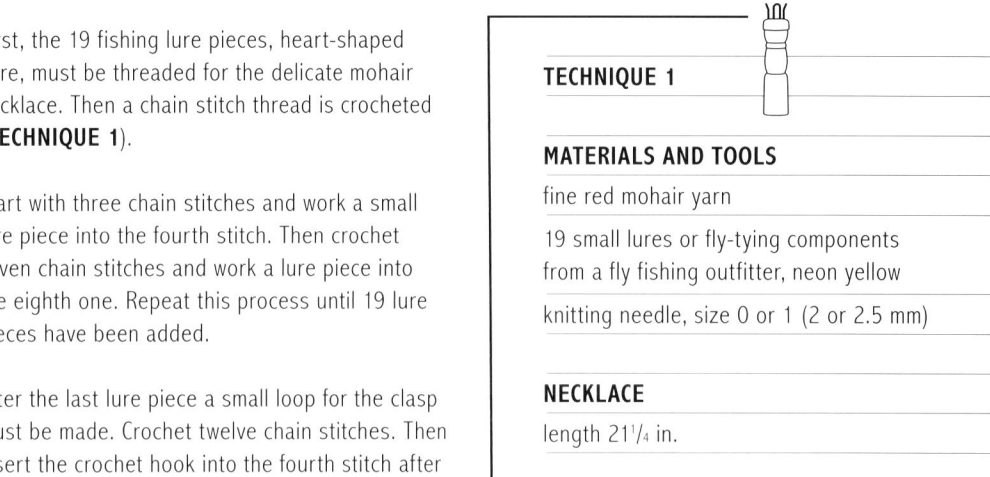

> **TIP:**
> This type of fluffy material should not be worked with a crochet hook, which is too thin.

TECHNIQUE 1

MATERIALS AND TOOLS

fine red mohair yarn

19 small lures or fly-tying components from a fly fishing outfitter, neon yellow

knitting needle, size 0 or 1 (2 or 2.5 mm)

NECKLACE

length 21¼ in.

3 HEART JINGLES

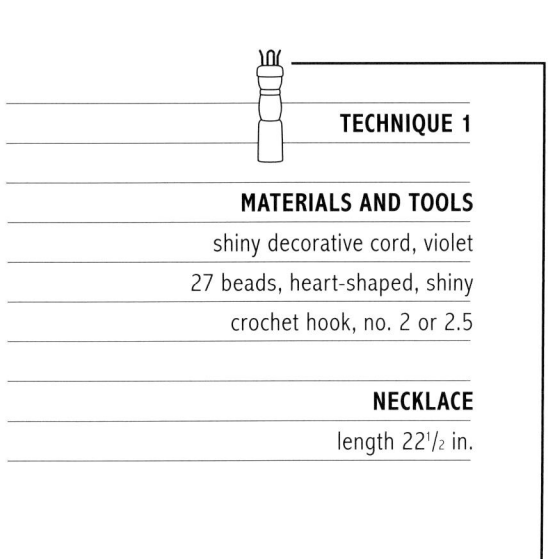

TECHNIQUE 1

MATERIALS AND TOOLS

shiny decorative cord, violet

27 beads, heart-shaped, shiny

crochet hook, no. 2 or 2.5

NECKLACE

length 22 1/2 in.

For this "hearty" necklace, the 27 beads are first threaded onto the decorative cord.

You start the chain stitch thread by making two stitches and working the first bead into the third stitch. Then you alternate between 26 rounds of three chain stitches without and one chain stitch with a bead.

Make a small loop for the clasp. Crochet eight chain stitches after the last bead. Then insert into the second stitch after the bead and pull the thread through this stitch with the crochet hook and, without picking up a new thread, through the last chain stitch (it still lies on the crochet hook). This results in a small ring and the last stitch lies on the crochet hook.

Last, the thread is cut off from the ball and the last stitch is widened enough so that the thread has slipped through entirely. Now the stitch is secured and cannot open up anymore. Sew the thread at both sides of the chain stitch in an unobtrusive way.

The last bead is used to close the necklace with the small loop.

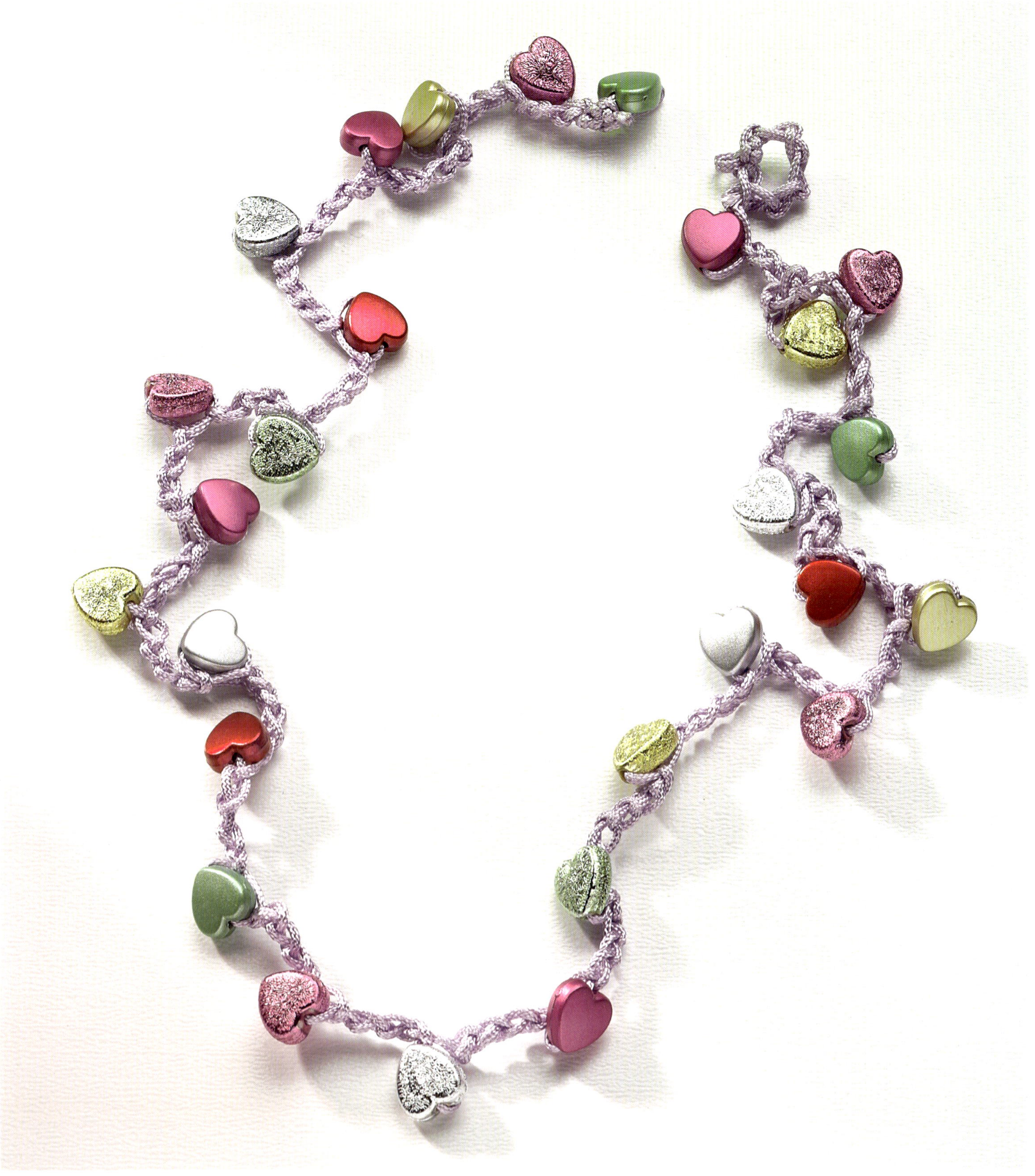

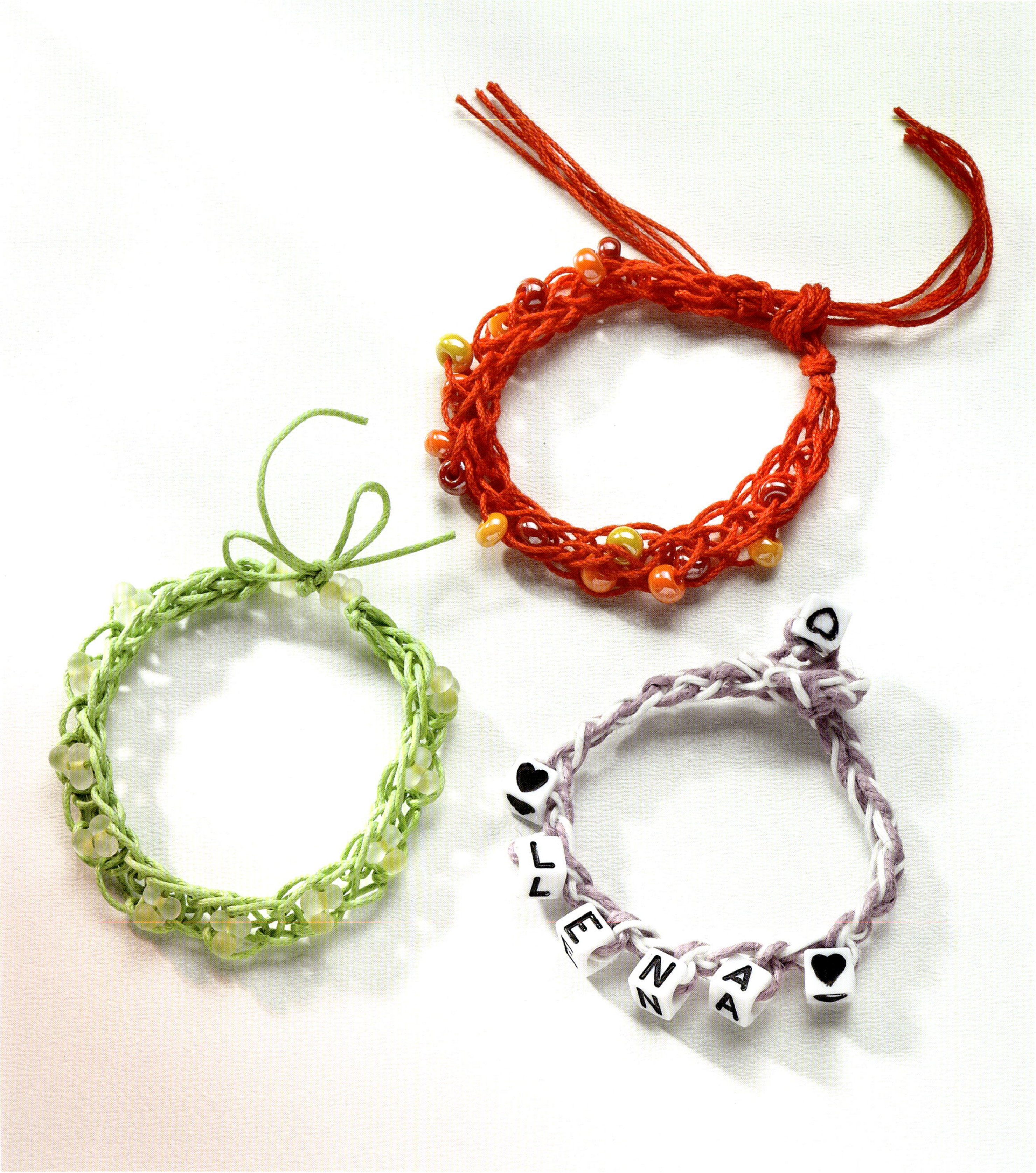
LENA

4 FRIENDSHIP

BRACELET WITH LETTER BEADS

In order to achieve a sort of melange effect both of the cotton threads are worked at the same time. Thread the beads onto **BOTH YARNS.** Order the beads so the name is spelled correctly.

You start with eight chain stitches. The bead with the heart motif is worked into the ninth stitch. The letter beads follow after one chain stitch without a bead. A letter bead is worked into every second chain stitch. After the last letter bead, make one more "empty" chain stitch and then crochet one with a heart bead.

For the remaining bracelet length and the closing loop you make another 14 chain stitches. The loop is closed by inserting into the eighth chain stitch after the last bead (see projects no. 2 and 3). For the clasp you thread a heart bead to the beginning of the chain stitch thread and knot it into the two starting threads.

Sew the remaining ends of the friendship bracelet in an inconspicuous way and cut off.

RED BRACELET

Thread 16 glass beads in alternating colors and work four winding and knitting rounds (**TECHNIQUE 2**).

Insert a glass bead each at the fifth winding round, after the first and third pegs. Then follows the fifth knitting round.
Then you work one winding and one knitting round without a bead. At the seventh winding round, you work in one glass bead each after the second and the fourth peg and continue with one knitting round. This way the beads are lying offset on the knitted mesh.

> **TIP:** Leave the beginning and the end of the thread fairly long.

Winding and knitting rounds with and without beads now alternate until all the beads have been worked in. Finish with four winding and knitting rounds without beads.

The two ends of the friendship bracelet are knotted with two threads, each about 2½ inches long. Both sides now feature fringes consisting of five threads. Cut them to the same length.

LIGHT GREEN BRACELET

Thread the 20 farfalle beads. Now work four winding and knitting rounds each (**TECHNIQUE 2**). You only use the first, second, and third pegs. Skip the fourth peg.

IMPORTANT: The fourth peg is always left empty.

Before the fifth winding round you push two farfalle beads to the third peg and then wind the first, second, and third pegs. Then follows a knitting round, then a winding and a knitting round without a bead. Alternate between a winding and a knitting round with and without a bead until ten rows of beads have been worked in. Finish with four winding and knitting rounds without beads.

Thread two beads each onto the ends of the threads on both sides, and affix with a knot. Shorten the ends so they can be used as closure ties.

TECHNIQUE 1

BRACELET WITH LETTER BEADS

length 6½ in.

MATERIALS AND TOOLS

cotton yarn, white and violet

beads with letters and hearts

knitting needle, no. 3

TECHNIQUE 2

RED BRACELET

length 6¾ in.

MATERIALS AND TOOLS

red cotton yarn

16 glass beads with large holes, red, orange, yellow, dia. 5.4 mm

4-peg wooden knitting loom

SEQUENCE OF BEADS

LIGHT GREEN BRACELET

length 6½ in.

MATERIALS AND TOOLS

cotton yarn, light green

24 farfalle beads, crystal, matte yellow, dia. 6.5 mm

4-peg wooden knitting loom

5 BEAD BAND

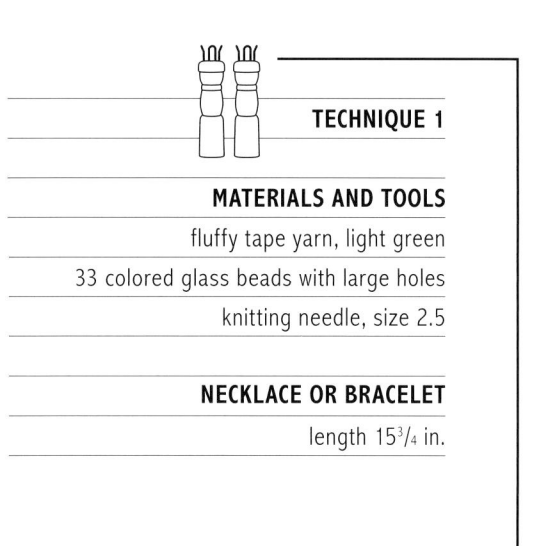

TECHNIQUE 1

MATERIALS AND TOOLS

fluffy tape yarn, light green

33 colored glass beads with large holes

knitting needle, size 2.5

NECKLACE OR BRACELET

length 15¾ in.

First you make a chain stitch thread where you alternatingly crochet two chain stitches without and one chain stitch with a bead. A total of 30 beads is crocheted in this way. You finish with two "empty" chain stitches.

Now a second row consisting of single crochets is crocheted into the chain stitch thread. Here the first single crochet is stitched into the chain stitch into which the last bead was crocheted. Then a single crochet is stitched into each chain stitch (including those with beads, see page 21). Finish with two chain stitches. You need them to "turn over" because now a second row of single stitches is crocheted the other way into the first row.

At the end of the second row with single stitches, six chain stitches are crocheted for the clasp and closed into a loop. The yarn is cut off from the ball and the rest of the thread is knitted.

At the other side of the band three beads are threaded onto the starting thread, and the thread is tightly sewn behind the beads at the end of the band. This causes the beads to form a kind of "button," which is passed through the closing loop to close the band.

The finished band can be worn as a necklace or as a bracelet; for that it is wrapped two or three times around the wrist. The fluffy material makes it comfortable to wear.

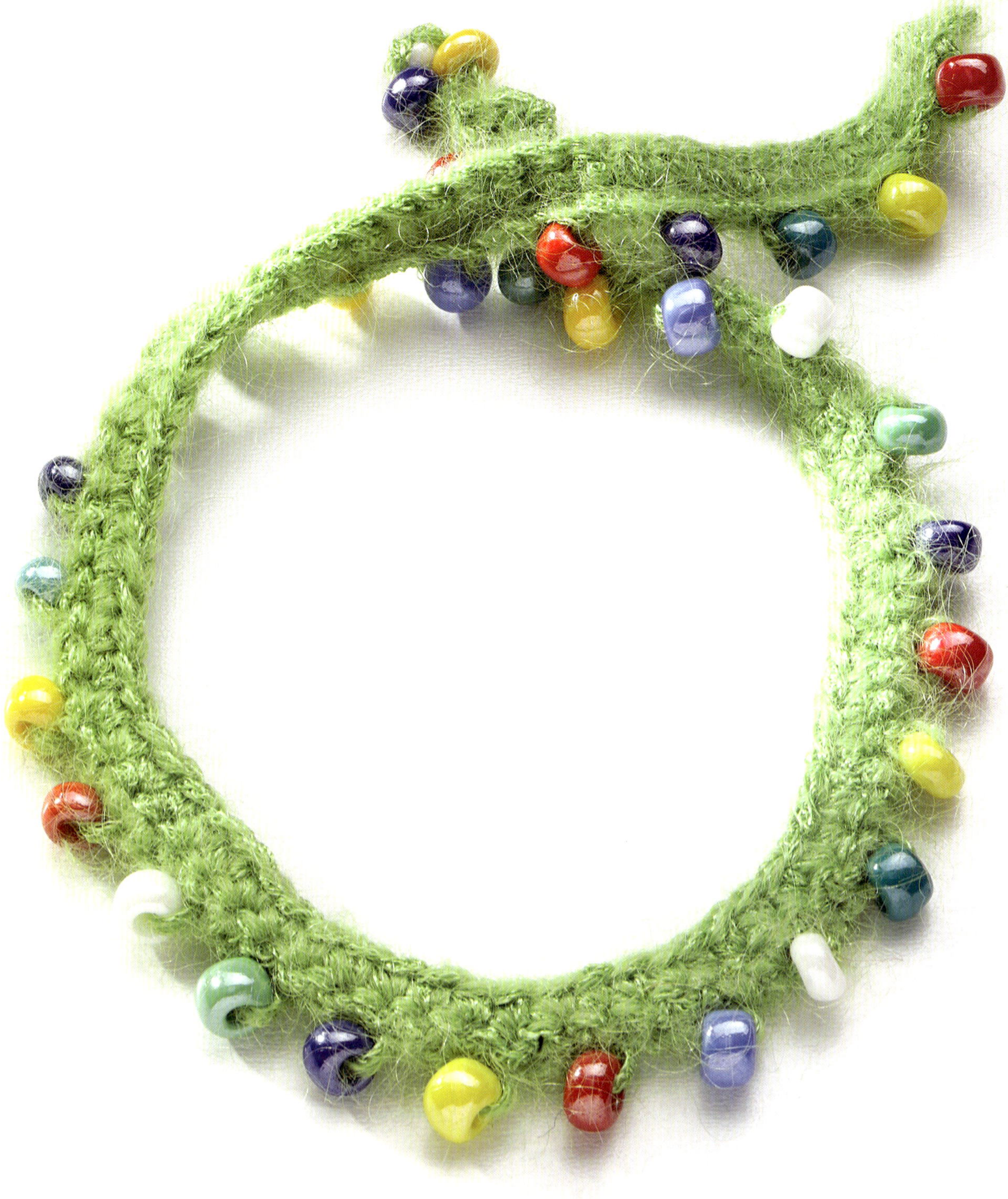

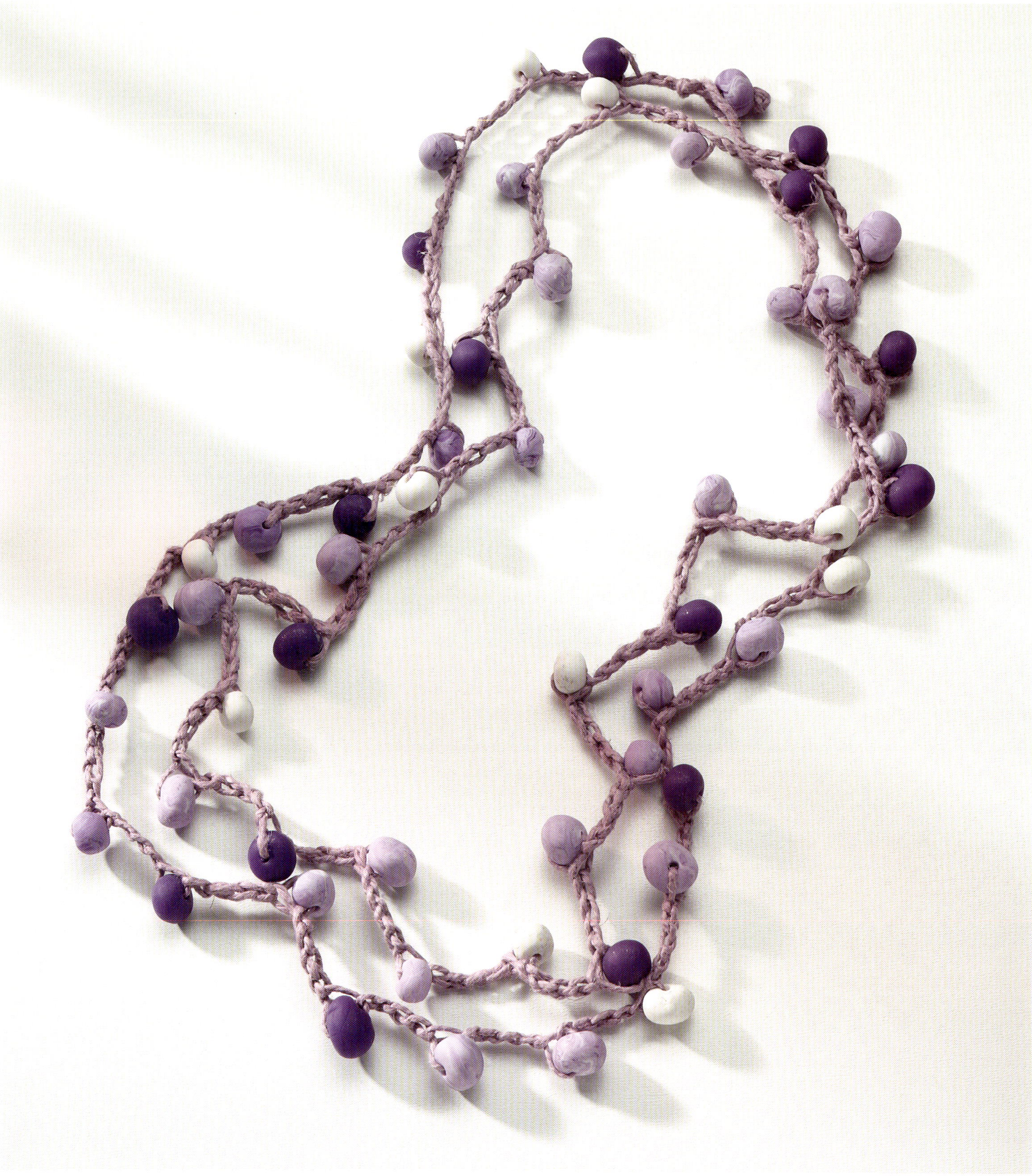

6 FIMO FABULOUS

First the beads must be made from Fimo modeling resin. Start with the white modeling resin so no bits of other colors get into the white resin. Knead about a fourth or a third of the Fimo slab until it is smooth and can be worked easily. Remove small amounts and use your fingers or the palms of your hands to shape spheres with a diameter of about 1/4 inch. Use a toothpick to punch holes into the centers.

IMPORTANT: Make sure the hole is large enough to allow the yarn or cord to be easily pulled through.

Now use the violet Fimo to make beads in the same way.

For marbled spheres, mix white and violet Fimo resin. This is best done by first rolling out a thin slab of each color and placing them on top of each other. Fold the slabs from the side and from the top or the bottom once, and roll the mass into a thin slab again. Repeat this process several times. Now the mass can be kneaded by hand until the desired amount of marbling has been achieved. Then make beads with a diameter of about 1/4 inch.

You need a total of about 50 beads for this project. After shaping them, you harden the beads in the oven.

IMPORTANT: Make sure you follow the manufacturer's directions when using and hardening the modeling resin!

After they cool, the beads are threaded onto the cord in the order you prefer. Make sure that you don't thread two beads of the same color next to each other.

Now work alternatingly four chain stitches without a bead and one chain stitch with a bead until the thread is 4 1/4 feet long. For the clasp, thread a Fimo bead onto the starting thread and affix it with a knot.

The ending thread is knotted into a loop which is large enough to hook over the Fimo bead.

TECHNIQUE 1

MATERIALS AND TOOLS

thin flax yarn or cord, violet, dia. 1.5 mm

Fimo modeling resin, violet, white

knitting needle, size 2.5

NECKLACE

length 22 in.

7 ZIGZAG

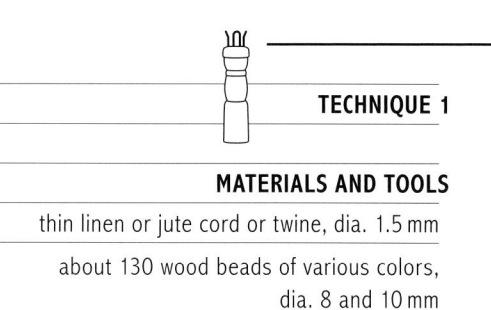

TECHNIQUE 1

MATERIALS AND TOOLS

thin linen or jute cord or twine, dia. 1.5 mm

about 130 wood beads of various colors, dia. 8 and 10 mm

2 earring hooks, brown

knitting needle, size 2

NECKLACE

length 22 in.

SEQUENCE OF BEADS

the wood beads can be threaded randomly with regard to color and size

NECKLACE

For this necklace four single chain stitches with a length of about 22 inches are made. Alternatingly crochet four chain stitches without beads and one chain stitch with bead. In order for the bead to be nicely balanced on the four strands, start with one chain stitch thread with two stitches, one with three, and one with four. At the end of the threads finish with as many chain stitches as needed on each so that the four threads are of equal length.

Since the cord is somewhat stiff, a small fold in the chain stitch is created with each bead. This results in a nice zigzag pattern, which provides added volume when the strands are joined.

To finish the necklace, place the four strands next to each other and slightly twist them. At one end, the four end threads of the chain stitch threads are knotted, a wood bead with a diameter of 10 mm is threaded onto the four threads, and a second knot is tied at a short distance away (about half an inch). The wood bead can be slightly shifted due to the distance between the two knots. Finally, cut off the threads at different lengths.

At the other end, the four end threads are also knotted. A second knot is made at a distance of about half an inch away without adding a bead. Due to the two knots, a loop results to hook over the closing bead. Finally, these four end threads too are cut off at different lengths.

TIP:
I put all of the beads into a small glass bowl and picked them out at random. This resulted in a nice mix. You just need to avoid putting two beads of the same color or size next to each other.

EARRINGS

For the earrings a 4 $^{3}/_{4}$-inch length of the cord is pulled through the jump ring of the earring hook. Now three wood beads, each with a diameter of 10 mm, are threaded onto the two halves of the thread (beige, light brown, dark brown) and secured by tying a knot directly below the last bead. The two ends of the cord are cut off at different lengths.

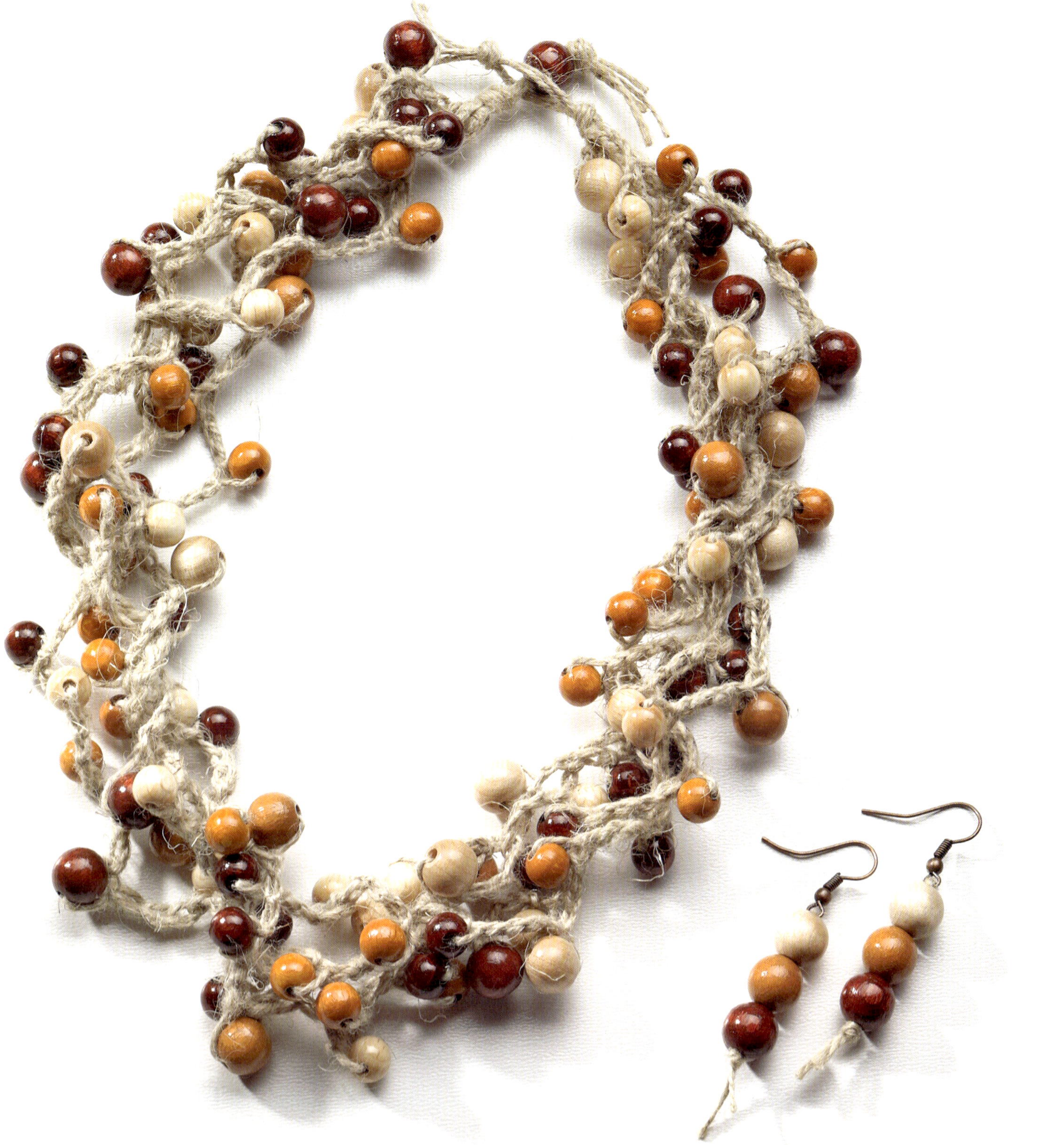

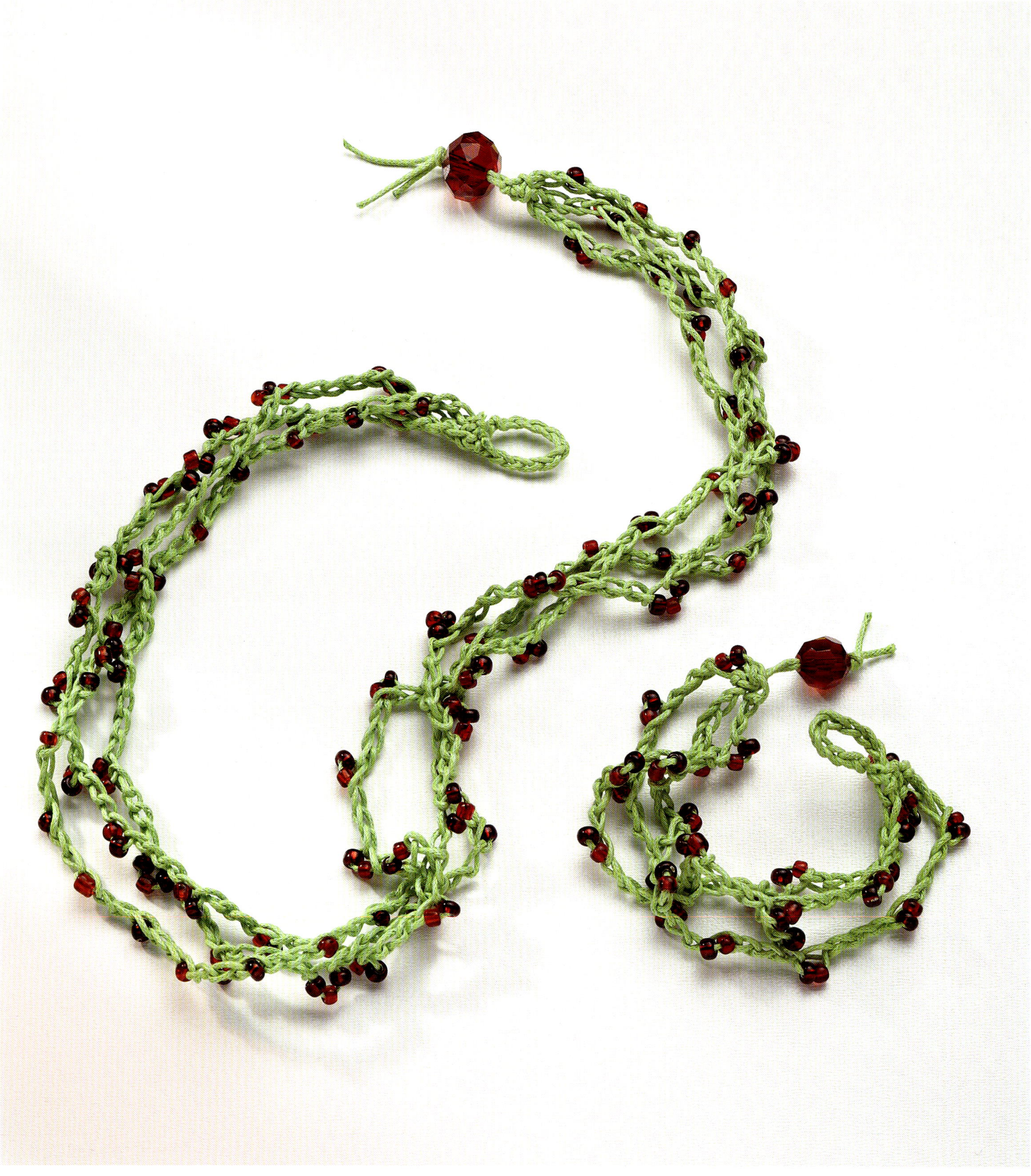

8 FROG KING

NECKLACE

For this necklace you crochet three chain stitches. You make two stitches for the first chain stitch and crochet a rocaille bead into the next chain stitch. Then alternatingly add two chain stitches with and one chain stitch without bead, until the 32 beads have been used. Finish with two chain stitches and cast off the thread; cut off from the ball.

Make three stitches for the second chain stitch thread and crochet in two rocailles into the next chain stitch. Now alternatingly crochet three chain stitches without and one with two beads, until the 52 beads have been used. Finish with three chain stitches and cast off the thread; cut off from the ball.

Make four chain stitches for the third chain stitch thread and then alternatingly make four chain stitches without a bead and one chain stitch with three rocailles. Use 60 beads this way and end with four chain stitches. Cast off the thread; cut off from the ball.

IMPORTANT: The ends of the threads should be about 11 inches long.

The three chain stitches should be of the same length now (about 20½ inches).

To finish the necklace, place the three chain stitch threads next to each other and twist them lightly. Then knot the end threads.

Thread the large faceted glass bead onto the three threads at one end and knot the three threads behind the bead. Cut off the threads at different lengths.

At the other end, secure two of the threads inconspicuously. Make twelve chain stitches with the long thread and close to form a loop where the three chain stitches meet. Secure the thread again. Now the large bead forms the closure using the loop.

BRACELET

For the bracelet, make three chain stitch threads with a length of about 6½ inches, alternating three chain stitches without bead and one chain stitch with two beads. A total of 52 beads is used. For the beads to not lie on all three strands at the same height, a chain stitch thread with two stitches, one with three, and one with four stitches are made. Finish the ends of the threads with as many chain stitches needed so that the three threads are of the same length.

To finish the bracelet, proceed as with the necklace. However, only ten chain stitches are needed for the closing loop since the closing bead is smaller.

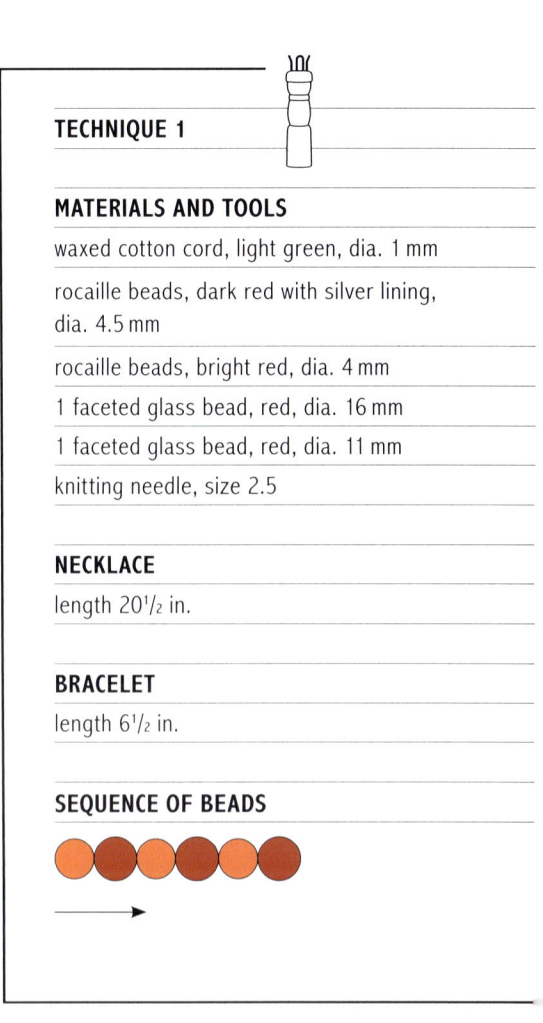

TECHNIQUE 1

MATERIALS AND TOOLS

waxed cotton cord, light green, dia. 1 mm

rocaille beads, dark red with silver lining, dia. 4.5 mm

rocaille beads, bright red, dia. 4 mm

1 faceted glass bead, red, dia. 16 mm

1 faceted glass bead, red, dia. 11 mm

knitting needle, size 2.5

NECKLACE

length 20½ in.

BRACELET

length 6½ in.

SEQUENCE OF BEADS

9 RED TONES

TECHNIQUE 1

MATERIALS AND TOOLS

Thin nylon yarn (e.g., yarn used for crocheting lace), black

about 130 glass beads in various red tones, clear and matte, dia. 8 mm

rocailles, orange-red, dia. 2 mm

rocailles, dark red with silver lining, dia. 2.6 mm

spherical magnet clasp, black, dia. 12 mm

knitting needle, size 2

NECKLACE

length 22¾ in.

SEQUENCE OF BEADS

First you thread the beads. With this rather thin yarn, that will only work by using a needle.

For this project seven chain stitches are crocheted. For the stitches to be nicely light and airy, you should use a crochet hook that is too large for the thin yarn. For the chain stitches, start with a different number between two and four so the beads of the finished necklace are nicely distributed. Now make five chain stitches without bead, alternating with one chain stitch with one glass bead or with five rocailles. The seven chain stitch threads should have a length of 21 inches each. You can even out the length with the number of chain stitches at the ends of the strands.

TIP: Place all of the 8-mm glass beads into a small glass bowl and pick them at random. This results in a nice mix all by itself. You should just make sure that you don't get two beads of the same color next to each other.

TIP: The more you twist the strands, the closer together the beads are. Notice that the necklace will also become somewhat shorter. Secure the threads individually, since that's less conspicuous.

To finish the necklace, the seven strands are placed next to each other and twisted.

Knot the end threads on each end with each other. Thread two glass beads onto all of the seven strands and run the threads through the jump rings of the magnet clasp. Run the threads back through the two beads and secure them where the strands meet.

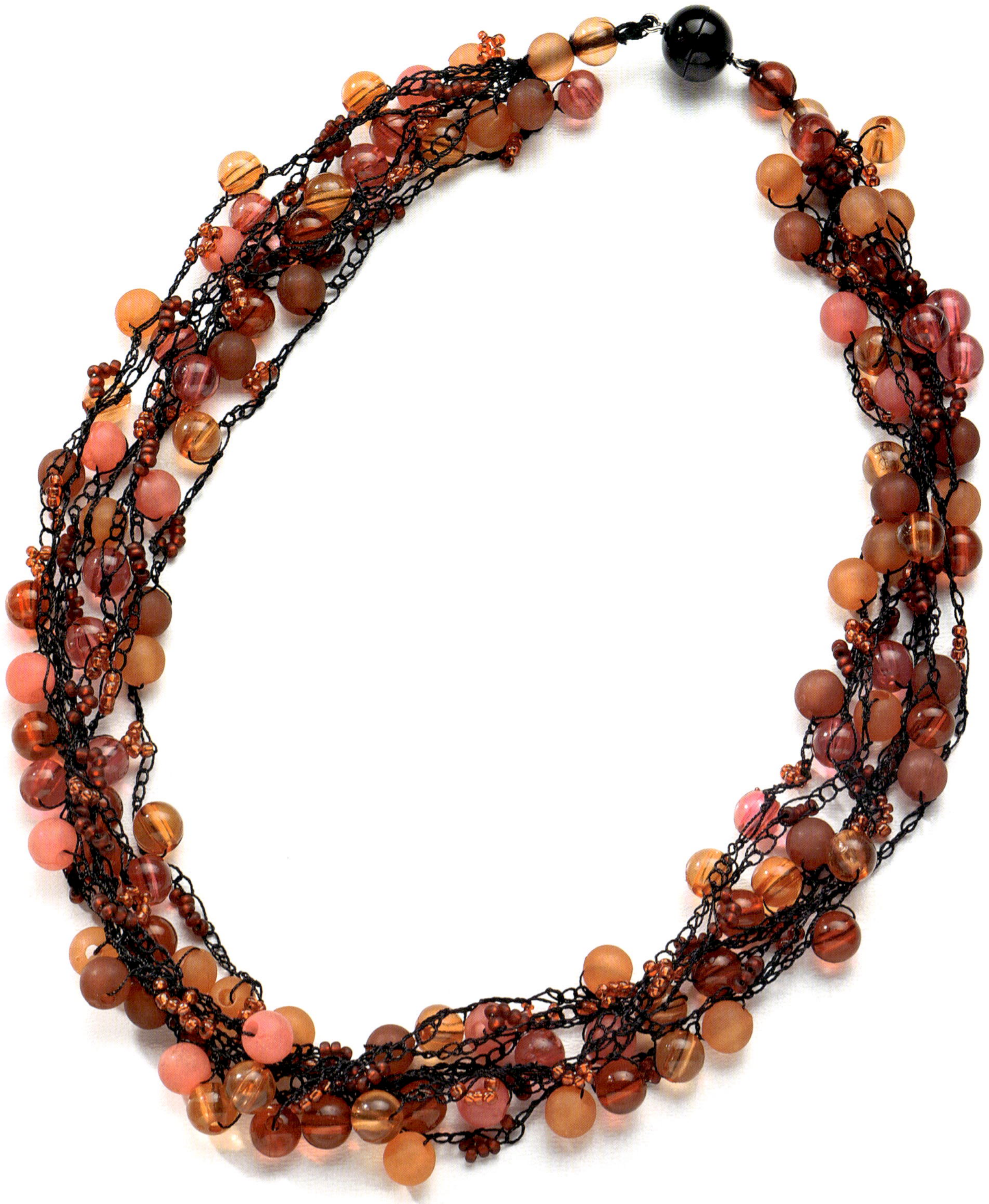

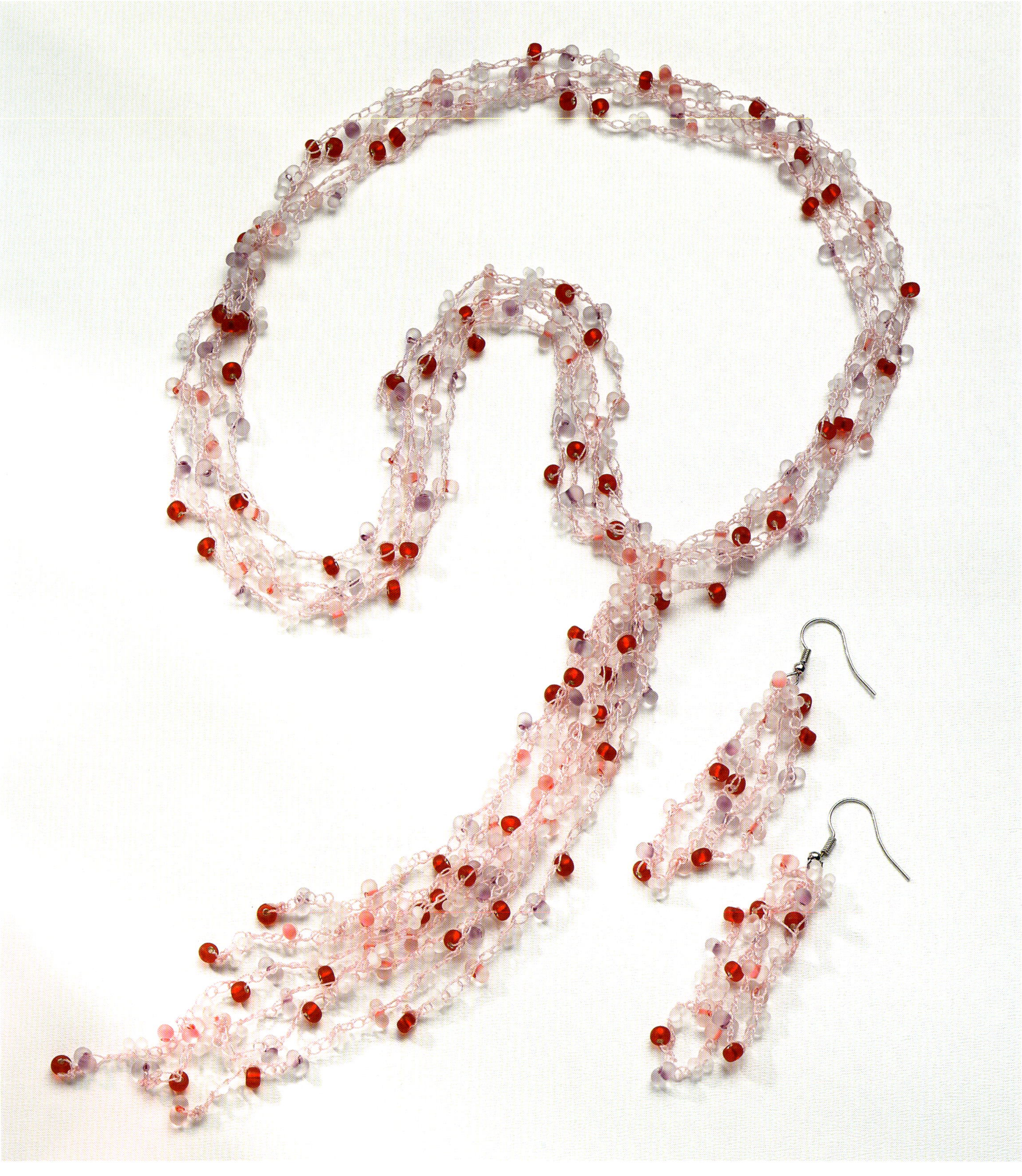

10 CHARLESTON

NECKLACE

Thread the beads according to the sequence shown. Now four chain stitches of lengths of about 36, 37, 39, and 41 inches are crocheted. Alternatingly stitch three chain stitches without bead and one chain stitch with one or two beads (see sequence).

IMPORTANT: Start the threads with a different number of stitches (from one to three) and make sure that you start with different beads. This way the beads are later nicely distributed.

When the four chain stitches are done, the ends of the threads can be secured.

Now place the chain stitches individually into a narrow U and shift the two sections so that one is 3/4 to 1 1/4 inches longer than the other one. Mark the new center with a thread or a safety pin.

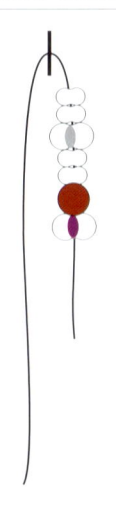

Once the four chain stitches have been marked, place them over each other at the marked sections and sew them together. This is the rear center of the necklace.

By shifting the individual strands, the ends of the four chain stitches are of different lengths.

Now sew all of the strands together once more, about 13 to 14 inches from the rear center, to close the necklace. Thread several beads and wind the thread with the beads around the strands of threads. This hides the sewn spot and the crossing point of the strands is somewhat emphasized. Secure the end of the thread inconspicuously.

EARRINGS

For the earrings, two chain stitches with a length of 9 1/2 inches are made. The sequence of the beads is the same as with the necklace. Between the beads crochet only two instead of three "empty" chain stitches. To make the mesh appear more delicate, the stitches should be crocheted with a somewhat firmer or a thinner crochet hook.

Close the chain stitch thread after a length of 9 1/2 inches and secure the ends of the threads. The chain stitch ring is now inserted at two locations (into two chain stitches) into the jump ring of the earring hook. Choose these two locations so that two loops of different lengths result from the ring.

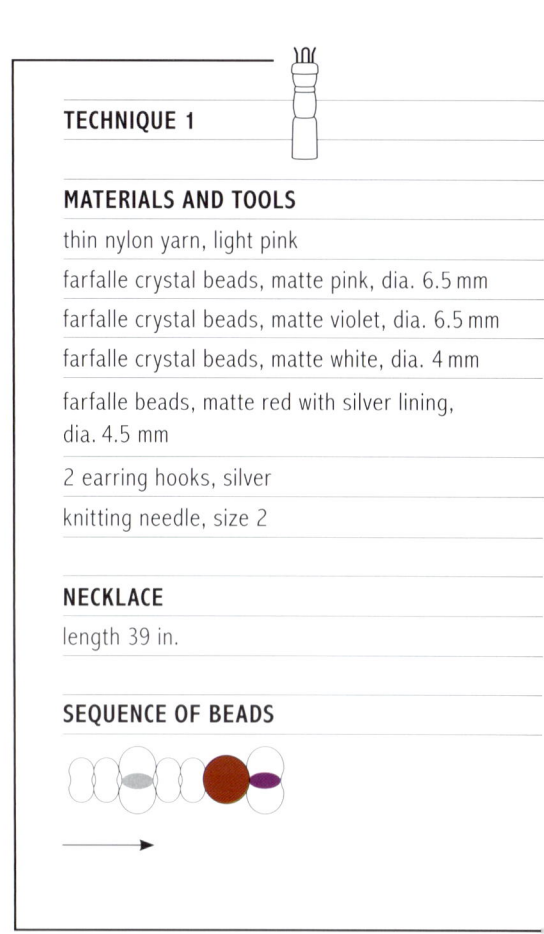

REAR CENTER

TECHNIQUE 1

MATERIALS AND TOOLS

thin nylon yarn, light pink

farfalle crystal beads, matte pink, dia. 6.5 mm

farfalle crystal beads, matte violet, dia. 6.5 mm

farfalle crystal beads, matte white, dia. 4 mm

farfalle beads, matte red with silver lining, dia. 4.5 mm

2 earring hooks, silver

knitting needle, size 2

NECKLACE

length 39 in.

SEQUENCE OF BEADS

Chapter 2 | Joyous Fashion Jewelry | Project 10

11 MOUNTAIN LILAC

TECHNIQUE 1

MATERIALS AND TOOLS

thin nylon yarn, violet

farfalle crystal beads, matte violet, dia. 6.5 mm

farfalle beads, matte white, dia. 4 mm

farfalle beads, dark red with silver lining, dia. 2.6 mm

rock crystal beads

lobster claw clasp with two jump rings, silver

knitting needle, size 2

NECKLACE

length 17 3/4 in.

SEQUENCE OF BEADS

One variation of the previous project is this necklace, which fits closely around the neck.

First thread the beads as shown in the sequence. Then make a chain stitch thread of 7.3 feet (!). Alternatingly make three chain stitches without and one chain stitch with one bead each, as described in the sequence for project no. 10.

Then the necklace is arranged into five strands of equal length. Place two pins 7 3/4 inches apart into a piece of cork or styrofoam and wind the chain stitch thread around the two pins without tension. The beginning of the chain stitch thread lies at one of the pins and the end of the necklace at the other pin.

Sew together the strands with the two ends of the threads where the pins are placed, and sew the thread ends inconspicuously.

For the clasp, a jump ring with a diameter of 1/4 inch is inserted into one end of the necklace, and the lobster claw clasp's jump ring is inserted into the other. Make sure that the jump ring runs through chain stitches of all the five strands.

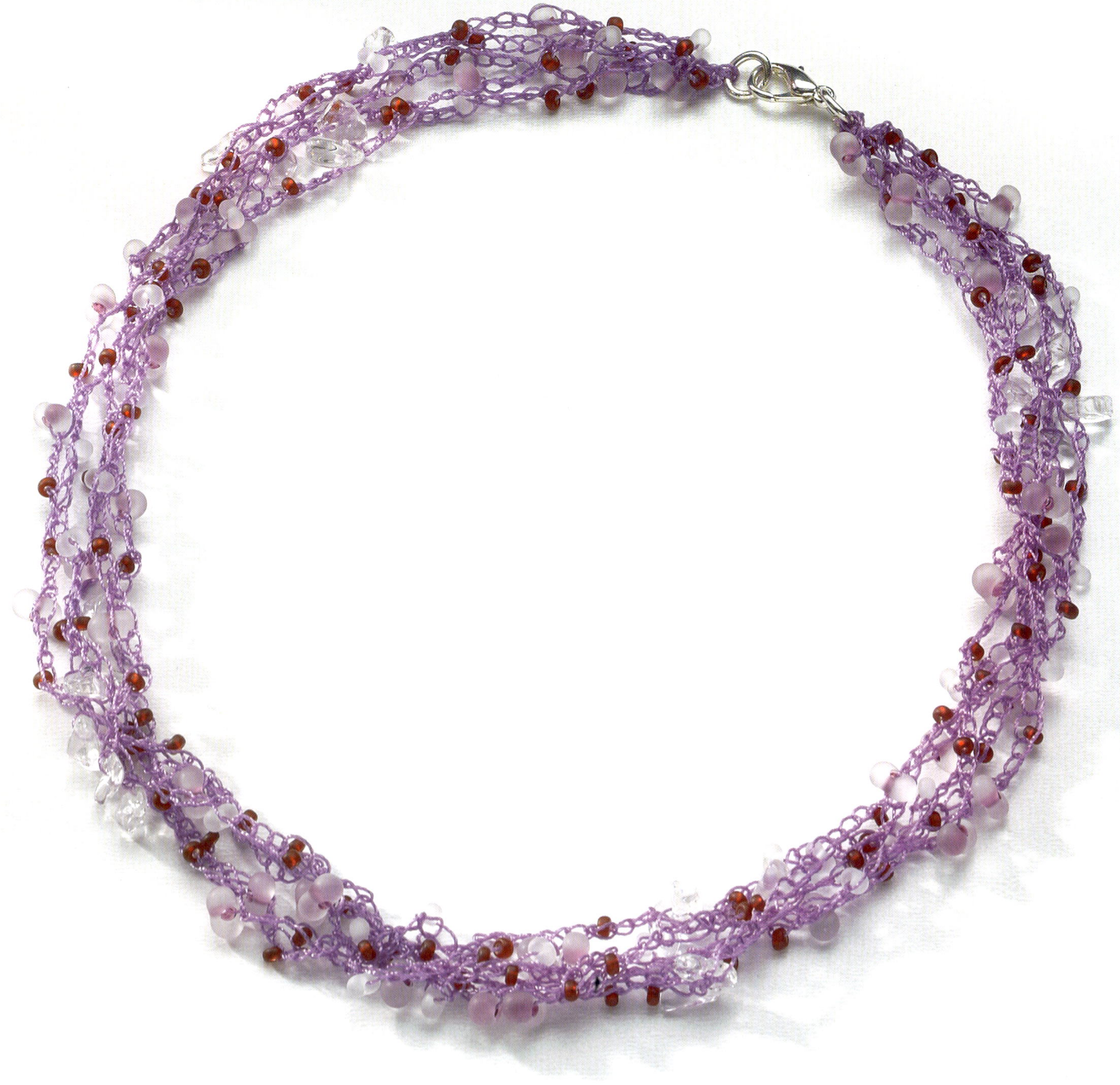

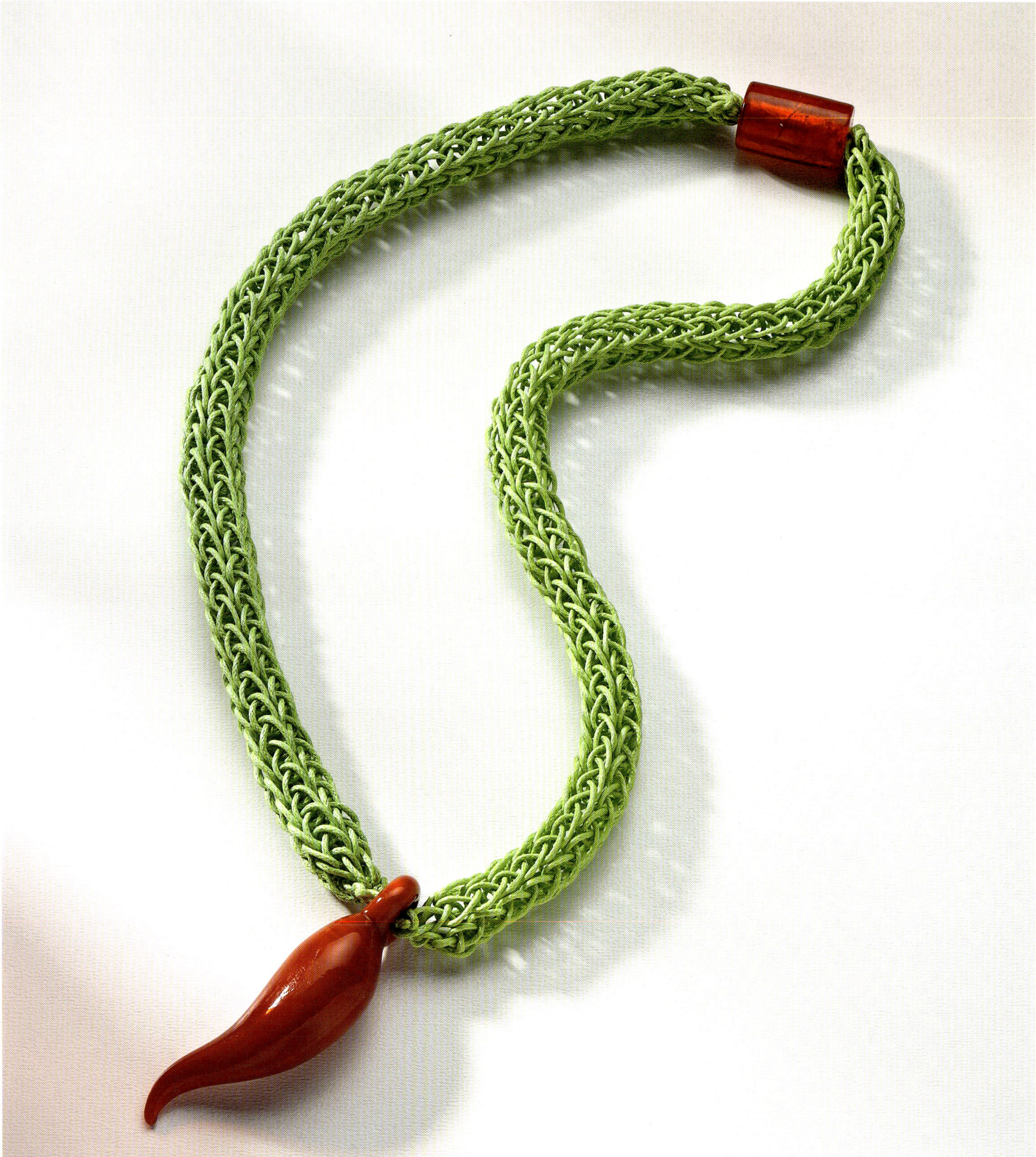

12 VENEZIA

For this project I used two nice glass objects I bought when I was on a trip to the famous glass-producing island of Murano, near Venice. Similar beads are found at antique shops or garage sales.

Make two knitted tubes, each 11½ inches long, in **SIMPLE** technique (**TECHNIQUE 2**). Cast off the end stitches of each tube and remove the tube from the loom. The end of the thread you used to cast off the end of the tube is used to pull the tube together. On the other side, thread the starting thread through the stitches so that the beginning of the tube can also be pulled together.

To attach the pendant, the thread ends of the two tubes are pulled through the jump ring from both sides. Run the threads through the last stitches of the opposite tube and then back through the jump ring to the exit side. Secure them there inconspicuously.

Do likewise to connect the other two ends of the knitted tubes through the glass bead at the rear center of the necklace. Since this necklace is long enough it doesn't need a clasp but can simply be pulled over the head.

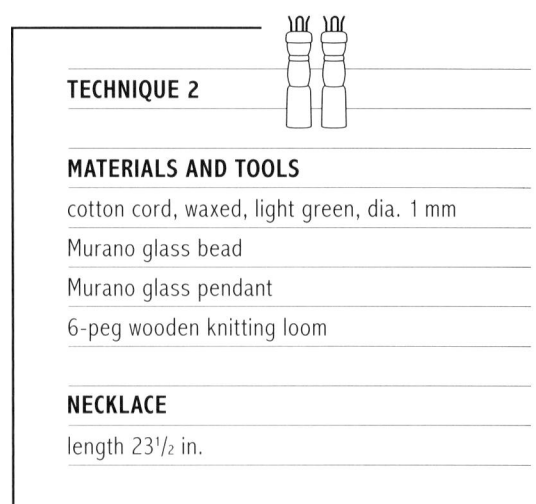

TECHNIQUE 2

MATERIALS AND TOOLS

cotton cord, waxed, light green, dia. 1 mm

Murano glass bead

Murano glass pendant

6-peg wooden knitting loom

NECKLACE

length 23½ in.

13 NETTED

TECHNIQUE 2

MATERIALS AND TOOLS

kitchen string, white

Fimo modeling resin, violet

craft knife

8-peg wooden knitting loom

NECKLACE

length 23 1/4 in.

First a 22-inch-long tube is made in **SIMPLE** technique (**TECHNIQUE 2**). Cast off the end stitches and remove the tube from the loom.

To make the decorative squares and the closure, the Fimo modeling resin is first kneaded until it is soft and can be worked easily. Then roll it out. The slab should be about 1/8 inch thick. Use a craft knife to cut out eight squares (1 x 1 inches) and one rectangle (1 1/8 x 1/4 inches). You will later need seven squares as decorative elements for the knitted tube, and one of the squares plus the rectangle will make up the closure.

Slightly bend up the decorative squares' edges at two opposite corners so the necklace will have extra depth.

For the closure, cut out of the remaining square a small square, 1/2 inch by 1/2 inch. Place this cutout so that one of the sides of the square is wider (about 5/16 inches). With a toothpick, make two holes through this edge of the square, and likewise make two holes in the center of the rectangle.

Harden all the decorative and clasp elements in the oven.

IMPORTANT: Make sure you follow the manufacturer's directions when using and hardening the modeling resin!

After cooling off the Fimo elements, insert them into the knitted tube. Since the knitted mesh is flexible the square elements are easy to insert. Make sure the distance between the elements and the closure is even. Once placed at the right location, the elements are held firmly in the tube and cannot move by themselves.

You can use the end of the thread you used to cast off the end of the tube to pull it together. At each end, the remaining thread is threaded through the holes of the corresponding closure section and sewn. By inserting the rectangular element into the square, the necklace is closed.

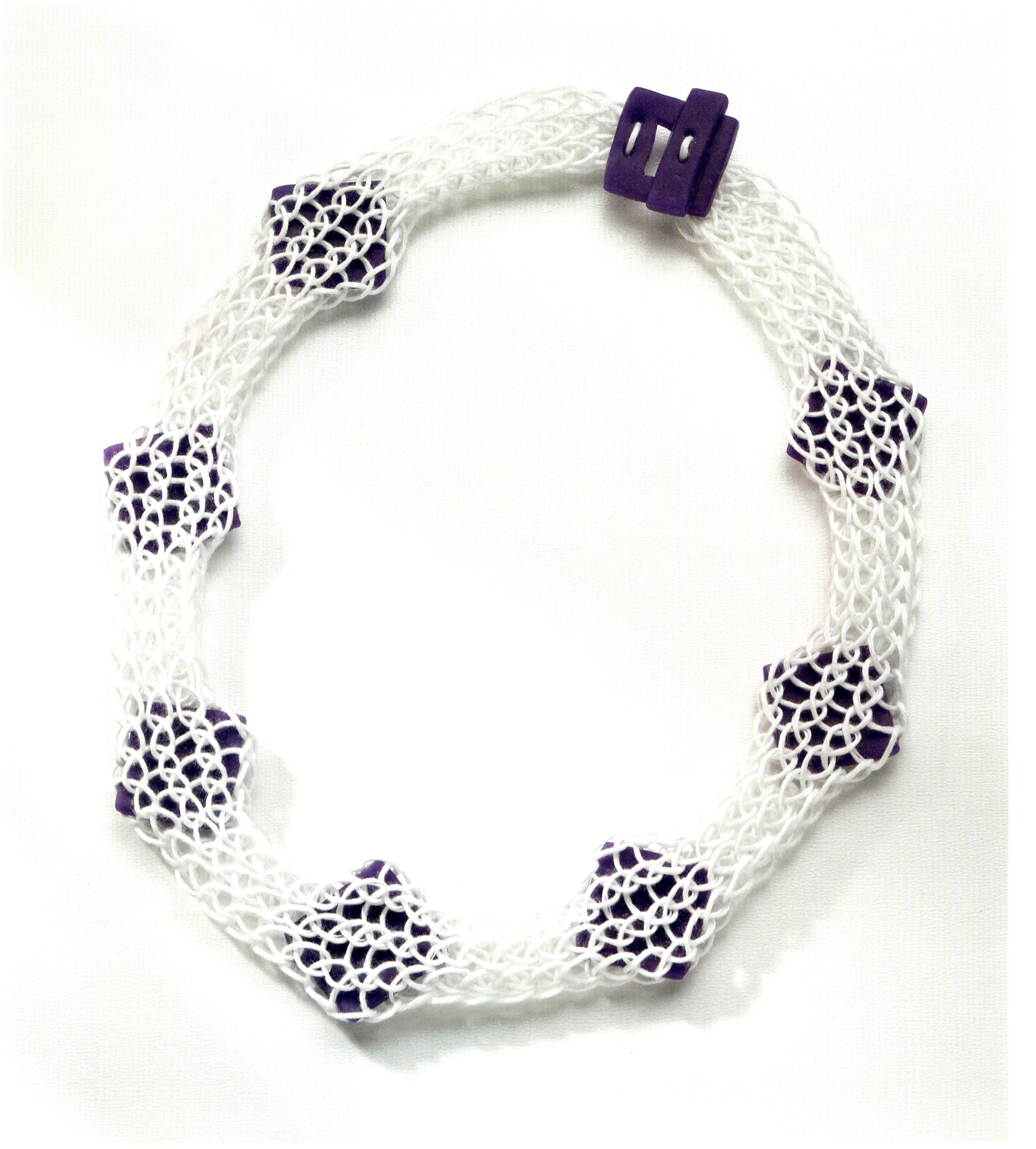

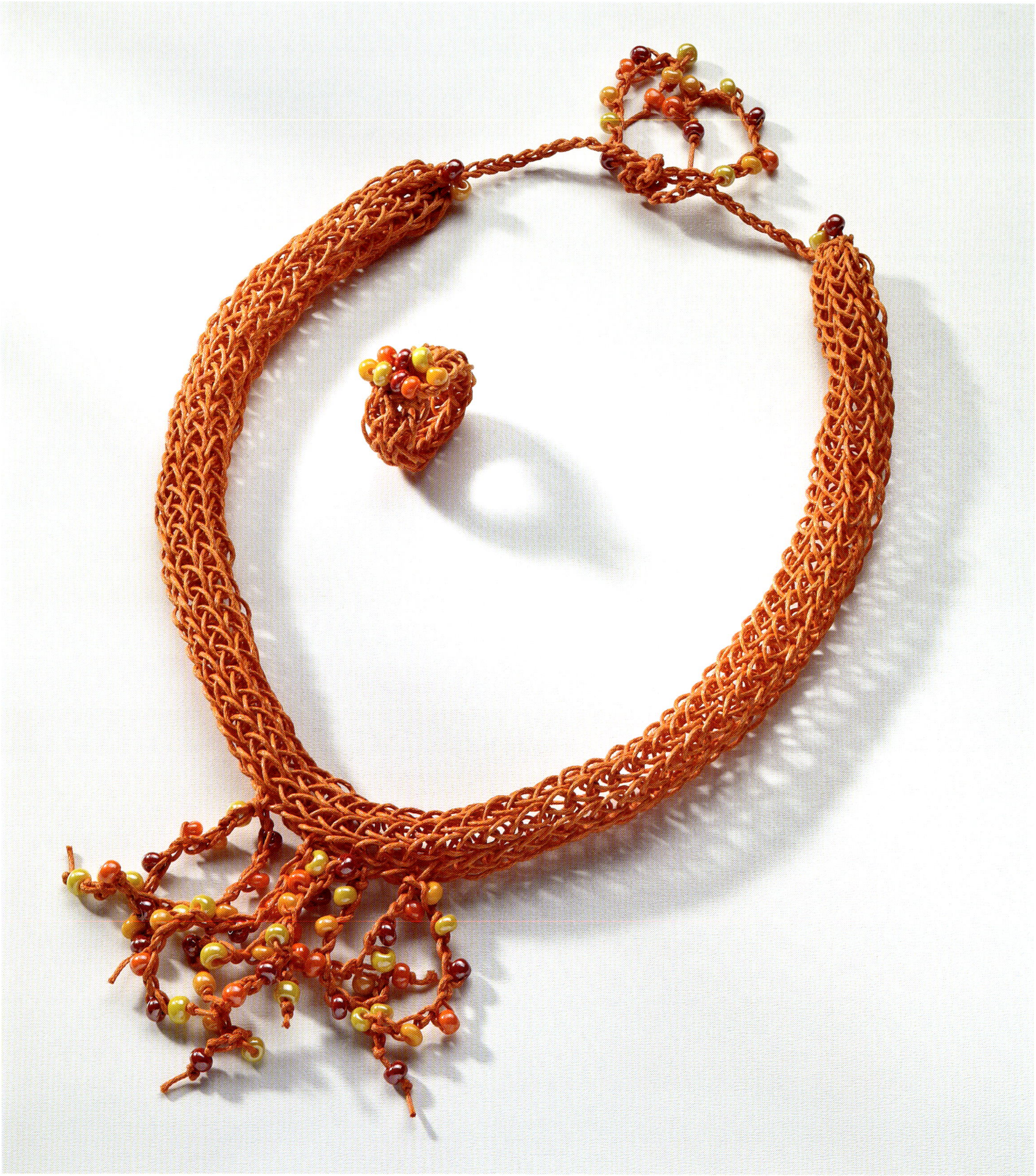

14 GYPSY

NECKLACE

For the necklace, work in **SIMPLE** knitting technique on the 8-peg loom to make a knitted tube 20 inches long (**TECHNIQUE 2**).

Cast off the end stitches and remove the tube from the loom. Pull both ends of the tube together as with projects no. 12 and 13.

IMPORTANT: Leave the beginning and end thread between 13 3/4 and 15 3/4 inches long!

Now the beads are threaded onto the cord following the sequence. This can be done without a needle since the beads have large holes.

For the closure make chain stitches from the beginning and end thread.

Before crocheting the first chain stitch, place the two beads at the end of the tube.

Then make 22 chain stitches without bead and crochet in seven glass beads so that there is an "empty" chain stitch between them. Finish with one chain stitch. Then cut off the cord and pull it entirely through the last stitch to cast off. Now another bead is threaded onto the cord and affixed with a knot. Cut back the rest of the thread to 3/8 inch long.

For the decorative fringes, crochet four chain stitches at the center of the necklace. Start with the threads as described in **TECHNIQUE 1.**

For the chain stitches always work alternating one chain stitch without bead and one with bead. To secure the chain stitch threads crochet the first thread directly to it. Once you have reached half of the length of the necklace, insert the crochet hook into the mesh of the knitted tube, grab the cord, and pull it through this stitch and the chain stitch which is still on the crochet hook. Then the second half of the chain stitch thread is finished.

Then the cord is cut off and cast off. Now add one more bead to both ends of the chain stitch thread and affix it with a knot. The rest of the cord can now be cut off.

RING

Using the 6-peg wooden loom, make a tube 3 1/8 to 3 1/2 inches long (depending on the size of the ring). Cast off the last stitches and remove the tube from the loom.

IMPORTANT: Don't pull the ends of the tubes together but press them flat so that the two ends of the cords are lying at the outer edges of the flat tube. Place the beginning and end of the tube together so that they don't overlap!

The beginning and end of the knitted tube should be sewn inconspicuously with one of the two ends of the cord. Thread four glass beads onto the other end of the cord and thread it through the stitch at the opposite edge. Add four more beads and run the cord back to its starting side and sew it. The beads now hide the seam. Make sure you have a nice-looking sequence of beads.

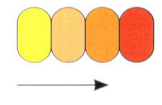

> **TIP:** Crochet the thread with different lengths (between 14 and 16 beads) to achieve a looser look.

TECHNIQUE 2

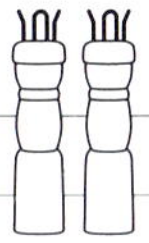

MATERIALS AND TOOLS

cotton cord, waxed, orange, dia. 1 mm

about 90 glass beads with large holes, yellow-orange, orange, red, opaque, dia. 5.4 mm

8-peg wooden knitting loom (necklace)

8-peg wooden knitting loom (ring)

crochet hook, no. 2.5

NECKLACE

length 20–23 1/2 in.

SEQUENCE OF BEADS

15 BAJAZZO

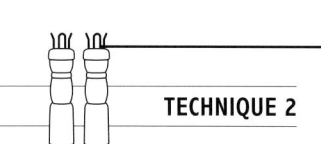

TECHNIQUE 2

MATERIALS AND TOOLS

yarn, violet, appropriate for crochet hook sizes 4 to 5

fringed yarn, various violet and gray tones

8-peg wooden knitting loom

crochet hook, no. 2.5

NECKLACE

length 22 in.

As described under **TECHNIQUE 2,** make a **SIMPLE** technique tube with a length of 21 1/4 inches. Cast off the end stitches and remove the tube from the loom.

Because the soft yarn tube tends to collapse after knitting I sewed a tube of cotton fabric (lining fabric) of matching color, using a piece of fabric 2 inches wide and 21 1/4 inches long, and inserted it inside the knitted tube to provide more firmness and volume.

TIP: To keep the sewn seams from being visible, you turn the fabric tube inside out after sewing it by using a safety pin. Using a safety pin is also a handy way to easily pull the fabric tube through the knitted tube.

Now the edges of the fabric tube are flipped inward and sewn. Pull together the two ends of the knitted tube.

For the clasp, crochet a chain stitch thread with twelve stitches from the end thread and close to make a loop. Now the start and end of the thread can be secured.

A small pompon is made for the other half of the closure. Make a chain stitch thread from fringe yarn, about 4 to 4 3/4 inches long, and close to a loop. Now pull this ring together at several places by inserting the crochet hook and pulling through the thread. Repeat this as many times as necessary until the mesh has formed a small and firm pompon. If the fringes get stuck pull them out with the crochet hook. The pompon is sewn to the end of the tube with the two ends of the thread.

For the decorative fringes at the center of the necklace, cut off several 4-inch lengths of the fringe yarn and knot them into the knitted tube.

Now grab the fringe thread at the center (the "fold") and pull it about 1/2 inch through the stitch of the knitted tube. The fringe thread now lies as a stitch on the knitting needle. Grab the two ends of the fringe thread with the knitting needle and pull through the stitch. This way the thread is secured to the tube. Do likewise to tightly knot the fringe threads in several rows into the knitted tube.

IMPORTANT: Make sure the fringes fan out symmetrically toward the center.

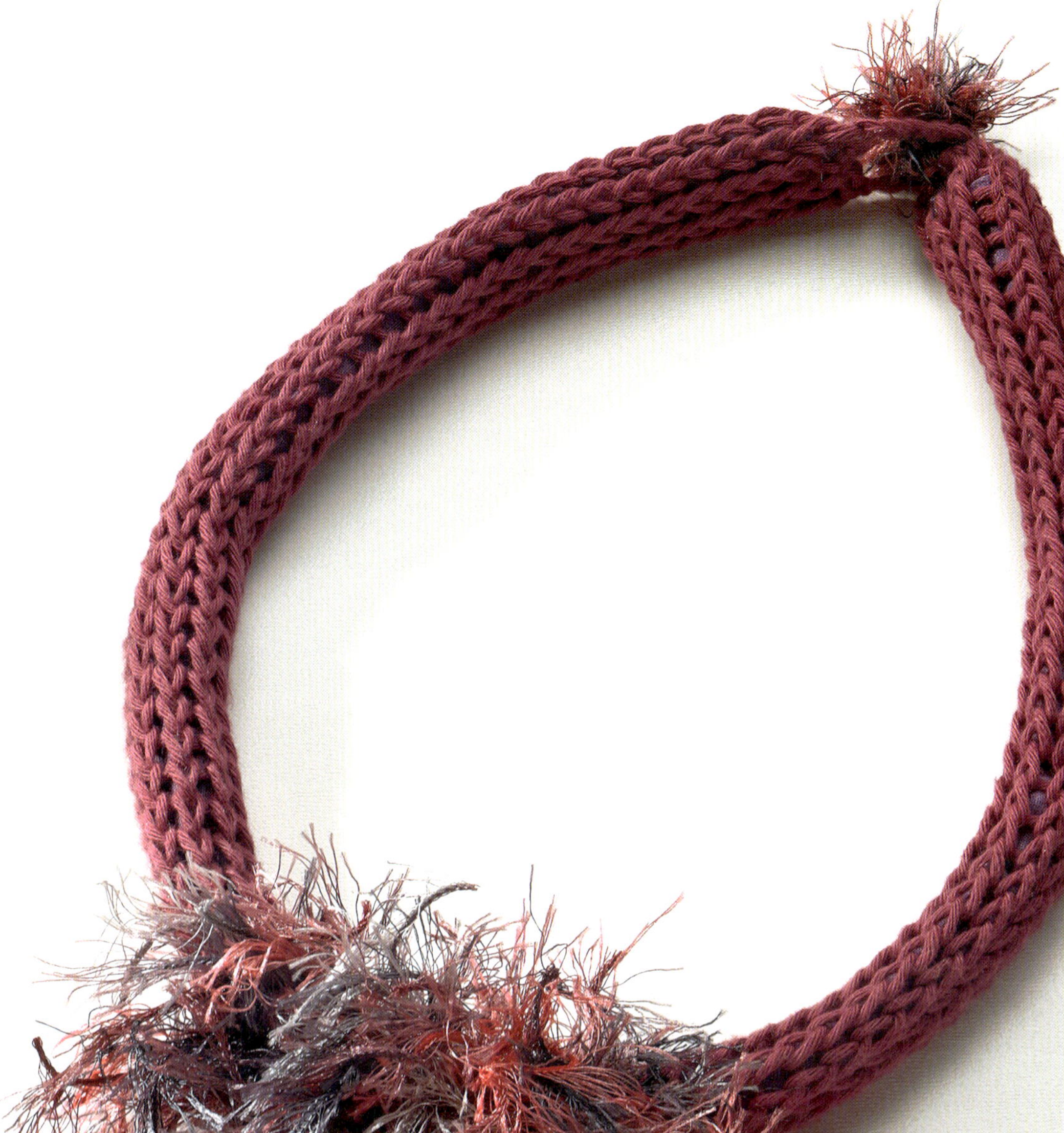

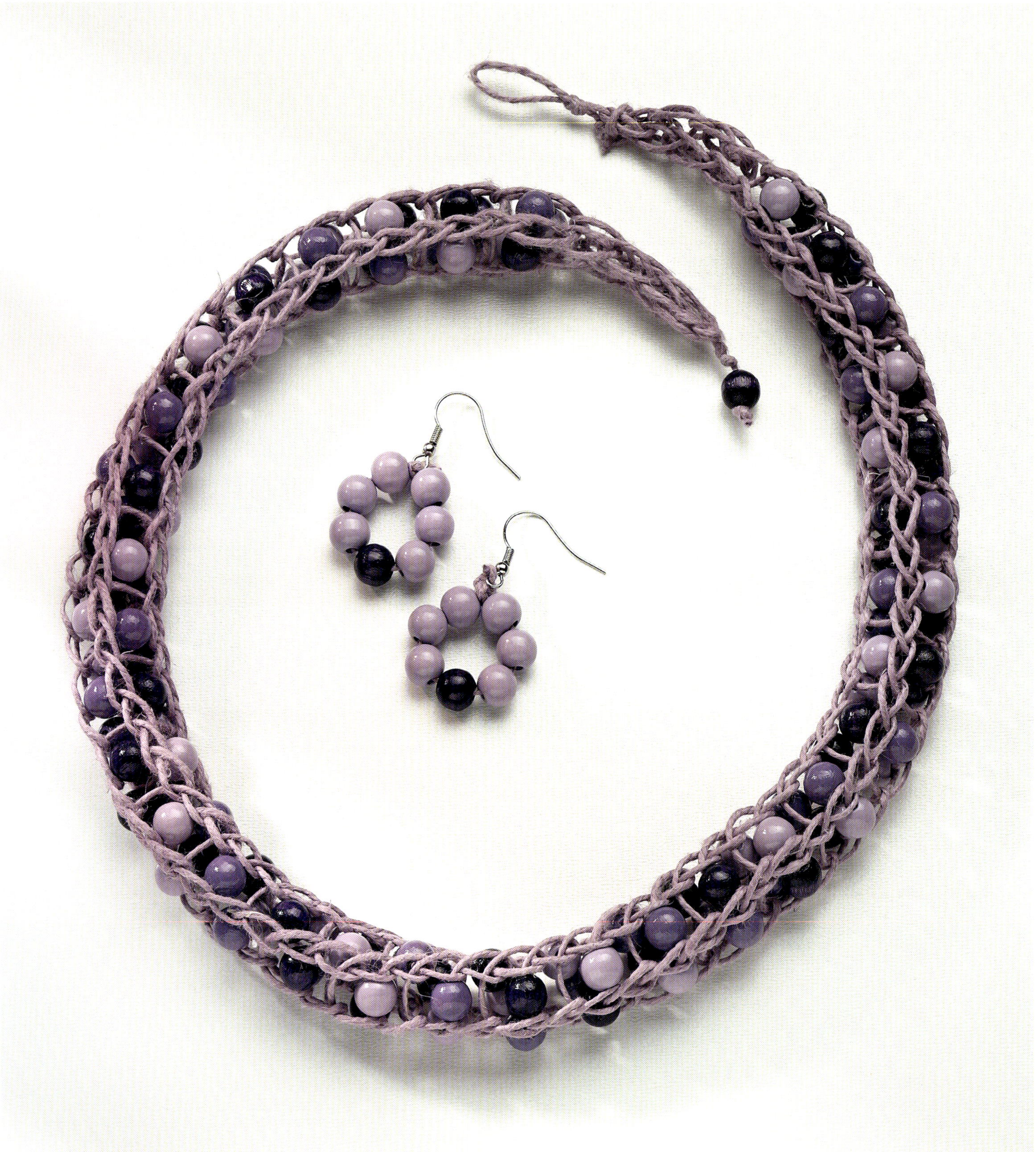

16 BEAD GAME

NECKLACE

Thread the beads as shown.

Now, using the 4-peg loom, knit in **SIMPLE** technique (**TECHNIQUE 2**) four rows without beads. Then one bead each is inserted between the pegs with each winding round (a total of four beads) and incorporated into the knitting round. Now another winding round follows, without beads, and another knitting round. From now on four beads are added at each second winding round until 32 winding rounds with beads have been made. Finally, four winding and knitting rounds without beads are made.

Cast off the stitches and remove the knitting tube from the loom. Both ends of the tube are now pulled together.

For the closure, make two knots on one end of the string, add a bead, and make another knot in order to secure it in place. Then cut off the end of the thread.

Knot the string on the other end into a loop, close to the end of the tube. Cut off the thread.

EARRINGS

For each earring, thread three light-colored, one dark, and three light beads onto a short length of string. Pull the ends of the string from both sides through the jump ring of the earring hook and knot both ends. Then cut off the remaining string.

TECHNIQUE 2

MATERIALS AND TOOLS

linen cord, violet, dia. 1.5 mm

143 wood beads in three shades of violet (light, medium, dark), dia. 8 mm

flax cord, violet, dia. 1.5 mm

2 earring hooks, silver

4-peg wooden knitting loom

NECKLACE

length 26 in.

SEQUENCE OF BEADS

17 ORANGE MELANGE

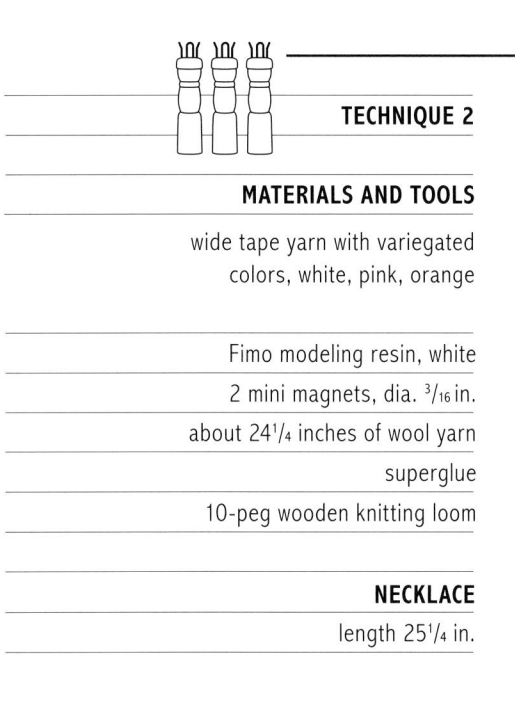

TECHNIQUE 2

MATERIALS AND TOOLS

wide tape yarn with variegated colors, white, pink, orange

Fimo modeling resin, white
2 mini magnets, dia. $3/16$ in.
about $24 1/4$ inches of wool yarn
superglue
10-peg wooden knitting loom

NECKLACE

length $25 1/4$ in.

Using the 10-peg wooden knitting loom, knit two tubes, each 17 inches long (**TECHNIQUE 2, SIMPLE** technique). Cast off both tubes but don't pull together the ends just yet.

For the decorative elements make three spheres, about $1/2$ inch in diameter, from Fimo modeling resin and press them into flat discs about $1 1/2$ inches wide. The discs only have to be roughly the same size and somewhat round. Bore a hole with a diameter of $1/2$ inch into the center of each (I have used an apple corer). Bend up the edges of the rings into a wavy shape.

Make two "hats" for the clasp. Start out again with a small sphere and press it into a flat disc. Then press the disc over the end of a pencil. This results in a type of funnel where you can later glue in the wool yarn. Bend the edge of the funnel in a wavy shape. Finally, press the mini magnet into the center.

IMPORTANT: Make sure the top side of the hat is not rounded but flat, and that both magnets are set flush with the Fimo resin so the two clasp sections will connect to each other later on.

The decorative elements and the two segments of the clasp are hardened in the oven (with the magnets). Make sure you follow the manufacturer's directions when using and hardening the modeling resin! If the magnets will not stick to the Fimo halves you can glue them in with superglue.

Now the wool yarn is inserted into the knitted tube (see page 14, image 12). This is easily done with a large safety pin. Then pull the three decorative elements and then the second knitted tube onto the wool yarn. Because the two knitted cords are longer than the yarn they are clinched while threaded. This provides more volume and gives a special look to the necklace.

Now pull together the knitted tubes at the ends and secure the ends of the threads.

Finally the wool yarn is glued into the two clasp sections. Use enough superglue to be sure of the hold.

Thanks to the clasp sections and the decorative elements, the ends of the knitted tubes are nicely hidden and the matte white elements coordinate perfectly with the color play of the yarn.

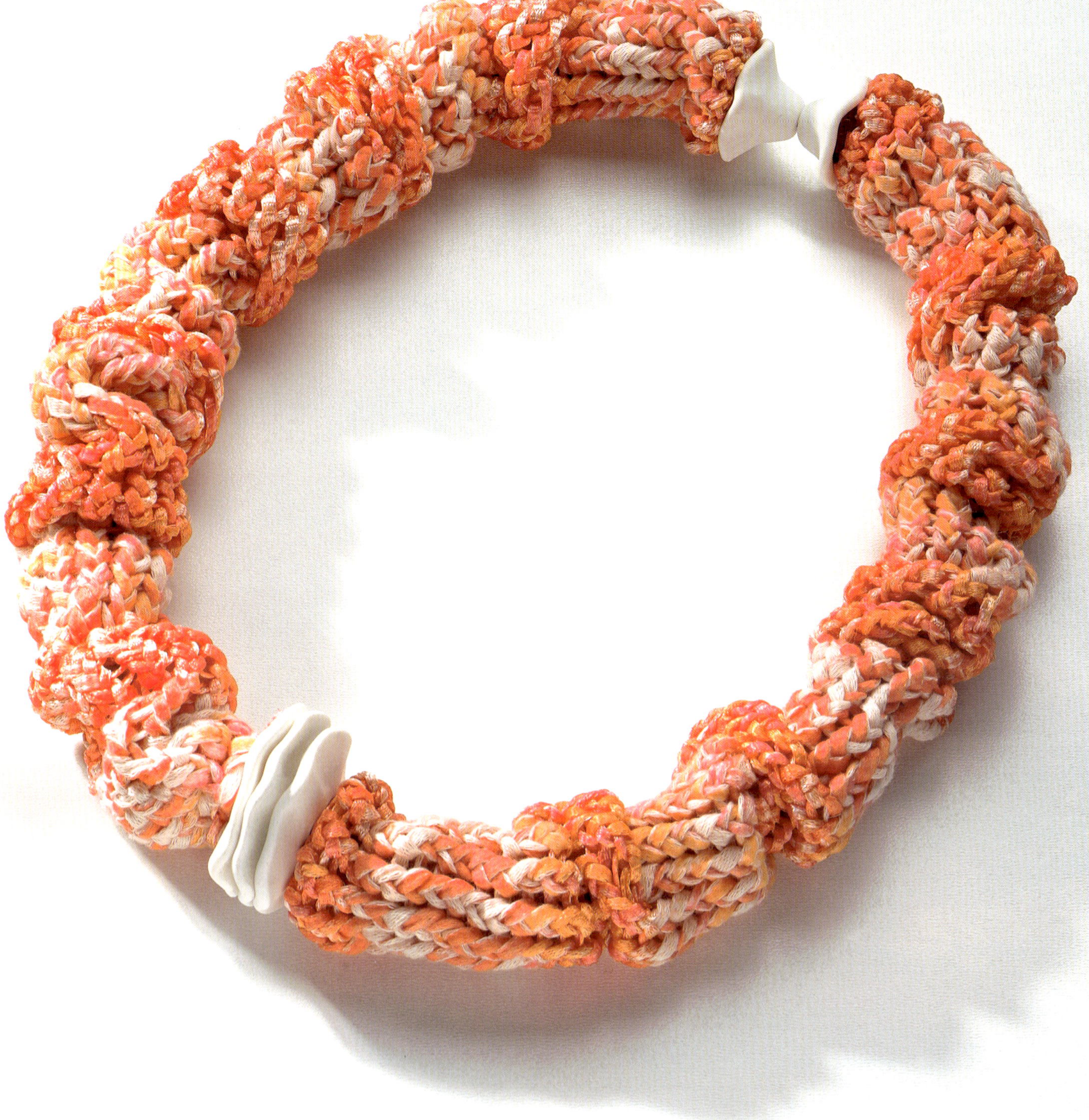

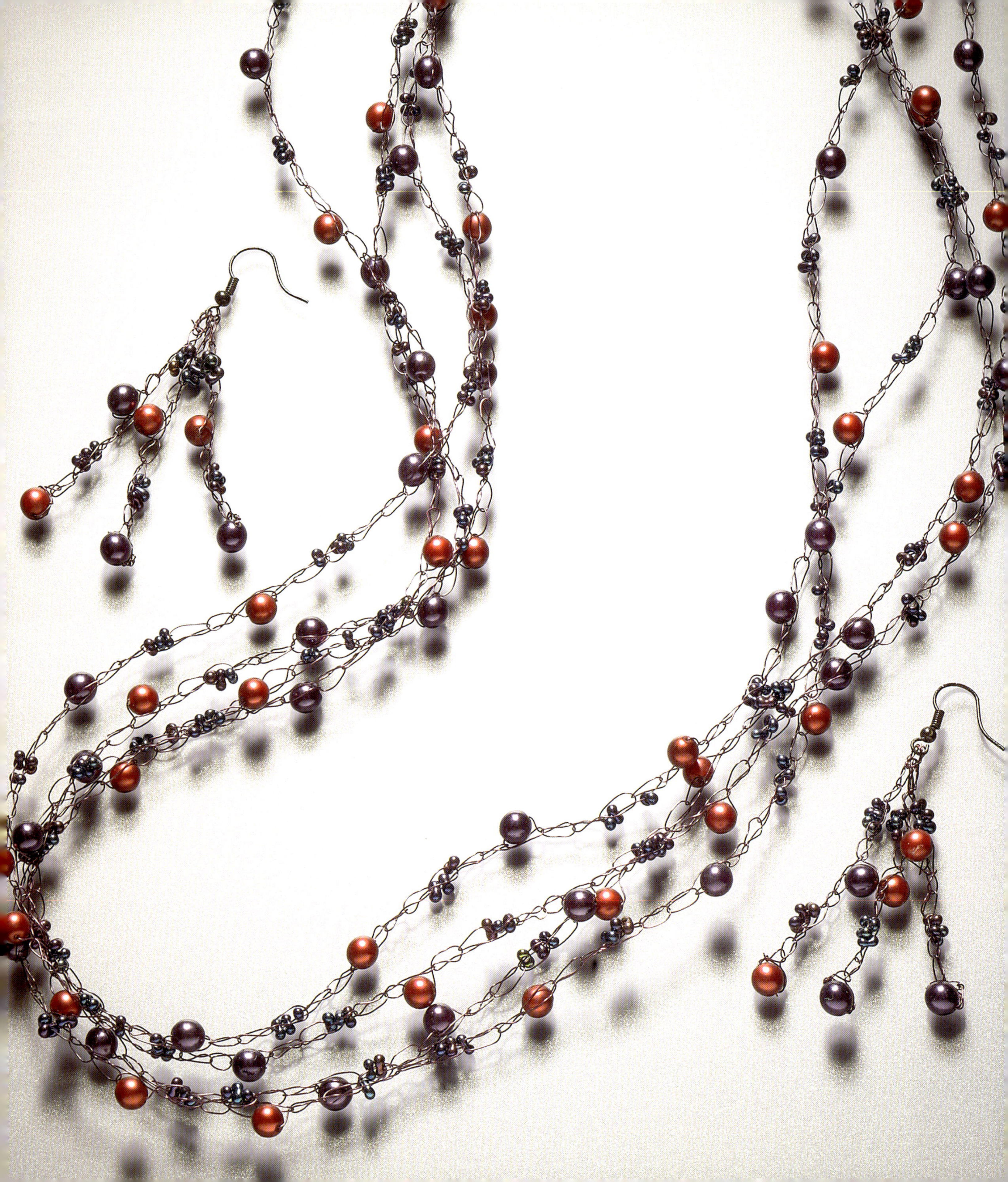

ELEGANT FASHION JEWELRY

"A WOMAN SHOULD DRESS EVERY DAY AS IF SHE COULD MEET THE LOVE OF HER LIFE."

Coco Chanel

18 MAIDEN

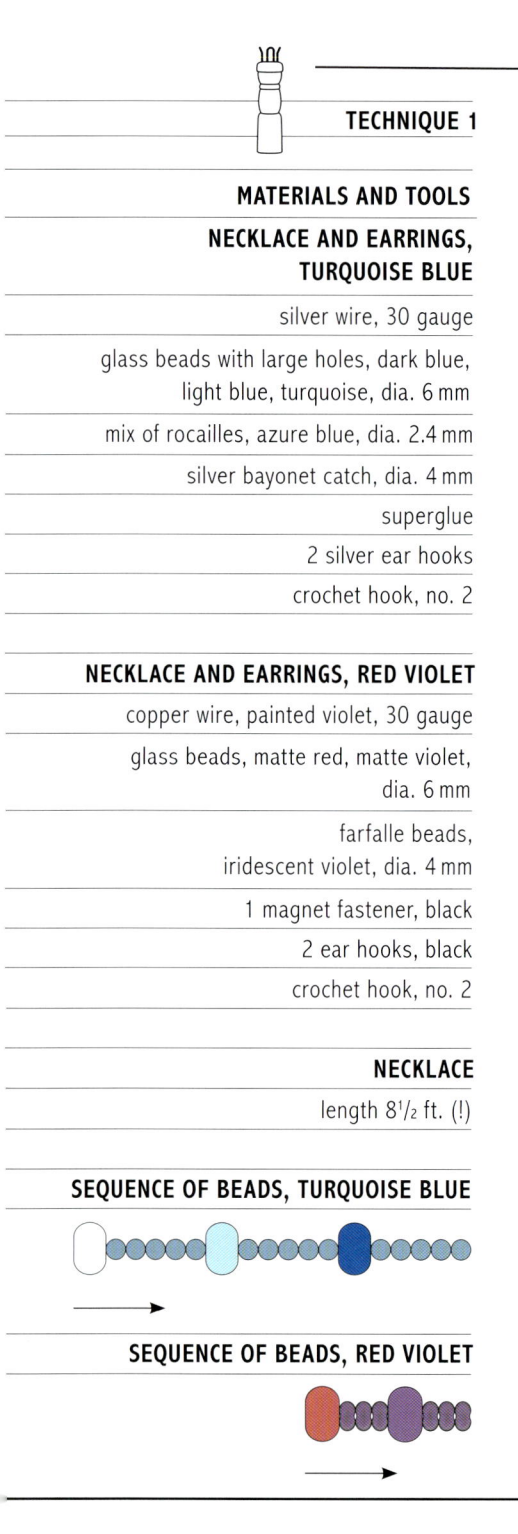

TECHNIQUE 1

MATERIALS AND TOOLS

NECKLACE AND EARRINGS, TURQUOISE BLUE

silver wire, 30 gauge

glass beads with large holes, dark blue, light blue, turquoise, dia. 6 mm

mix of rocailles, azure blue, dia. 2.4 mm

silver bayonet catch, dia. 4 mm

superglue

2 silver ear hooks

crochet hook, no. 2

NECKLACE AND EARRINGS, RED VIOLET

copper wire, painted violet, 30 gauge

glass beads, matte red, matte violet, dia. 6 mm

farfalle beads, iridescent violet, dia. 4 mm

1 magnet fastener, black

2 ear hooks, black

crochet hook, no. 2

NECKLACE

length 8½ ft. (!)

SEQUENCE OF BEADS, TURQUOISE BLUE

SEQUENCE OF BEADS, RED VIOLET

NECKLACE

I created these necklaces and earrings for my two daughters using their favorite colors.

Start with six chain stitches (**TECHNIQUE 1**) without beads for the chain stitch thread. Then crochet while alternating one chain stitch with bead (or rocaille/farfalle) and two chain stitches without bead. The wire is cast off at the last stitch.

The entire necklace has a length of 8½ feet! Depending on how many times you wrap it around the neck it can be worn at different lengths.

If wrapped only three or four times the look is very delicate. With several (shorter) loops the play of colors becomes more prominent because of the number of beads next to each other.

The necklace features a catch so it can also be worn tightly around the neck. For the turquoise-blue necklace I have used a bayonet catch which is attached to the ends of the threads with superglue.

The red-violet necklace features a black magnet catch with jump rings. Here the wire ends of the thread are wound through the jump ring several times and back to the thread. Twist it and shorten.

EARRINGS

Three chain stitch threads of about 2 inches long are crocheted for the earrings. With each thread, start with three chain stitches and work in two rocailles or farfalle and two beads. Between them are two chain stitches each without beads. After the second bead crochet another chain stitch and cast off. Twist the end of the wire at the last bead and shorten. Do likewise with the end of the wire at the other side.

The three small threads are each hooked into the jump ring of the ear hook with the first of the three chain stitches. Close the jump ring tightly so the thin wire won't slip.

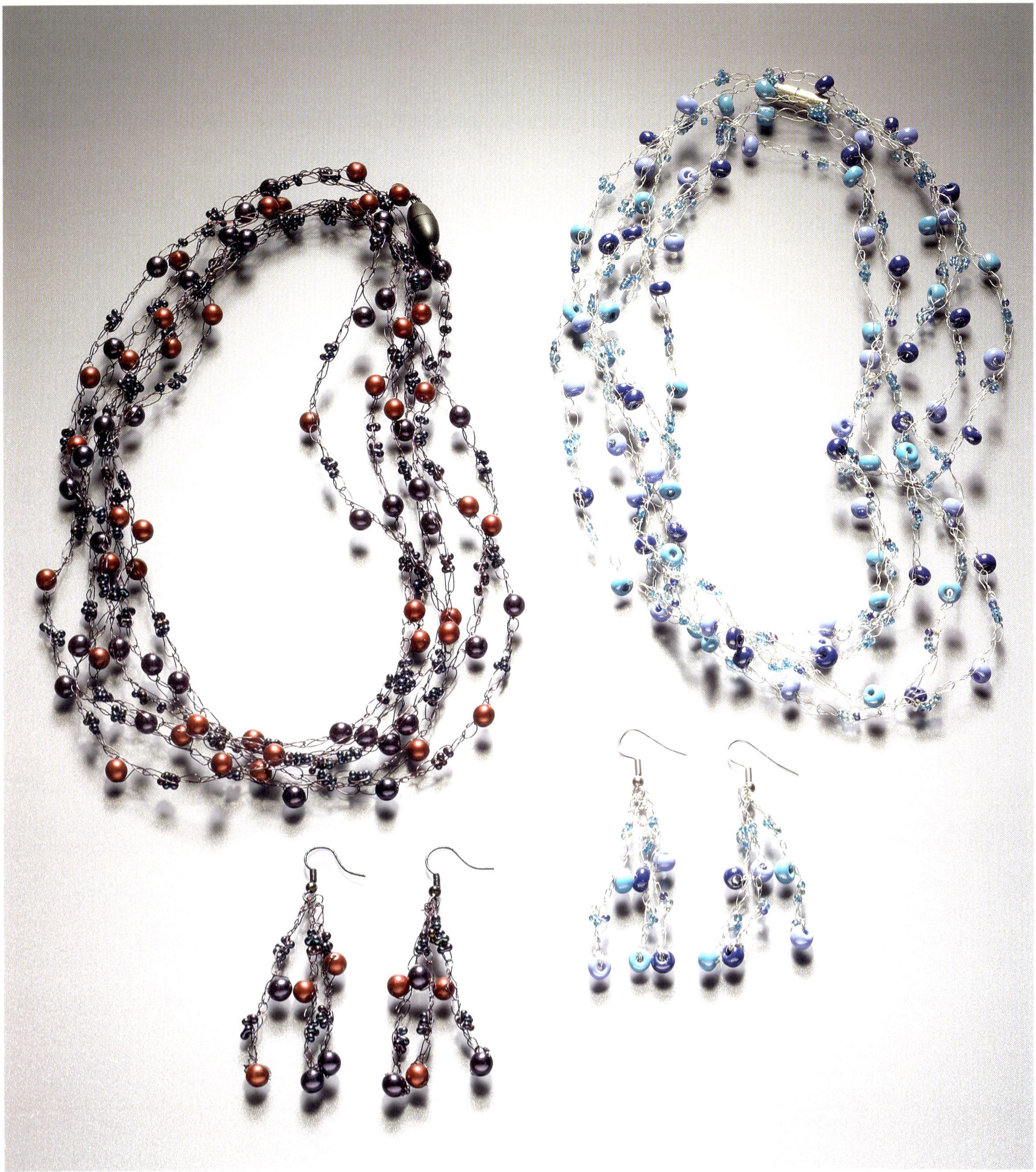

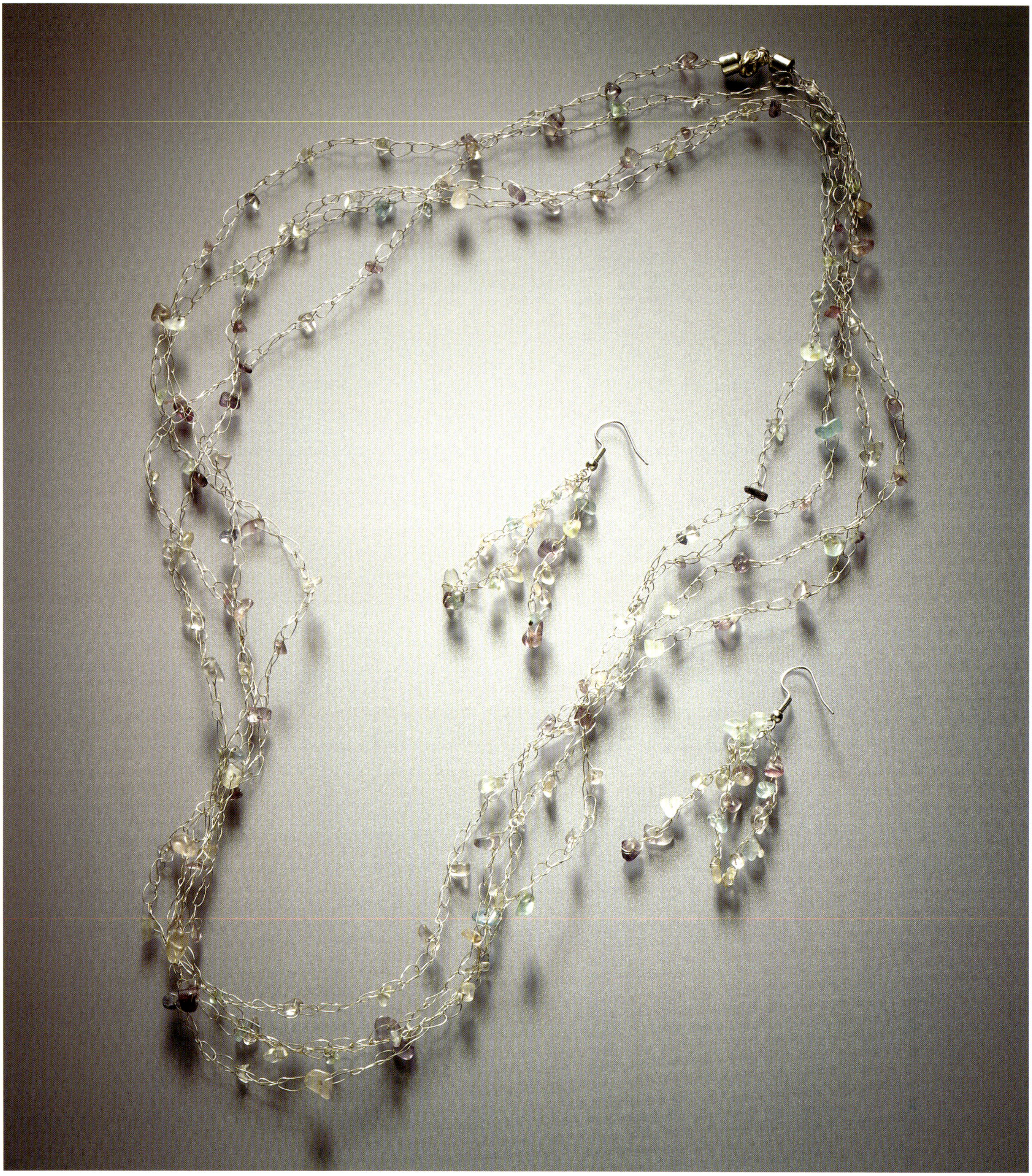

19 AQUARELLE

NECKLACE

After making the "maiden" necklaces, I also made a version for myself.

This delicate necklace comes alive from the changing color play of the fluorite beads, from white, light green, light blue, and light pink to violet.

First the beads are threaded onto the silver wire. Use a crochet hook (no. 2.5) to knit relatively large chain stitches, which add further lightness to the necklace.

Start with four chain stitches and then crochet alternatingly three chain stitches without and one chain stitch with a bead. The total length of the chain stitch thread should be about 6 1/2 feet. The ends of the wires are twisted and shortened.

At both ends of the thread the last three stitches are twisted together into a twine and glued into the cylinder caps of the lobster claw clasp with superglue.

The necklace can be worn long with two loops. However, due to the catch it is also possible to wear the necklace close to the neck with many loops. In this case the color play of the fluorites is particularly attractive.

EARRINGS

For the earrings three small threads are made. I have selected the smallest fluorite beads and threaded them onto silver wire.

Use the thin hook (no. 1.5) to alternatingly crochet two chain stitches without and one chain stitch with a bead until the seven beads have been worked in. After the last bead, one more chain stitch is made. Twist the ends of the thread, shorten them, and hook the small threads into the ear hooks with the first chain stitch.

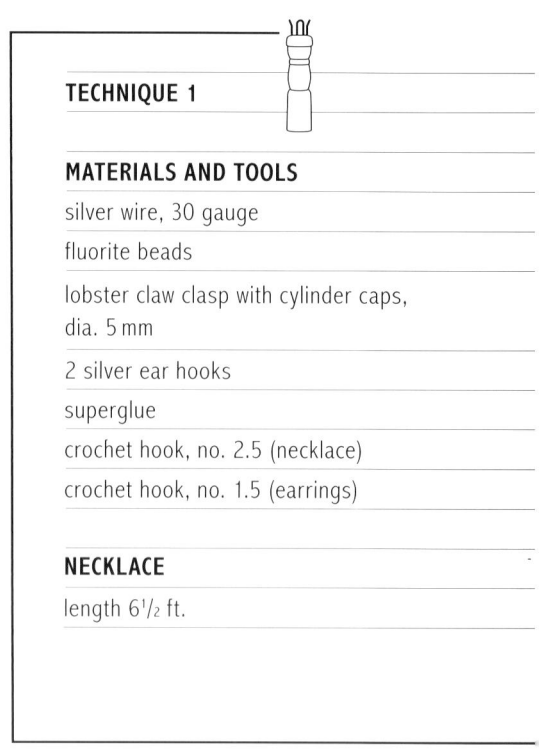

TECHNIQUE 1

MATERIALS AND TOOLS

silver wire, 30 gauge

fluorite beads

lobster claw clasp with cylinder caps, dia. 5 mm

2 silver ear hooks

superglue

crochet hook, no. 2.5 (necklace)

crochet hook, no. 1.5 (earrings)

NECKLACE

length 6 1/2 ft.

20 SPRINGTIME AWAKENING

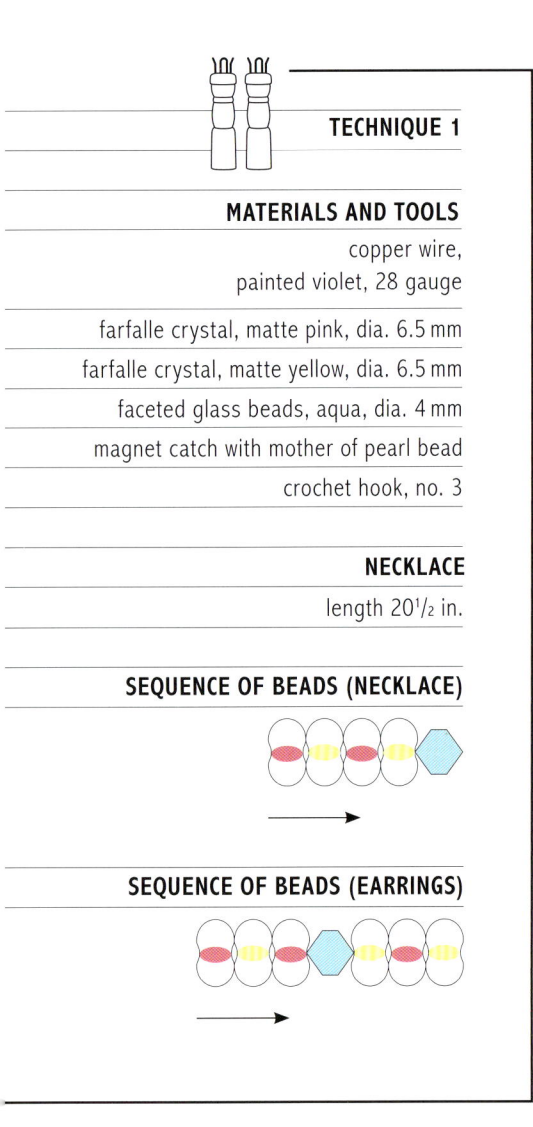

TECHNIQUE 1

MATERIALS AND TOOLS

copper wire,
painted violet, 28 gauge

farfalle crystal, matte pink, dia. 6.5 mm

farfalle crystal, matte yellow, dia. 6.5 mm

faceted glass beads, aqua, dia. 4 mm

magnet catch with mother of pearl bead

crochet hook, no. 3

NECKLACE

length 20½ in.

SEQUENCE OF BEADS (NECKLACE)

SEQUENCE OF BEADS (EARRINGS)

NECKLACE

For this necklace five individual chain stitch threads are crocheted, between 9¼ and 9¾ inches long.

First thread the beads as shown in the diagram. Then you start with two to four chain stitches for the individual threads and work a bead into every other stitch. So there is an "empty" chain stitch between each bead.

Once all the five threads have been made, the wire ends on one side are twisted, run through the jump ring of the magnet catch, and twisted behind the jump ring so an 8-mm wire peg is created. Shorten all the wires.

Now slightly twist the five chain stitch threads around each other. Due to the slightly different lengths of the individual threads the result is a nice curve and the necklace gets additional volume.

Then secure the magnet catch to the ends of the wires on the other end as well, as described previously.

TIP:
Start each thread with a bead of a different color so the colors of the beads are evenly distributed along the piece of jewelry. Also make sure the chain stitches aren't too small. Otherwise the chain stitch threads will look somewhat stiff. With larger stitches the look is more loose and airy.

EARRINGS

For each of the earrings, the sequence of the beads must be threaded as described so the faceted glass bead lies at the lower center inside of the loop.

Start the chain stitch thread with three chain stitches and work a bead into every other chain stitch. Finish with three chain stitches. Twist the two ends of the wires and run them through the jump ring of the ear hook. Twist the wires below the jump ring so a small peg of about 5 mm is created. Tightly close the jump ring so the thin wire can't slip.

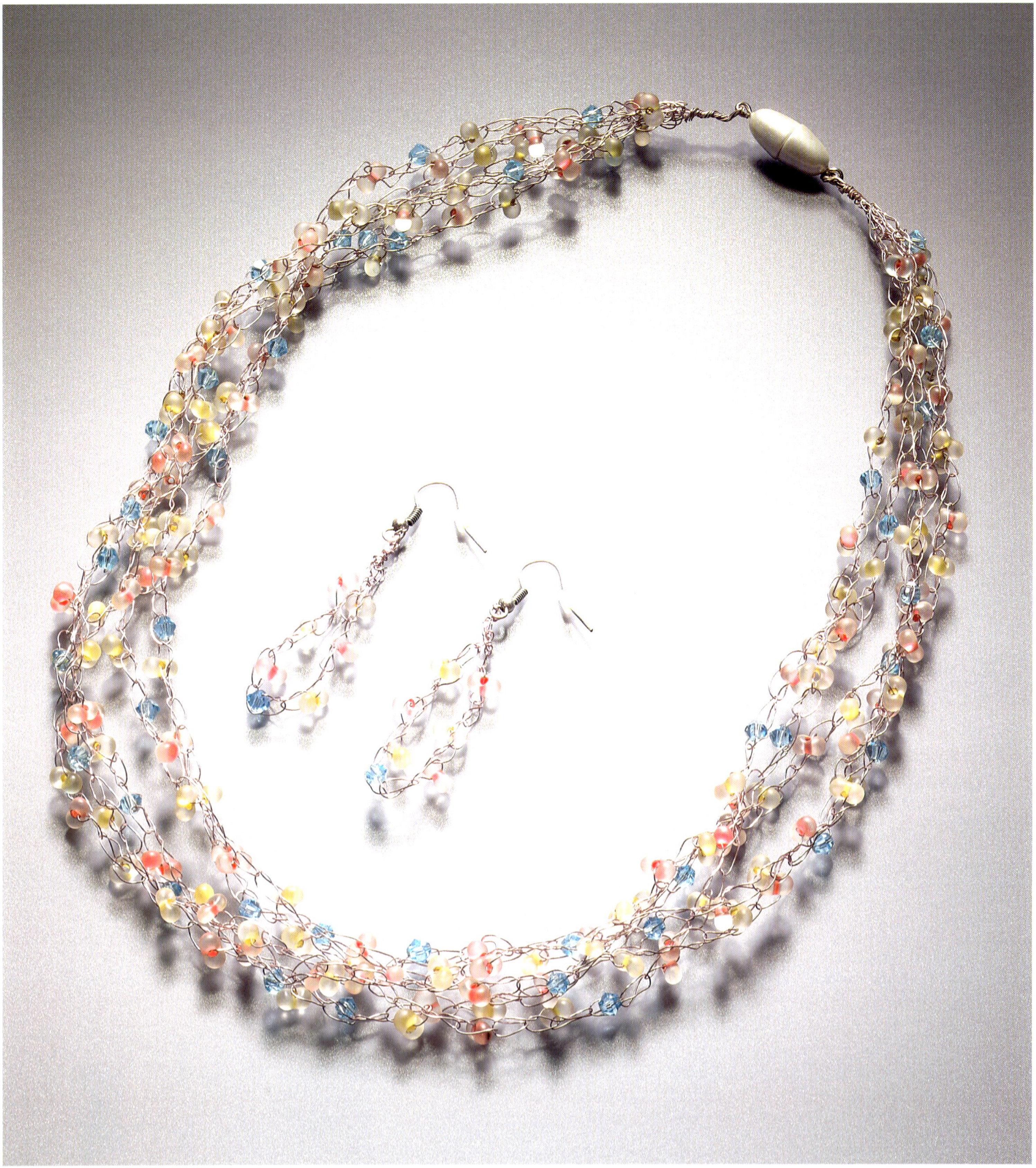

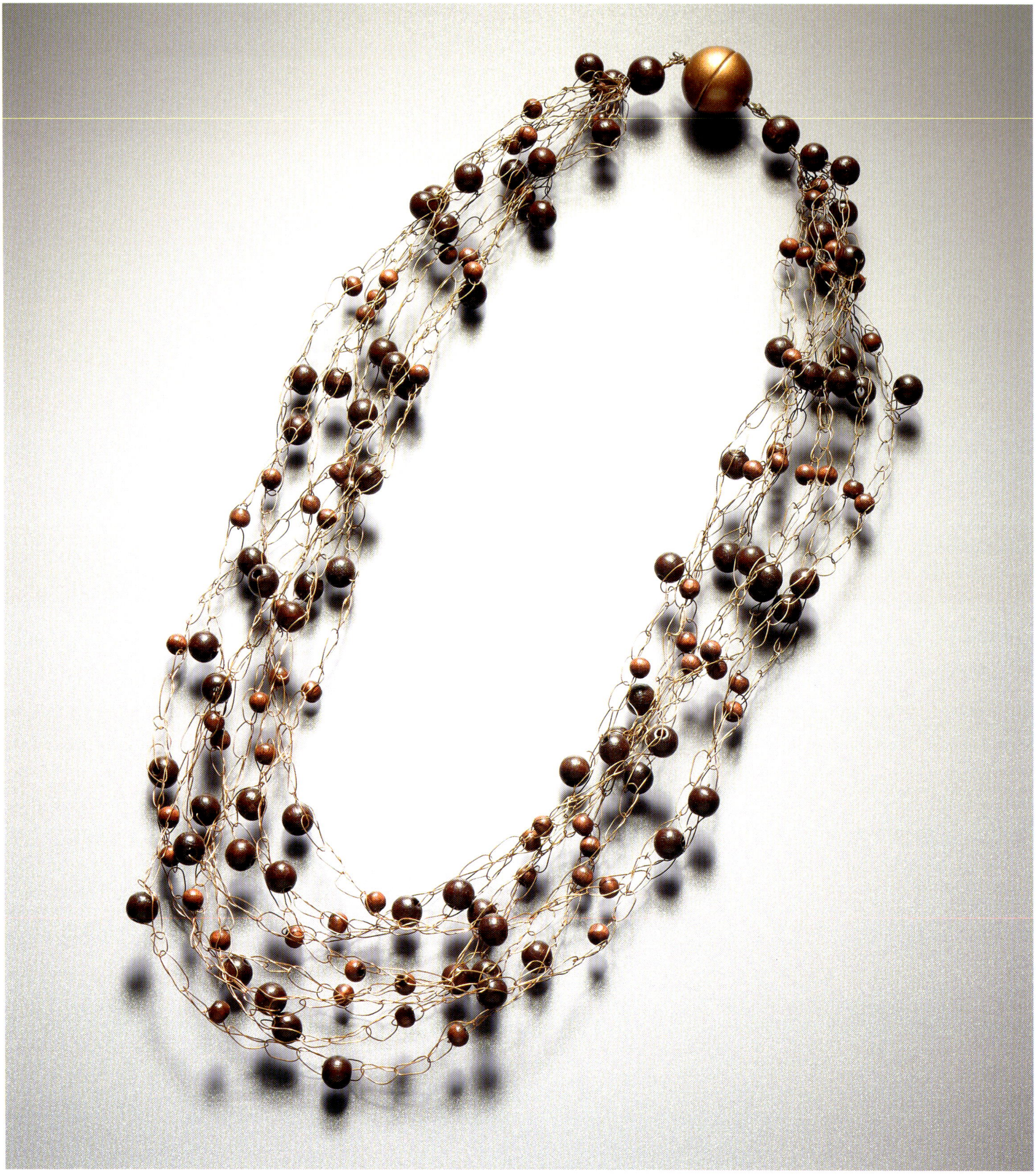

21 WOOD TONES

First thread the beads following the sequence shown, and then make a chain stitch thread with a length of 12 1/2 feet (!).

Alternatingly crochet three chain stitches without and one chain stitch with a bead. Start and end the chain stitch thread with three chain stitches each.

IMPORTANT: Using a no. 3 crochet hook results in nice loose stitches. This prevents the wire from becoming too stiff and the mesh gets a light look despite the dark beads.

To form the long necklace, stick two pins 18 1/2 inches apart into a piece of cork or styrofoam. Start at one peg with the end of the thread, and wind it four times around the pins so that each new round lies outside the previous one. This results in each round being slightly longer and provides more volume to the necklace. The beginning and end of the thread will meet at the first pin.

Then attach the eight strands together at the point which lies at the beginning/end pin. To attach one end you can use the beginning and/or end thread. For the other end, cut a piece of wire 4 inches long from the spool, run it through a chain stitch, and twist the beginning with the stitch.

IMPORTANT: Run the wire on both sides through the chain stitches so it catches all of the eight strands.

To attach the magnet catch, the wires on both sides are first run through the large wood bead, then through the jump ring of the magnet catch and back to the bead. After the wood bead, the ends of the wires are twisted with the remaining wire and shortened.

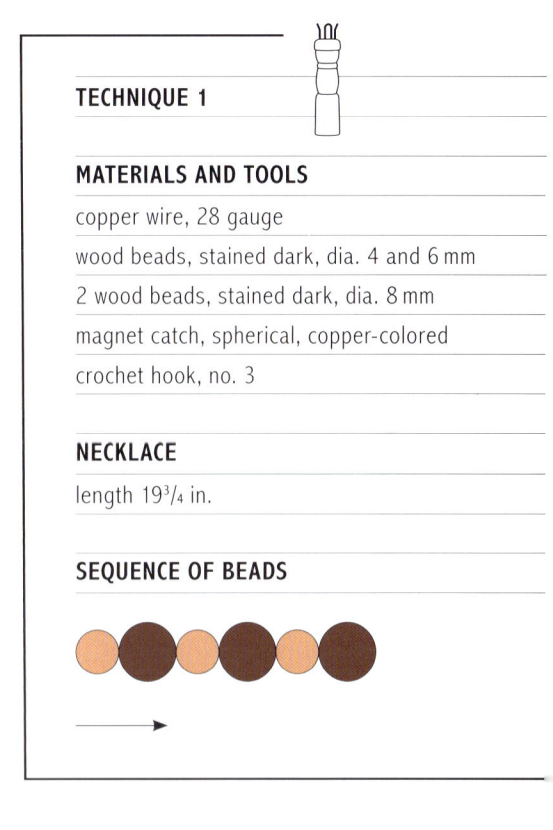

TECHNIQUE 1

MATERIALS AND TOOLS

copper wire, 28 gauge

wood beads, stained dark, dia. 4 and 6 mm

2 wood beads, stained dark, dia. 8 mm

magnet catch, spherical, copper-colored

crochet hook, no. 3

NECKLACE

length 19 3/4 in.

SEQUENCE OF BEADS

22 POMPONS

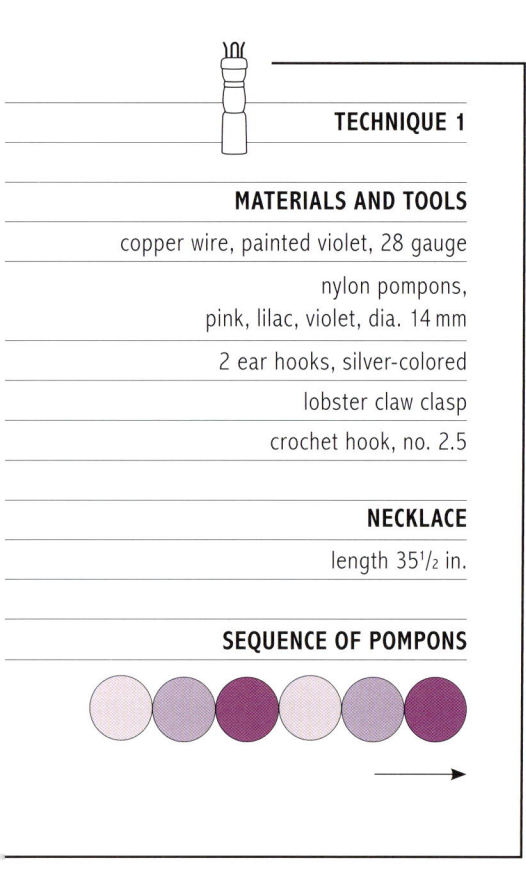

TECHNIQUE 1

MATERIALS AND TOOLS

copper wire, painted violet, 28 gauge

nylon pompons,
pink, lilac, violet, dia. 14 mm

2 ear hooks, silver-colored

lobster claw clasp

crochet hook, no. 2.5

NECKLACE

length 35½ in.

SEQUENCE OF POMPONS

NECKLACE

First thread the pompons according to the sequence shown. This is best done with a large sewing needle with a wire threaded into it.

IMPORTANT: The pompons should be pierced at the exact center so the wire will hold well.

Now crochet one chain stitch thread (**TECHNIQUE 1**). Start with three chain stitches and then alternatingly crochet four chain stitches without and one chain stitch with a pompon. When you have reached a length of 35½ inches, one final chain stitch follows after the last pompon which is used to close the thread into a loop. Make sure the color sequence from the last to the first pompon is correct.

Then cast off the wire and twist both ends of the wires so they lie under the pompon. Shorten the ends of the wires.

EARRINGS

Small threads are crocheted for the earrings. Start with two chain stitches, then add a violet pompon, one chain stitch, one lilac pompon, one chain stitch, and one pink pompon.

Now the pompons lie close to each other. The two ends of the wires are twisted and shortened.

The small thread is hooked into the jump ring of the ear hook at the first chain stitch.

BRACELET

For the bracelet, make a 6¼-inch-long chain stitch thread. Start with three chain stitches and crochet only two instead of four empty chain stitches between the pompons.

This results in the pompons lying closer together. Finish with another three chain stitches. Make sure the color sequence between the last and the first pompon is correct.

Run the ends of the wires through a 6-mm jump ring on both sides, twisted and shortened.

Work a lobster claw clasp into one of the jump rings as a fastener.

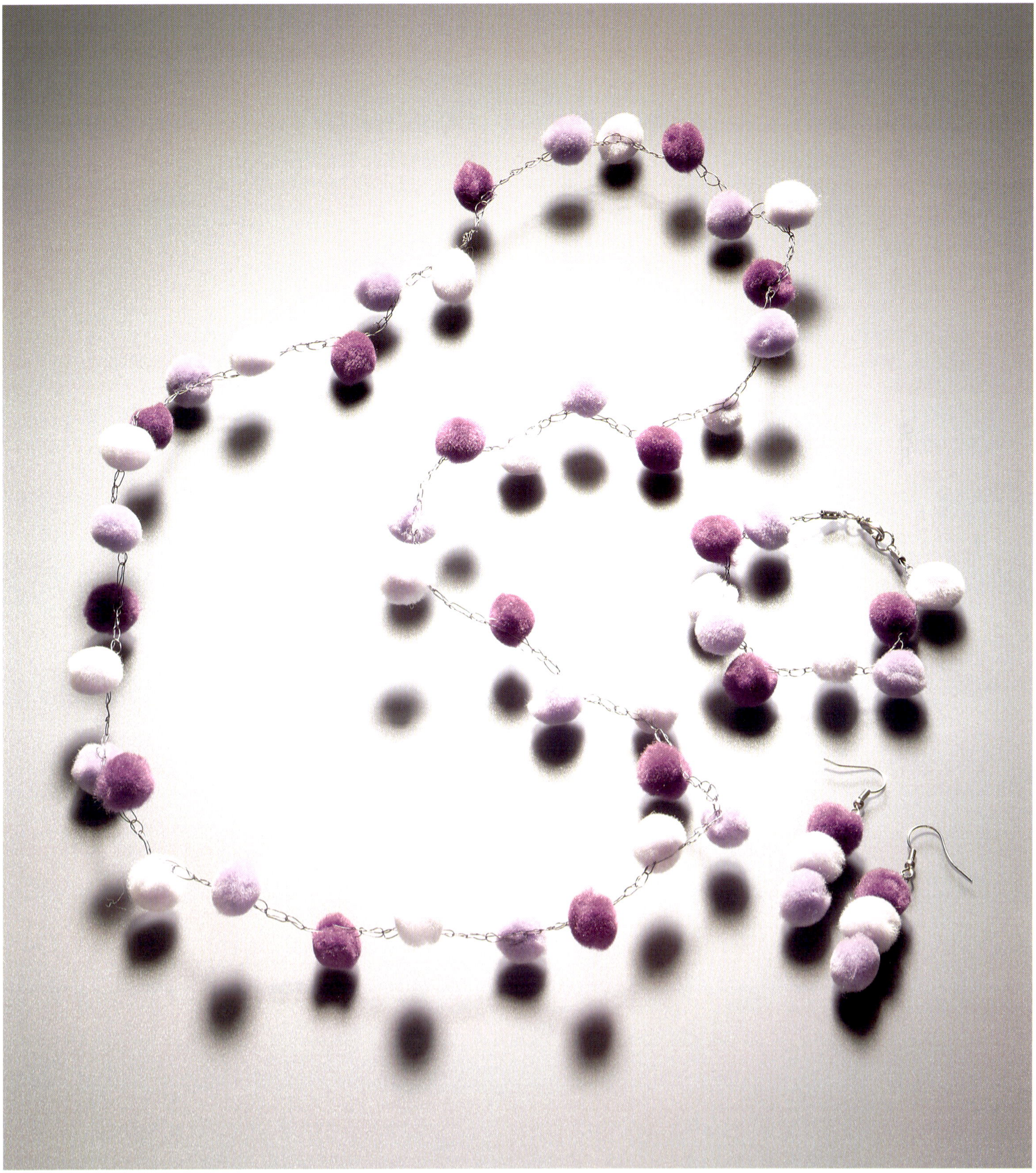

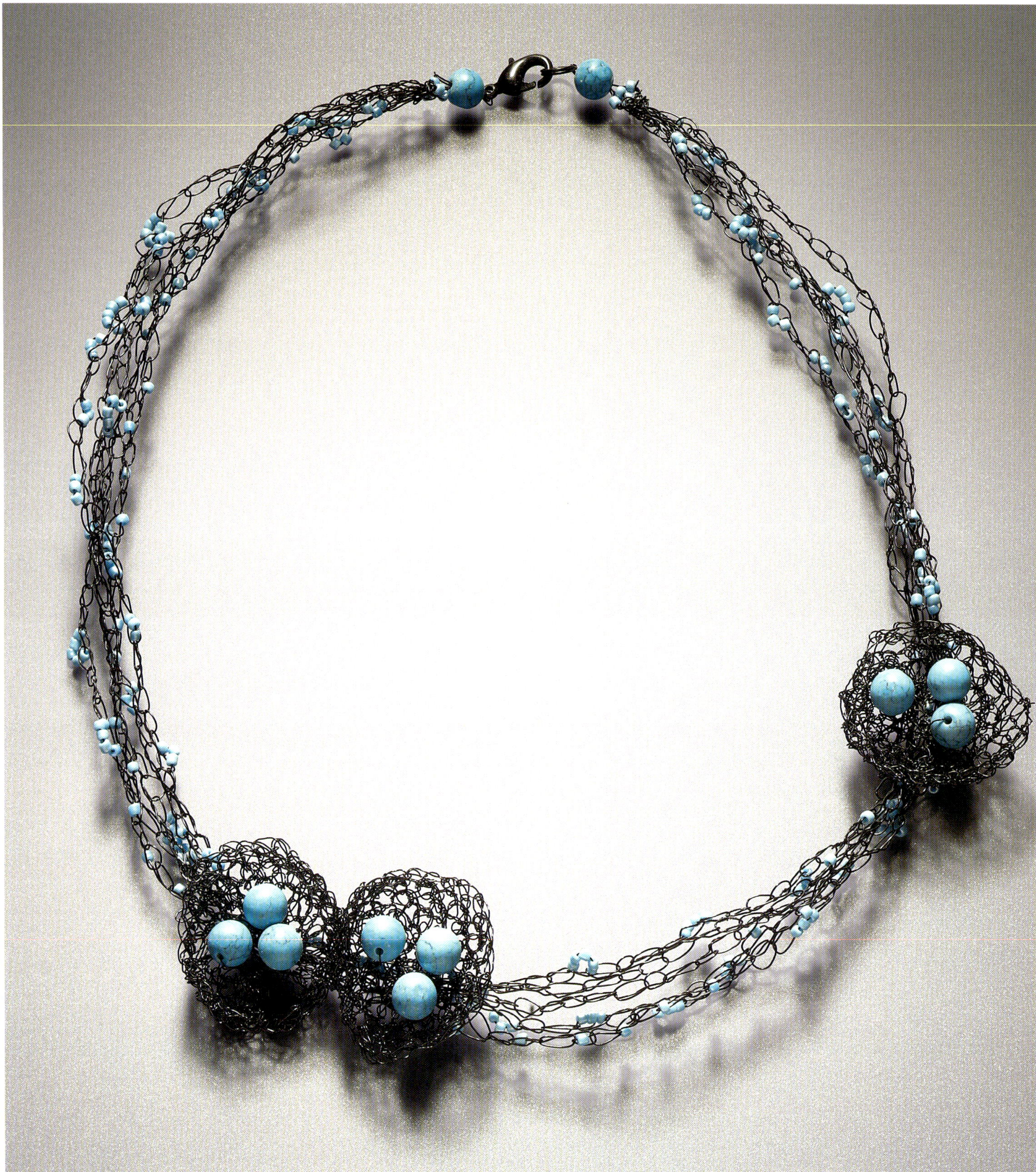

23 NESTS

Five chain stitch threads, each 20½ inches long, are crocheted for the necklace. Two chain stitch threads are crocheted without beads. On one chain stitch thread, one chain stitch without a rocaille alternates with a chain stitch with a rocaille. One chain stitch thread is crocheted with three chain stitches without bead and one chain stitch with three rocailles; and one chain stitch thread is created with five chain stitches without and one chain stitch with five rocailles.

Place the threads next to each other and slightly twist them. At both ends of the thread all five strands are united with one of the wire ends by running the wire through the last chain stitch of each strand.

Then thread one rocaille bead each onto all of the five wires at both ends of the thread, and run the five wires first through a turquoise bead and then through the jump ring at the lobster claw clasp and through the jump ring, respectively. Run the wires through the turquoise bead and the rocailles back again, and twist them at the end of the thread strands. Then shorten the ends of the wires.

For the nest make three rosettes (**TECHNIQUE 1**). Allow the initial thread to be at least 7⅞ inches long.

After the end of the wire has been twisted and shortened at the last stitch, the rosette is sewn to the necklace with the end of the wire. Run the wire at each of the five chain stitches through one chain stitch, respectively. Then turn the wire toward the center of the rosette again and sew three turquoise beads one by one into the rosette. Twist the end of the wire at the bottom of the rosette and shorten it.

TECHNIQUE 1

MATERIALS AND TOOLS

copper wire, painted black, 26 gauge

copper bullion wire, painted black, 28 gauge

11 turquoise beads

rocailles, turquoise, dia. 2.4 mm

lobster claw clasp with jump ring, dia. 7 mm

crochet hook, no. 2

NECKLACE

length 22 in.

24 COUNTRY DEER

TECHNIQUE 3

MATERIALS AND TOOLS

copper wire, painted red, 28 gauge

magnet catch, silver-colored

deer motif pendant

2 silver jump rings, dia. 8 mm

superglue

9-peg metal loom, dia. 1 3/16 in/30 mm

NECKLACE

length 21 1/2 in.

The charming pendant for this country-style necklace doesn't come from the mountains, but from a stand at the Spitalfields Market in London! A reminder that it's a good idea to keep your eyes open and to allow yourself to be surprised and inspired.

The red thread is done with a metal knitting loom with a diameter of 1 3/16 inches and with nine pegs. Work in **OFFSET** technique (**TECHNIQUE 3**) with the uneven number of pegs. Knit a thread with a length of 20 7/8 inches.

Cast off the stitches and remove the knitted thread from the loom. You can use the piece of wire you utilized to cast off the end of the tube to pull the tube together. On the other end, the end of the wire is threaded through the stitches so that the start of the tube can be pulled together.

Use superglue to glue both ends of the tube into the magnet catch.

IMPORTANT: Make sure that no glue gets onto the outside of the catch or on the area where the parts meet.

My pendant already had two holes, at the antlers of the deer. This is where I hooked the pendant to the necklace with two silver jump rings. If you want to re-create this necklace with a different pendant you might have to drill the appropriate holes.

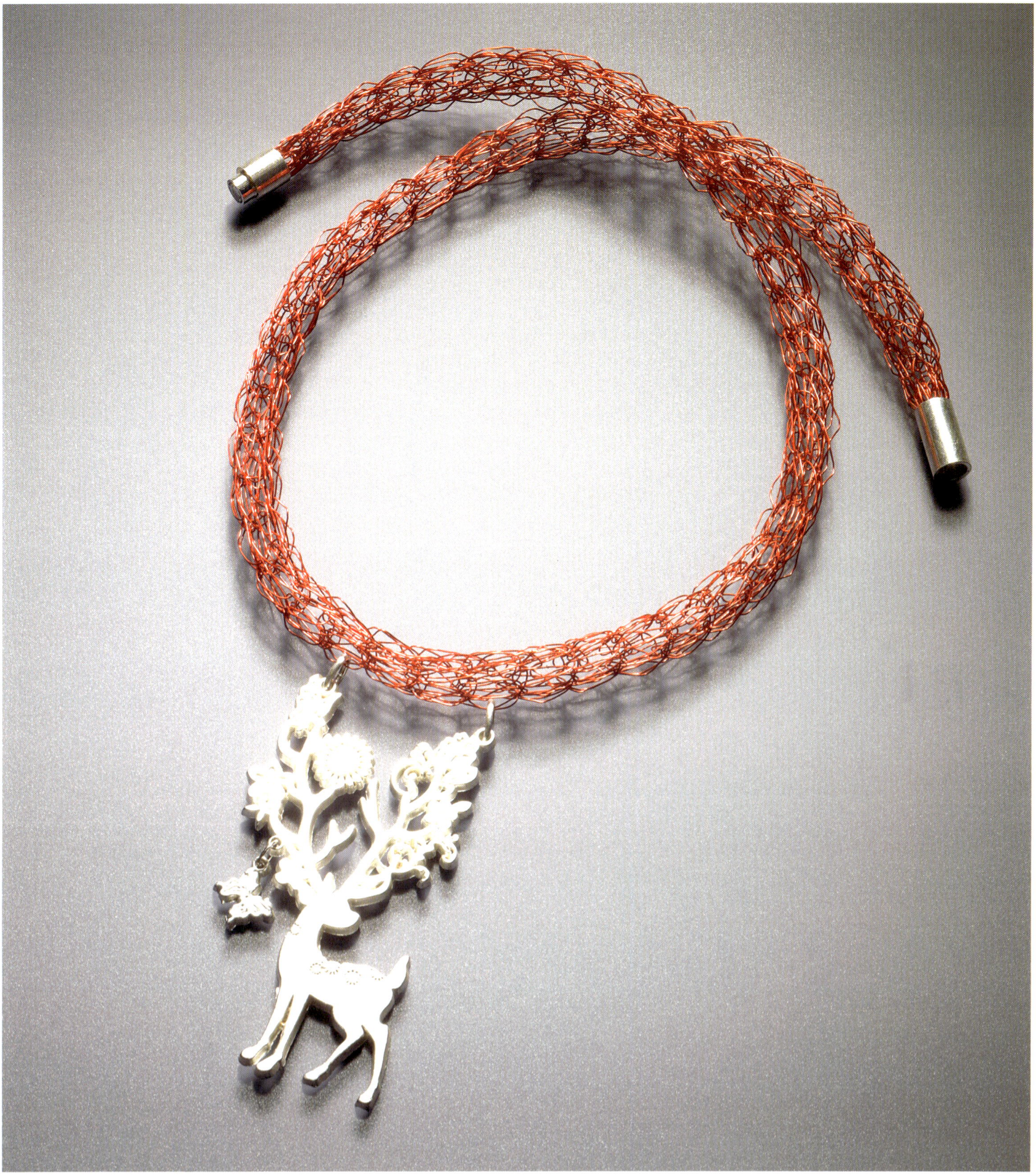

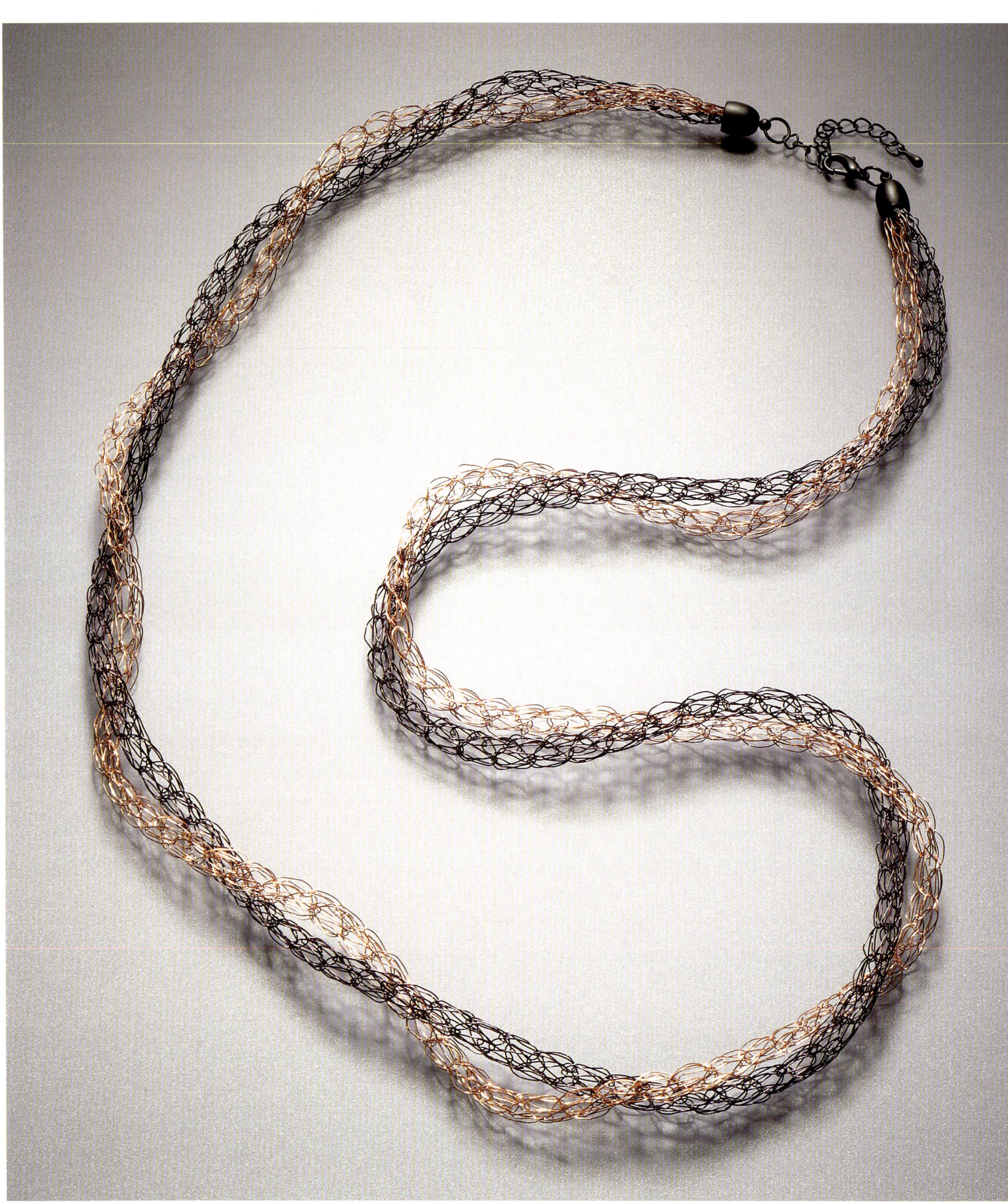

25 DOUBLE PASS

This attractive necklace is made in **SIMPLE** technique (**TECHNIQUE 2**) by knitting two identical threads from painted and non-painted copper wire with the 4-peg wooden knitting loom.

You knit two threads with a length of 34$^1/_2$ inches, and pull them after knitting until they are 36$^1/_4$ inches long. While pulling, the thread is still hooked into the wooden loom.

After pulling, the stitches are cast off and the knitted tube is removed from the loom. Place the two threads next to each other and loosely wrap them around each other.

Then hold the two threads at the ends and sew them together. Twist and shorten the wires. Glue the ends of the wires into the caps of the catch with superglue.

The necklace can be worn long or short. The total length can be somewhat adjusted with the extension chain at the catch.

TECHNIQUE 2

MATERIALS AND TOOLS

copper wire, 28 gauge

copper wire, painted violet, 28 gauge

lobster claw clasp with extension chain, black

4-peg wooden knitting loom

superglue

NECKLACE

length 36$^1/_2$ in.

26 CATERPILLAR

TECHNIQUE 1 AND 2

MATERIALS AND TOOLS

copper bullion wire, 28 gauge

fringed yarn, black

magnet catch, black, dia. 18 mm

6-peg wooden knitting loom

crochet hook, no. 2.5

NECKLACE

length 36½ in.

First make a knitted tube in **SIMPLE** technique (**TECHNIQUE 2**) on the 6-peg wooden knitting loom. While knitting, pull the tube slightly.

When the thread has reached a length of 26½ inches, the stitches are cast off and the tube is removed from the loom.

Make a chain stitch thread with a length of 26¾ inches from the yarn. (I cast on 110 chain stitches.) Now make a row of single stitches over the chain stitch thread. This way the thread turns out somewhat shorter. Make sure the stitches of this second row don't turn out too tight or the thread might end up being too short.

In order to be able to thread the yarn thread into the wire thread, I fabricated a pulling wire. I cut a length of about 31½ inches from thicker wire (dia. about 2.5 mm) and bent one end into a jump ring.

Now the pulling wire is carefully threaded through the copper tube with the jump ring first. One end of the yarn thread is hooked into the jump ring and the wire is carefully pulled back through the knitted tube.

IMPORTANT: Make sure the jump ring is closed so it won't get caught by the stitches of the wire tube.

Then the yarn and wire threads are sewn to each other at the ends. Use the crochet hook to pull the fringes of the yarn outward through the wire stitches.

To attach the catch, the copper wire is run several times through the jump ring of the magnet hemispheres, then twisted and glued.

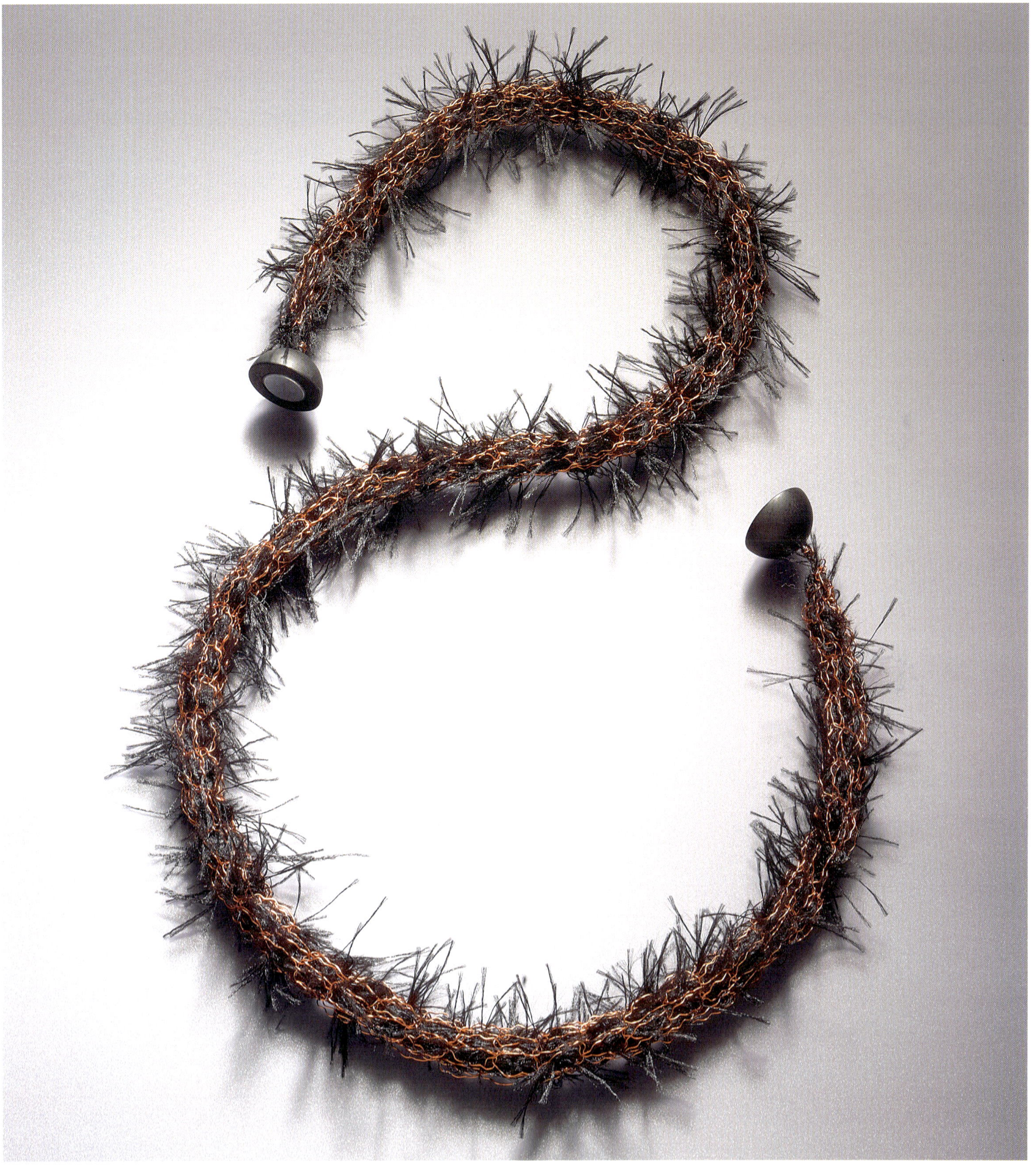

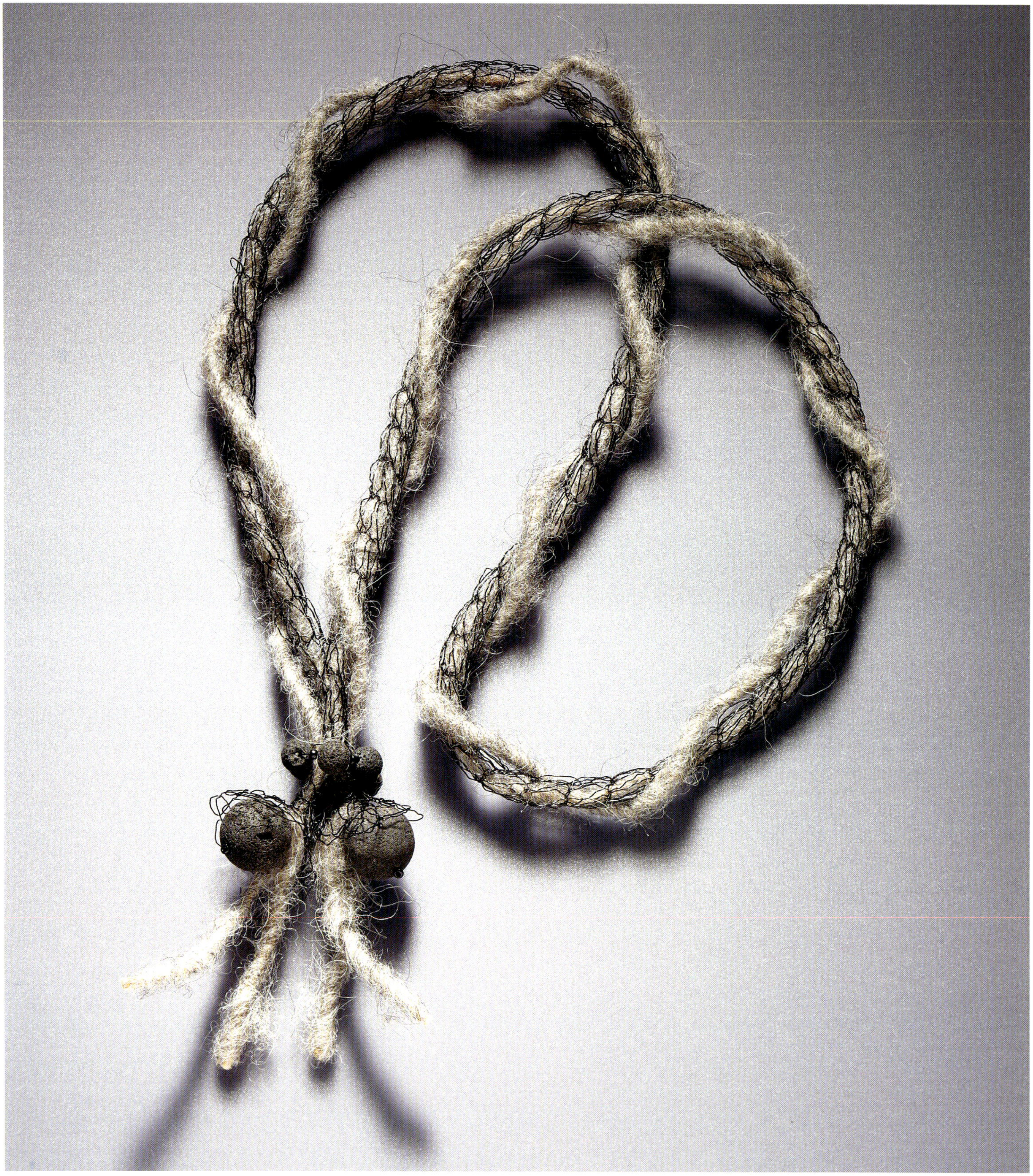

27 MATTED

Make a tube with a length of 35½ inches in **SIMPLE** technique (**TECHNIQUE 2**).

IMPORTANT: When casting on the stitches, leave the end of the wire with a length of at least 7⅞ inches, and later on, do the same with the end of the wire when casting off.

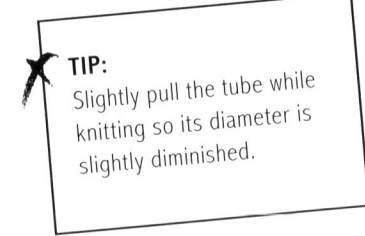

TIP: Slightly pull the tube while knitting so its diameter is slightly diminished.

After casting off, the tube is removed from the loom and the felted string is inserted with the help of a pulling wire as described in project 26. After you insert it, shorten the felted string so its ends are about 2 inches longer than the wire tube.

The remaining felted string is loosely wrapped around the wire tube. Run both ends of the felted string at the end of the wire tube through a wire stitch toward the inside and again outward at the open end. Here as well, leave about 2 inches of extra felted string and cut off.

Run the ends of the wires of the knitted tube in an inconspicuous way through the stitches about half an inch toward the back, and wrap the wire tightly around the knitted tube twice. Then run the wire through the felted string toward the other side and back. This attaches the felted string so it cannot slip back inside the tube.

Then run the ends of the wires through the knitted tube to the outside again, and thread a large lava bead and a rocaille bead each. The wire is run back through the lava bead and is then twisted inconspicuously around a stitch of the knitted tube and glued.

Now carefully bend up the ends of the knitted tube so they lie around the bead and the two felt strings like a calyx.

Thread the small lava beads and the rocailles alternatingly onto a 6-inch-long piece of wire. This thread is placed around both of the wire tubes, and the ends of the wires are twisted and shortened to ¼ inch. To keep the ends of the wire invisible, run them through the lava beads next to them.

TECHNIQUE 2

MATERIALS AND TOOLS

bullion wire, black, 28 gauge

felted string, gray, dia. 5 mm, length about 6½ ft.

2 lava beads, dia. 16 mm

6 lava beads, dia. 7 mm

8 rocailles, black, dia. 2.4 mm

8-peg wooden knitting loom

NECKLACE

length 37½ in.

28 FIRESTONE

TECHNIQUE 2

MATERIALS AND TOOLS

copper wire, painted black, 26 gauge

pebble stones, white

lobster claw clasp with cylinder caps (dia. 10 mm) and extension chain

superglue

8-peg wooden knitting loom

NECKLACE

length 24 3/4 to 26 in.

The white pebble stones provide a nice contrast to the black wire, and can be easily inserted into the knitted tube because of their round shape.

IMPORTANT: Before knitting, you should test whether the stones fit easily through the knitting loom. Keep in mind that the inner diameter of the loom will be further reduced by the knitted tube inside of it.

Knit seven rows in **SIMPLE** technique (**TECHNIQUE 2**) with the 8-peg loom. Then place the first stone into the loom. Slightly press it into the knitted mesh so it won't fall out when you continue to knit.

Now knit nine or ten rounds (depending on the size of the stones) and place the next stone into it. In our project nine stones were knitted in.

> **TIP:**
> An uneven number of stones is usually better, so one stone lies at the front center of the necklace.

Finish the knitted tube with seven winding and knitting rounds after the last stone. The thread sections between the stones can be pulled by hand so the diameter is somewhat diminished.

The sections with the stones are more pronounced, and the stones are fixed in position securely.

Cast off the stitches and pull together the tube at both ends. Tightly wrap the ends of the wires around the end of the tube two to three times. Then twist and shorten the wire.

Use superglue to join the caps of the lobster claw clasp with the ends of the tubes.

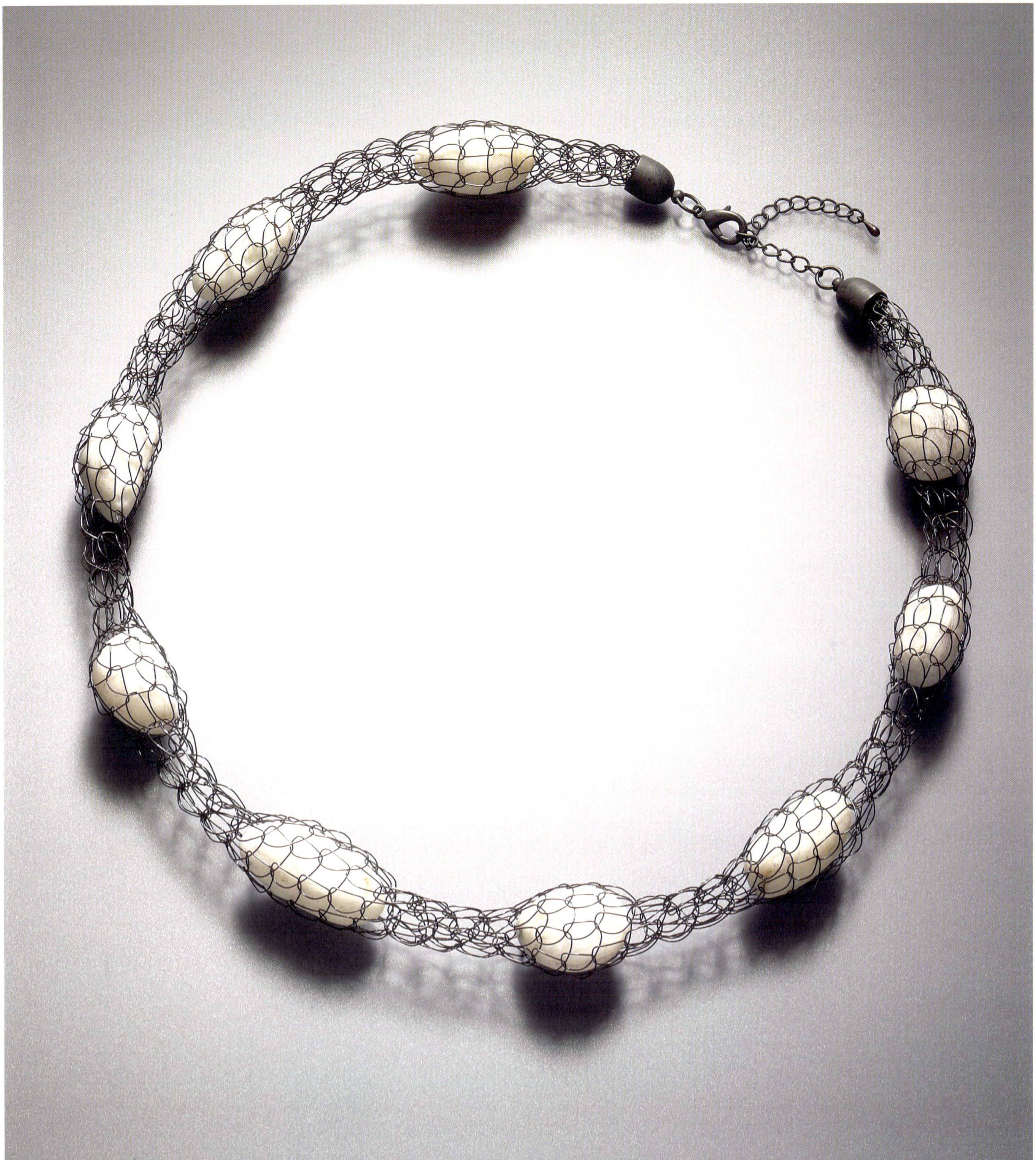

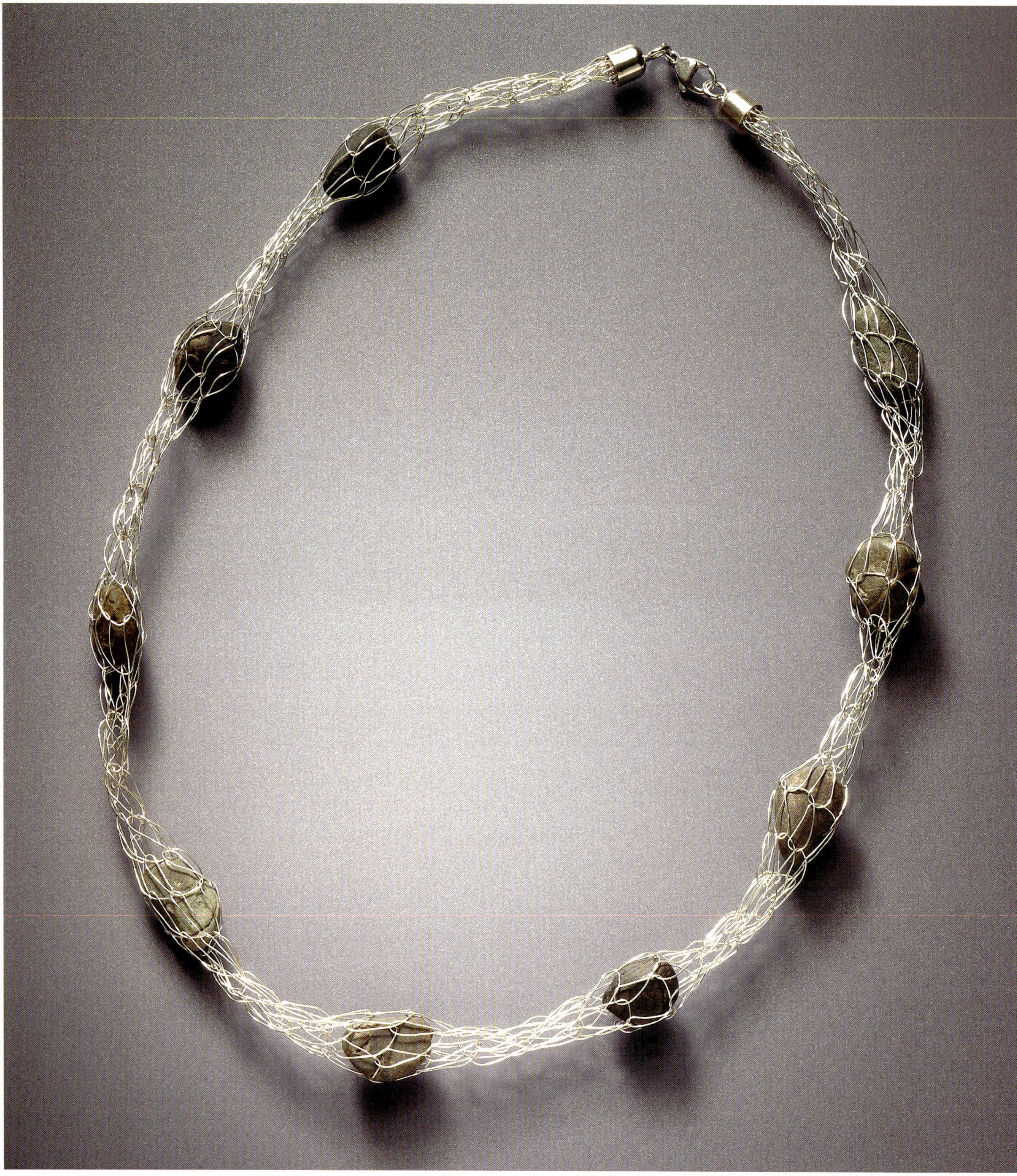

29 BLACK PEBBLE

I collected small black pebbles for this necklace. The dull matte surface provides a nice contrast to the shiny silver wire.

IMPORTANT: Before knitting, check whether the stones fit through the knitting loom!

Seven rows are knitted in **SIMPLE** technique (**TECHNIQUE 2**) with the 4-peg knitting loom. Then place the first stone into the loom. Slightly press it into the knitted mesh so it doesn´t fall out when you continue knitting.

Now knit six rounds and place the next stone inside, until nine stones are set; or, depending on the desired length, more or fewer stones.

TIP:
An uneven number of stones is usually better, so one stone will lie at the front center of the necklace.

Finish the knitted tube with seven winding and knitting rounds after the last stone.

Cast off the stitches and pull the tube together at both ends. Tightly twist the ends of the wires two to three times around the end of the tube. Then it is twisted and shortened.

Using superglue, join the caps of the lobster claw clasp with the ends of the tubes.

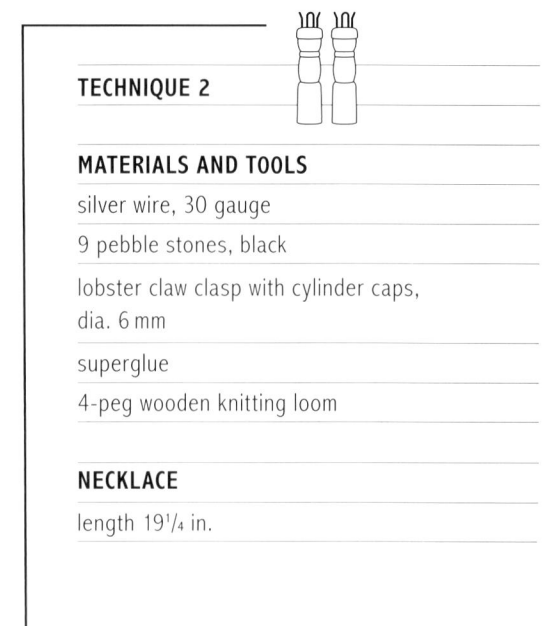

TECHNIQUE 2

MATERIALS AND TOOLS

silver wire, 30 gauge

9 pebble stones, black

lobster claw clasp with cylinder caps, dia. 6 mm

superglue

4-peg wooden knitting loom

NECKLACE

length 19 1/4 in.

30 TANGO

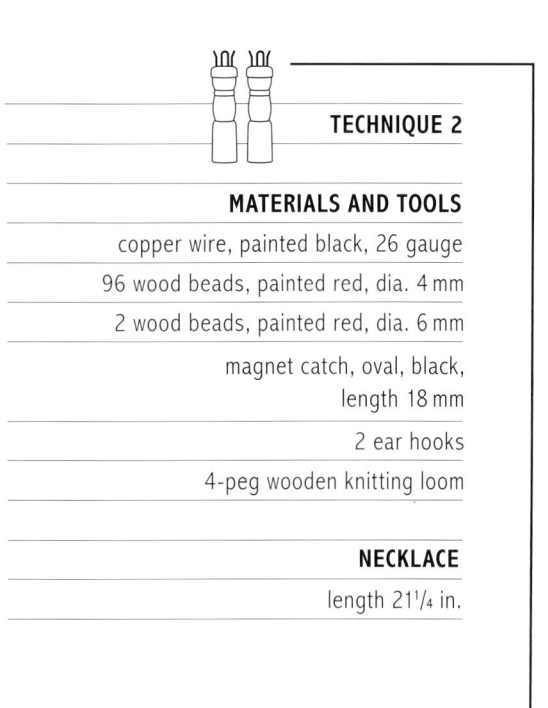

TECHNIQUE 2

MATERIALS AND TOOLS

copper wire, painted black, 26 gauge

96 wood beads, painted red, dia. 4 mm

2 wood beads, painted red, dia. 6 mm

magnet catch, oval, black, length 18 mm

2 ear hooks

4-peg wooden knitting loom

NECKLACE

length 21 1/4 in.

NECKLACE

Before knitting, 72 wood beads (dia. 4 mm) are threaded onto the wire. Then knit in **SIMPLE** technique (**TECHNIQUE 2**) six winding and six knitting rounds without beads.

Continue with four winding and four knitting rounds with beads. When winding, one bead each is inserted at the first and third round after the first and third pegs, in the second and fourth round of winding after the second and fourth pegs. In total you knit eight beads so they are offset on top of each other.

Now follow another four winding and knitting rounds without beads.

Continue alternating four winding and knitting rounds without and four winding and knitting rounds with beads. After nine sections with beads, finish with six rounds without beads.

The knitted tube is cast off and removed from the knitting loom. Pull both ends of the tube together. One large wood bead each (dia. 6 mm) is threaded onto the ends of the wires; then the wire is run through the jump ring of the magnet catch and back again through the bead. Run the wire through the end of the tube and back again through the bead and jump ring. Then twist the end of the wire and shorten it.

EARRINGS

For the earrings, do as with the necklace and knit two short threads. Start with two winding and knitting rounds without beads. Then follow with four winding and knitting rounds with beads, and finally two more winding and knitting rounds without beads.

Thread a small wood bead onto both ends of the wires, then pull the ends of the tubes together. Twist the wire at the lower end of the earring. At the top end, run it through the jump ring of the ear hook (perhaps twice) and also twist and shorten it.

RING

For the ring, make a small tube 3 1/8 to 3 1/2 inches long (depending on the desired size of the ring) as described previously. Start and end with five to six winding and knitting rounds without beads. At the center make three winding and knitting rounds with beads (a total of six).

Remove the knitting tube from the loom **WITHOUT** casting off the stitches and press the tube flat. Sew the beginning and end stitches into a loop to close the tube so that the end stitches won´t open.

> **TIP:**
> If you knit the sections which you need for the earrings and the ring to the knitted tube right away you save yourself to cast on the stitches again. Simply knit two to three "empty rows" between the individual objects. You can separate the sections with a cutter and "back-knit" the extra rows by hand. The resulting ends of the wires are usually sufficient to complete the objects.

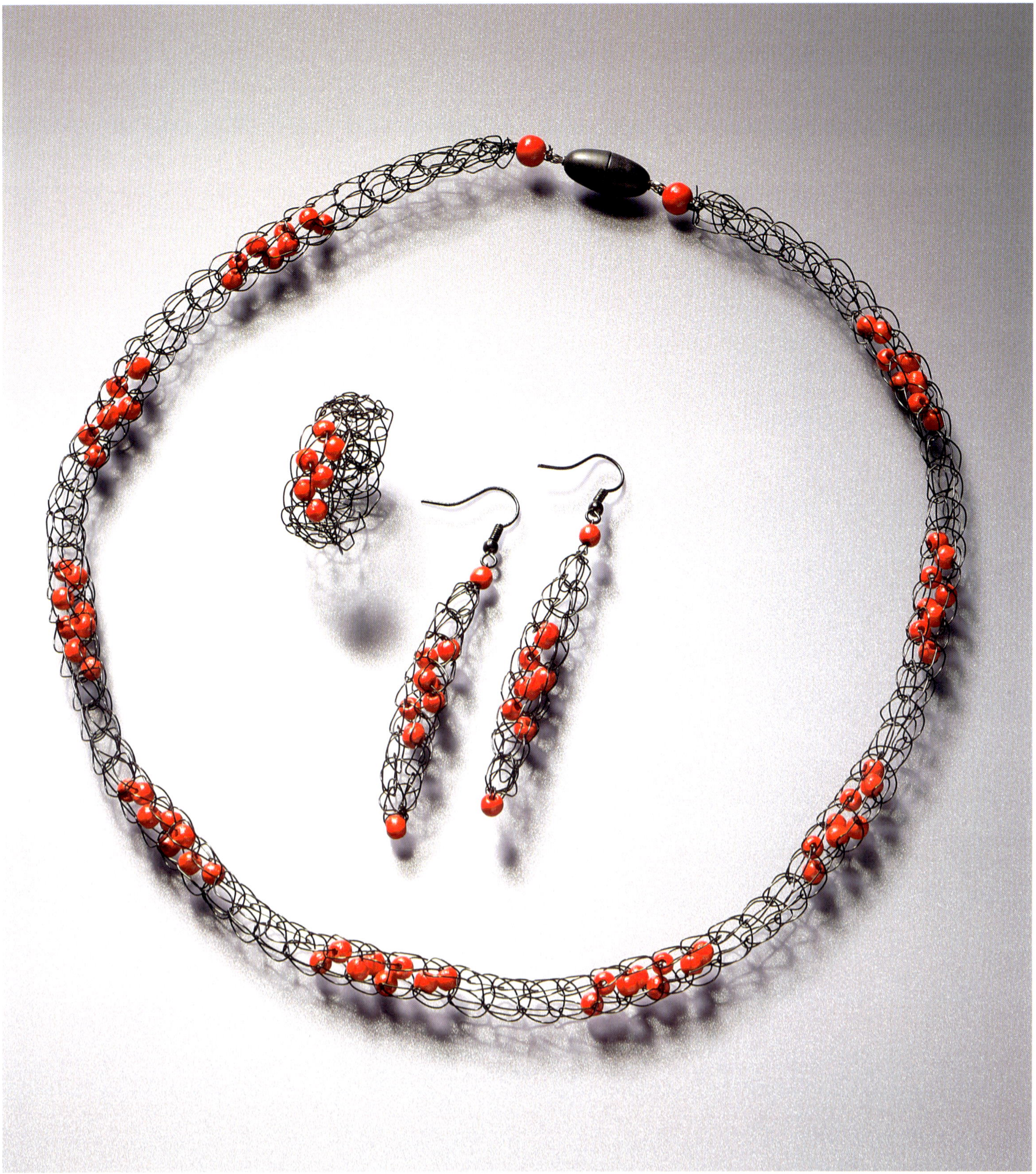

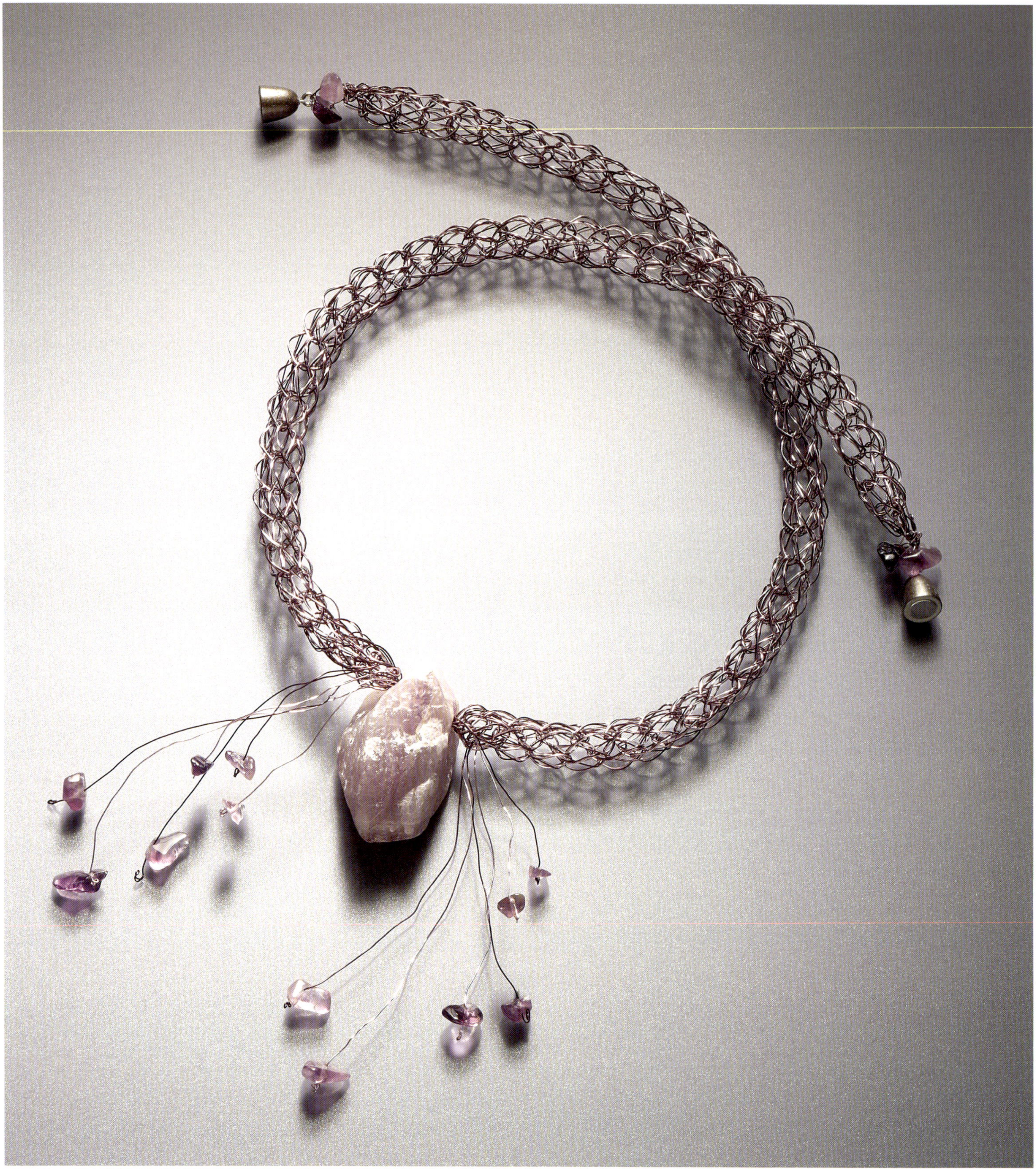

31 STONE DANCE

The two violet tones of the necklace nicely complement each other. So I worked both wires simultaneously and emphasized their color play.

Knit two tubes with a length of 10 1/2 inches in **SIMPLE** technique (**TECHNIQUE 2**). Work with both wires at the same time and leave the ends of the wires with a length of at least 7 7/8 inches.

IMPORTANT: Make sure both wires are wound around the pegs and that you pick up both wires when lifting the stitches over the pegs. Otherwise the stitch of the following round cannot be cast off.

The end stitches of both tubes are cast off and the ends of the tubes are pulled together.

In order to attach the large amethyst, both wires at the cast-off end are run through the drill hole of the stone. Then run the wires through the last stitches of the opposite tube and back again through the hole of the side you started out from. Twist the wires so they'll be inconspicuous.

Three sections of wire of different length in both colors are attached to the knitted tube at both sides (run them through the stitches and twist). A small amethyst is threaded onto each piece of wire, and the end of the wire is bent into a small spiral. This way the amethysts can move freely on the wire but won't slip over the end of the wire.

At the other end of the two thread tubes, attach the magnet catch. Thread a small amethyst onto both ends of the wires, then run the wire through the jump ring of the magnet catch and back again through the amethyst. The end of the wire is run through the last stitches of the knitted tube, twisted, and shortened.

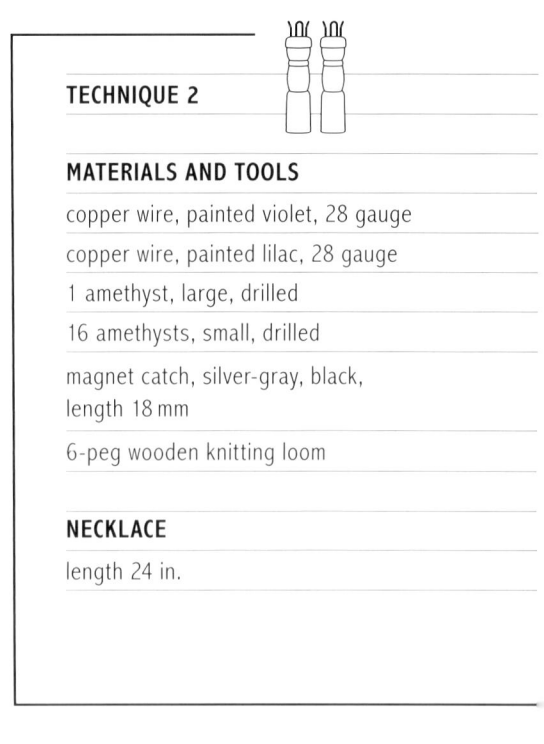

TECHNIQUE 2

MATERIALS AND TOOLS

copper wire, painted violet, 28 gauge

copper wire, painted lilac, 28 gauge

1 amethyst, large, drilled

16 amethysts, small, drilled

magnet catch, silver-gray, black, length 18 mm

6-peg wooden knitting loom

NECKLACE

length 24 in.

32 GOSSAMER

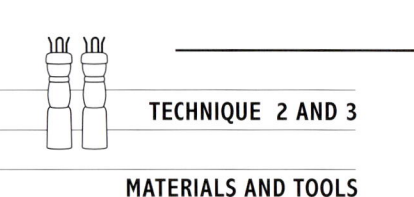

TECHNIQUE 2 AND 3

MATERIALS AND TOOLS

copper bullion wire, painted light green, 28 gauge

72 farfalle beads, matte white, dia. 6.5 mm

72 farfalle beads, matte white, dia. 4 mm

2 glass beads, dia. 8 mm

2 eyeglass chains, clear, silver-colored

magnet catch, white

9-peg metal knitting loom, dia. 1 3/16 in/ 30 mm (bracelet)

9-peg metal knitting loom, dia. 3/8 in/ 10 mm (ring)

4-peg wooden loom (eyeglass chain)

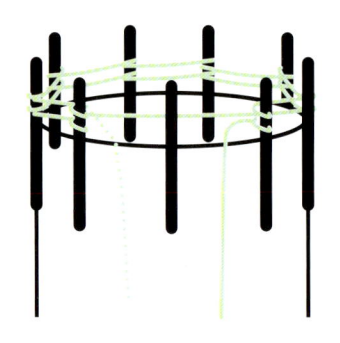

(TECHNIQUE 3)

BRACELET

Thread 72 farfalle beads onto the bullion wire. The wire is cast on the metal knitting loom (dia. 1 3/16 inches) so that the ninth peg is left out. So the wire runs between the eighth and the first peg. This is where the farfalle beads are later threaded.

First make three winding and knitting rounds without beads in **SIMPLE** technique (**TECHNIQUE 3**). You can see the three tensioned wires between the eighth and the first peg.

Six farfalle beads are pushed toward the eighth peg before the fourth winding round, the winding round starts at the first peg. The following knitting round binds the farfalle beads into the mesh.

Now alternate between two winding and knitting rounds without and one winding and knitting round with beads until ten rows of beads have been made. Finish with three winding and knitting rounds without beads. The length of the knitted tube is now about 6 inches long.

Cast off the stitches and remove the tube from the loom. The stitches are pulled together with the ends of the wires. Press the knitted tube flat. Now the beads lie at the center of the top. Six farfalle beads each are threaded onto both ends of the wires and are pulled together into a small loop by running the wire through the last stitches of the tube. In order to attach the magnet catch the ends of the wires are once again run through three of the six farfalle beads and through the jump ring of the catch.

Run the wire through the other three farfalle beads downward again, and twist and shorten it.

RING

For the ring, you proceed just as with the bracelet, however, use the metal knitting loom (dia. 3/8 inch). Leave the end of the wire at about 12 inches.

Three farfalle beads are worked into every other row between the eighth and the first peg so there is always an empty piece of wire and a row of farfalle beads visible. A total of 14 rows are knitted with farfalle beads. Remove the tube from the loom without casting off the stitches. Press it flat and make sure the farfalle lie nicely at the center. Beginning and end of the tube are sewn together with the end of the wire and inserted into the end stitches so they won't open.

Three farfalle beads are now threaded onto the long end of the wire. Run the wire close to the starting point through a stitch at the seam. The three farfalle form a "pile." Thread another three farfalle and thread the wire through a stitch at the seam. Continue likewise until the entire seam has been covered and the beads form a nice pile. The remaining piece of wire is twisted and shortened.

EYEGLASS CHAIN

The 4-peg wooden knitting loom is used for the thin eyeglass chain. A knitted tube of 27 1/2 inches is made with **TECHNIQUE 2** in **SIMPLE** technique. Stretch the tube while knitting by pulling gently. The large stitches that result from the 4-peg loom easily yield when pulled. This results in a filigree knitted thread. After casting off both ends of the tube are pulled together and one bead each is threaded onto the ends of the wires. Run the end of the wire through the rubber loop of the eyeglass chain and then back through the beads. Twist the wire at the end of the tube and shorten it.

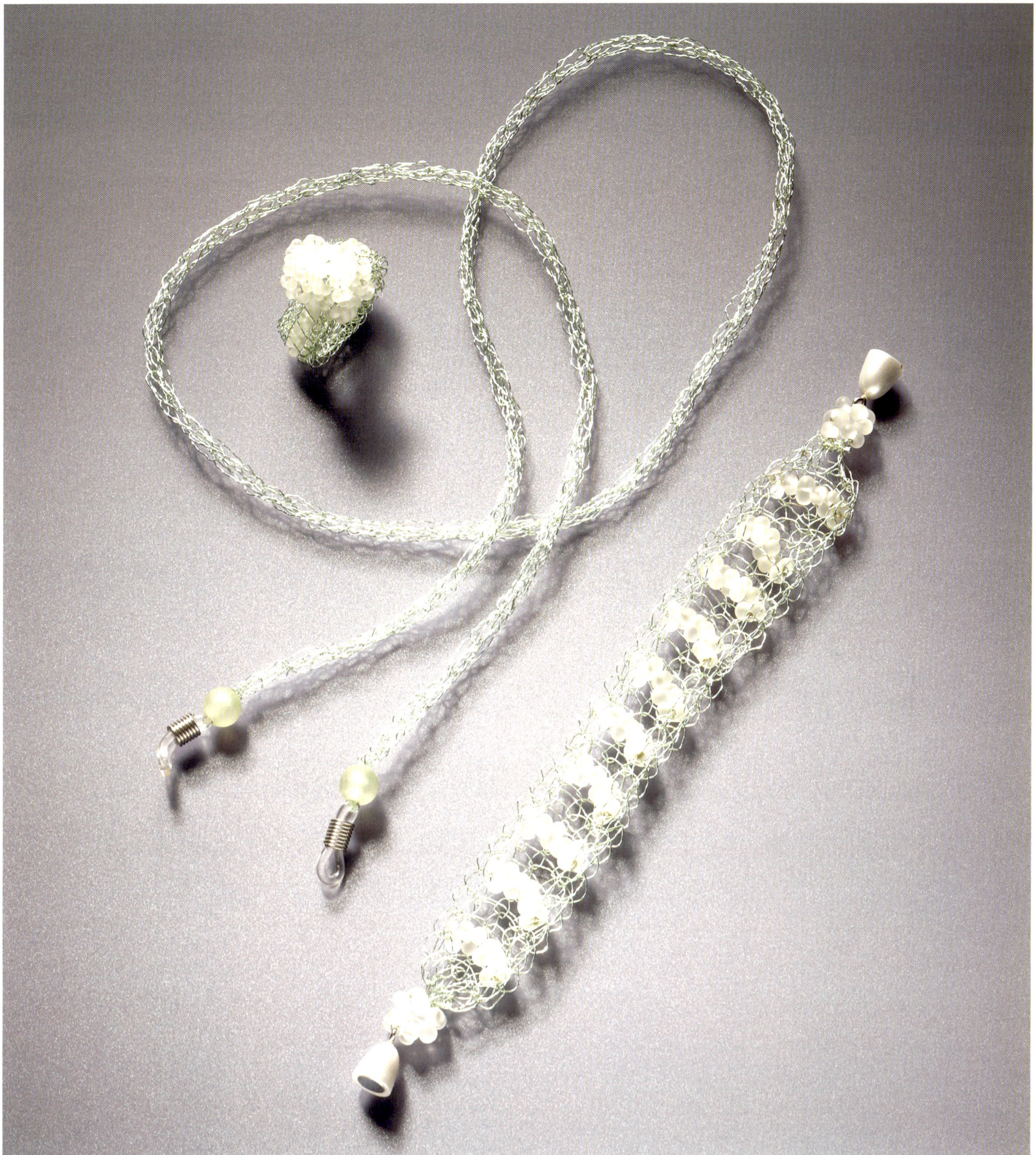

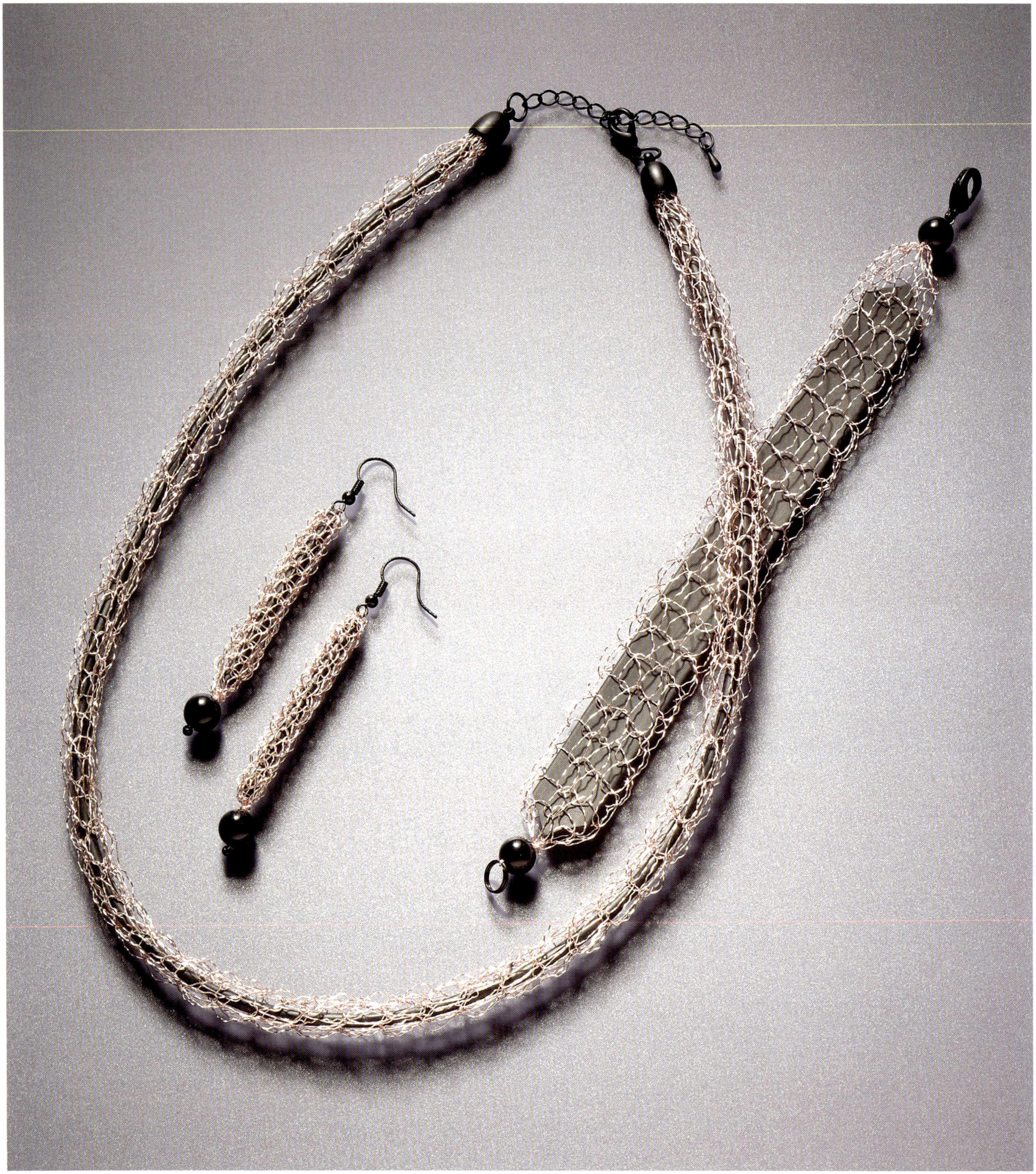

33 PARISIENNE

NECKLACE

The thread is knitted **OFFSET** (**TECHNIQUE 3**) with the metal knitting loom (dia. 1³/₁₆ in). The thread is pulled slightly while knitting to reduce the diameter somewhat and to make the mesh pattern more regular. Cast off the stitches after 21 inches and remove the tube from the loom. Usually the 3 mm natural rubber string can be pushed through the tube without tools. Cut off the string so it ends flush with the knitted tube on both sides. Then wrap the ends of the wires several times tightly about the end of the tube to secure the rubber string and glue the ends of the tubes into the caps of the catch.

IMPORTANT: Before glueing the tube into the caps of the lobster claw clasp, check that the wire loops are not visible but lie under the caps.

EARRINGS

Knit a 4³/₄ inch-long-tube in **OFFSET** technique (**TECHNIQUE 3**) with the metal knitting loom (dia. ³/₈ in) for both earrings.

The tube is cut in half at the center with the cutter and both halves are "knitted back" (pulled open) until they are 2 inches long. The now free ends of the wires are used to grab the stitches and to pull them together.

Then thread one onyx bead and one rocaille bead and run the thread back through the onyx bead to the end of the tube. Then the wire is twisted and shortened.

Now push the rubber string into both tubes and shorten it as necessary. At the side of the tube that's still open, the stitches are pulled together with the end of the wire. Run the wire through the jump ring of the ear hook. It is twisted and shortened at the end of the tube.

BRACELET

The knitted tube for the bracelet is made with the 8-peg wooden knitting loom (**TECHNIQUE 2**). The tube is knitted in **SIMPLE** technique. It should have a length of about 6³/₄ inches, depending on the circumference of the arm.

IMPORTANT: Pull the tube carefully through the knitting loom so its diameter won't become too small.

The cast-off tube is removed from the loom and carefully pressed flat.

IMPORTANT: Make sure four entire stitches lie on the top and bottom sides, respectively, so a nice edge forms at the rim of the band.

The cast-off side of the knitted tube is pulled together so an even tip results. Also cut the 15-mm-wide PVC band so it is pointed. This makes it easier to insert into the knitted tube and push it into its tip.

Shorten the PVC band according to the length of the knitted tube and also cut a tip on this side. The stitches are also pulled together with the end of the wire and are shaped into an even tip which nicely fits to the PVC band.

Now thread an onyx bead onto both ends of the wire. At one side the wire is run through the jump ring of the lobster claw clasp, at the other side through the 7 mm jump ring and then back through the bead. Twist and shorten the wire at the end of the tube.

TECHNIQUE 2 AND 3

MATERIALS AND TOOLS

copper bullion wire, painted antique pink, 28 gauge

string made of natural rubber, dia. 3 mm, length 25¹/₂ in.

PVC band, black, 6³/₄ x ¹/₂ x ¹/₁₆ in.

4 onyx beads, dia. 8 mm

2 rocailles, black, dia. 2.4 mm

lobster claw clasp with extension chain, black, with caps dia. 8 mm

superglue

lobster claw clasp, with jump ring dia. 7 mm

2 ear hooks, black

9-peg metal knitting loom, dia. 1³/₁₆ in/ 30 mm (necklace)

9-peg metal knitting loom, dia. ³/₈ in/ 10 mm (earrings)

8-peg wooden knitting loom (bracelet)

NECKLACE

length 21¹/₄ to 23¹/₂ in.

34 SEA ANEMONE

TECHNIQUE 3

MATERIALS AND TOOLS

copper wire, painted metallic pink, 28 gauge

farfalle beads, violet, dia. 4 mm

cylindrical silver magnet catch

superglue

9-peg metal knitting loom, dia. 1 3/16 in/ 30 mm (necklace)

9-peg metal knitting loom, dia. 9/16 in/ 15 mm (decoration)

NECKLACE

length 36 1/4 in.

NECKLACE

Two tubes are knitted in **OFFSET** technique (**TECHNIQUE 3**) with the metal knitting loom (dia. 1 3/16 inches) for this necklace. One tube gets a length of 16 1/2 inches, the other of 18 7/8 inches. While knitting the tubes are already pulled slightly so the mesh pattern looks regular and even.

Once the knitted tube has reached the intended length, cut off the wire after about 9 3/4 inches. Carefully remove the tube from the loom **WITHOUT (!)** casting off the stitches. The tube on this side already has a trumpet-like shape.

Four farfalle beads are threaded onto the end of the wire and the wire is run through the first open stitch of the final round. Then thread another four farfalle beads and run the wire through the second open stitch. Continue likewise until nine times four farfalle beads have been worked in and all of the open stitches have been cast off. Twist the end of the wire with a stitch and push it through the four last farfalle beads to hide it.

At the other side of the knitted tube the stitches are pulled together and the end of the wire is twisted and shortened. Then press the ends of the tubes together slightly and glue them with superglue into the cylinder halves of the magnet catch.

DECORATION

The smaller metal knitting loom (dia. 9/16 inch) is used for the decorative "trumpets." Knit in **SIMPLE** technique (**TECHNIQUE 3**).

Each one of the small trumpets is removed from the loom after ten rows without casting off the stitches. As described before, insert two farfalle beads each between the open stitches so you cast off the end stitches at the same time.

At the other side of the trumpet, the stitches are pulled together with the end of the wire. When attaching the first trumpet on the thread you attach the two long knitted threads to each other at the same time. The other two trumpets are secured close to the first one on the tubes. Finally, twist and shorten the ends of the wires.

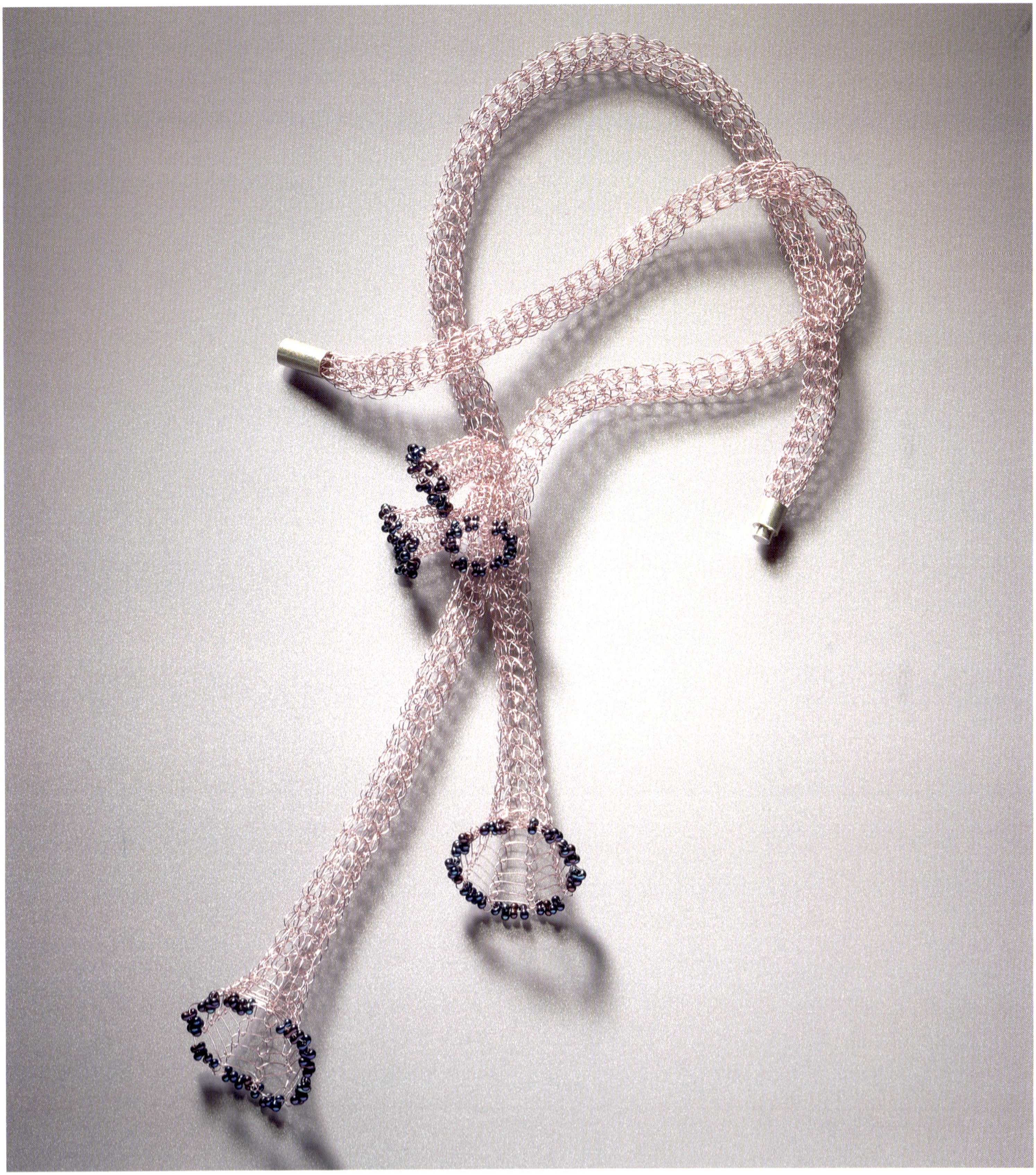

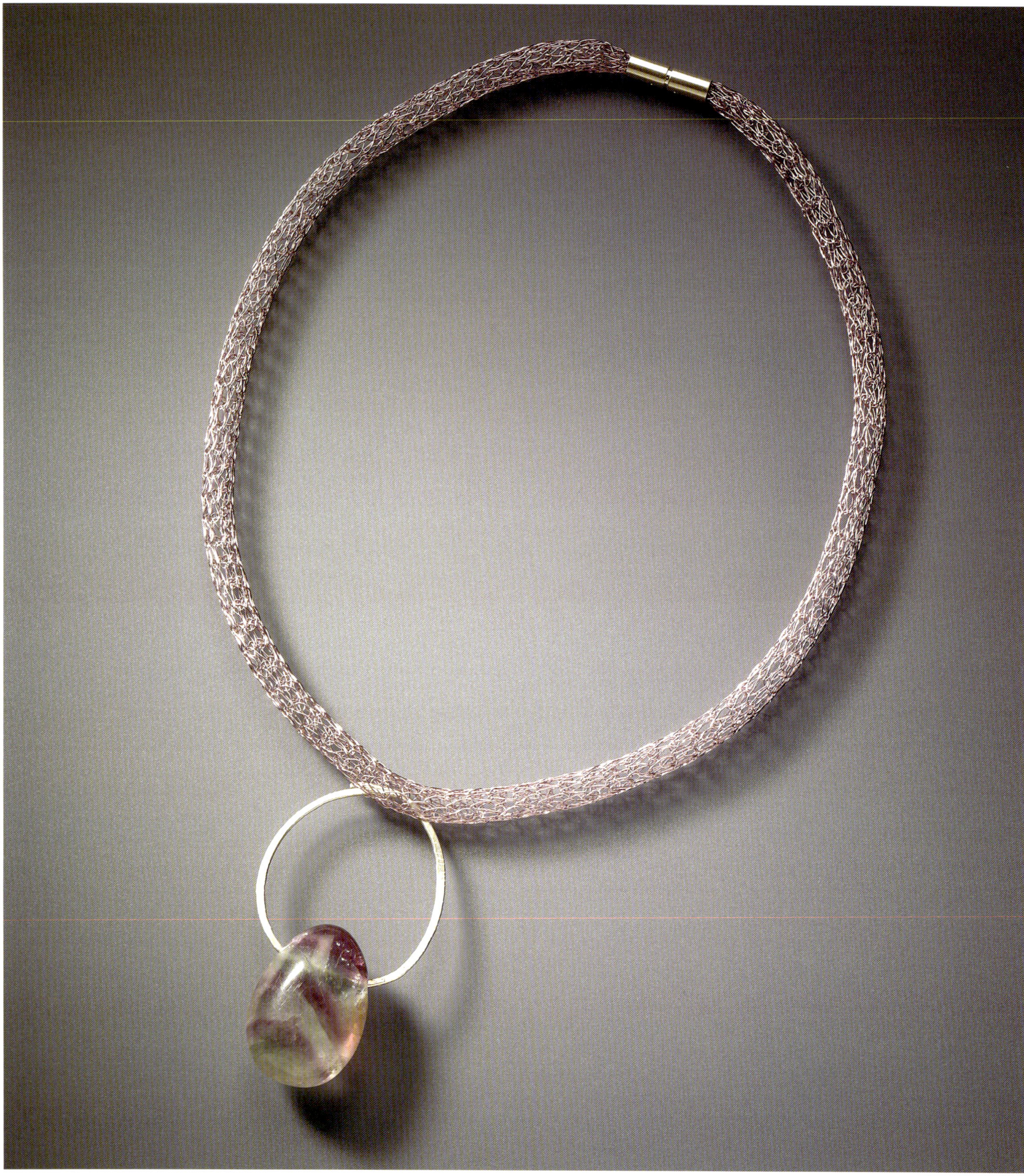

35 VEILED STONE

A knitted tube with a length of 19 inches is made with the wooden knitting loom (**TECHNIQUE 2**). Knit in **SIMPLE** technique. The mesh looks very airy because the stitches are fairly large.

When pulling in the loom, the diameter already diminishes significantly because the large stitches slip into each other.

IMPORTANT: Don't pull too hard or the tube might not decrease its diameter along its entire length evenly, but only at certain places. Instead of a nice necklace you would get an irregular tube.

To make the thread thinner and even, pull it by hand through the draw plate (**TECHNIQUE 4**). Pull the thread through increasingly smaller holes.

IMPORTANT: Do not leave out a hole but reduce the diameter in the sequence of the holes.

When pulling by hand, it may happen that individual stitches "fall" inward and the mesh pattern is not even. To prevent this from happening, use metal cores for the last two or three passes through the draw plate. The metal rods sustain the stitches from the inside (see also page 13).

After the last pass (hole with dia. 7 mm) the thread is 21 inches long. The end stitches are cast off and the two ends of the tube are pulled together and glued to both parts of the plug catch.

The silver wire is bent into a ring with a diameter of $1^{1}/_{2}$ inches for the mounting of the amethyst. This is best done when you bend the wire around a core, such as a round piece of wood, a glass, etc.

Since the wire has a length of $2^{3}/_{8}$ inches the ends of the wires overlap $^{3}/_{8}$ inch. Run the wire through the opening of the amethyst.

Use a hammer to flatten the wire at both ends over a hard surface. The traces of the hammer result in a finely structured surface which scatters the light nicely. The edges and the ends of the wires are broken with a fine file and slightly rounded.

Hook both ends of the ring into the mesh of the necklace. Both ends of the wires overlap inside of the thread and are secured there.

TECHNIQUE 2

MATERIALS AND TOOLS

copper wire, painted lilac, 28 gauge

silver wire, 15 gauge, length $2^{3}/_{8}$ in.

silver plug catch

superglue

1 amethyst, drilled

8-peg wooden knitting loom

hammer

fine file

NECKLACE

length $21^{1}/_{4}$ in.

36 ZEPPELIN

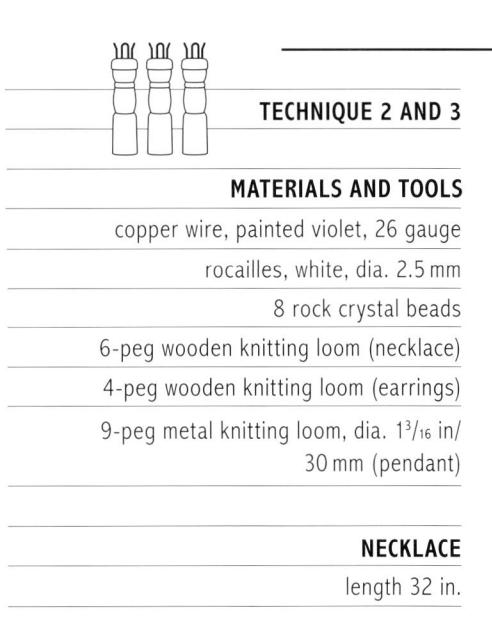

TECHNIQUE 2 AND 3

MATERIALS AND TOOLS

copper wire, painted violet, 26 gauge

rocailles, white, dia. 2.5 mm

8 rock crystal beads

6-peg wooden knitting loom (necklace)

4-peg wooden knitting loom (earrings)

9-peg metal knitting loom, dia. 1 3/16 in/ 30 mm (pendant)

NECKLACE

length 32 in.

NECKLACE

First a 30 1/4-inch-long knitted tube is made in **SIMPLE** technique (**TECHNIQUE 2**) with the 6-peg wooden knitting loom. Pull the thread slightly while knitting so the mesh pattern turns out more even.

Cast off the end stitches and pull the two ends of the tubes together.

PENDANT

White rocaille beads are threaded onto the wire for the pendant with a zeppelin shape and a cylinder is made in simple technique with the metal knitting loom.

Start out with three rounds of winding and knitting without beads. During the fourth round of winding four rocailles are inserted after the first, fourth and seventh pegs. During the fifth round of winding the rocailles lie after the second, fifth and eighth pegs. And during the sixth round of winding after the fourth, sixth and ninth pegs. The seventh round of winding and knitting is knitted without beads.

Repeat this sequence four times and finish with three rounds of winding and knitting without beads. Cast off the stitches and remove the cylinder from the loom.

Due to the gauge of the wire, it is not easy to pull the ends of the cylinder together. Rather, you have to shape a nice top by hand on both sides. Bend the cylinder until the ring closes completely. The shape is secured with both ends of the wire by running the wire through the end stitches and then twisting and shortening them.

In order to attach the pendant to the necklace first three rock crystal beads each are threaded onto the ends of the wire. Then the wire is run through the end stitches of the cylinder and is twisted and shortened.

EARRINGS

A winding and knitting round without beads is made with the 4-peg wooden knitting loom in **SIMPLE** technique. At the second round two rocailles each are inserted behind the first and the third pegs. The third round is left without beads. At the fourth round they lie behind the second and the fourth pegs. The fifth row is once again knitted without beads.

TIP:
Work both of the earrings with three to four "blind rows" in between. There the tube is divided with a cutter and both halves are "knitted back" to the desired size (see Tango, page 110).

Then cast off the end stitches. Thread three rocailles onto the starting wire. The wire is run through the jump ring of the ear hook and twisted above the rocailles. Run the wire back through the three rocailles and shorten it.

Finally, thread one rock crystal bead onto the end wire and twist and shorten the wire at the end of the tube.

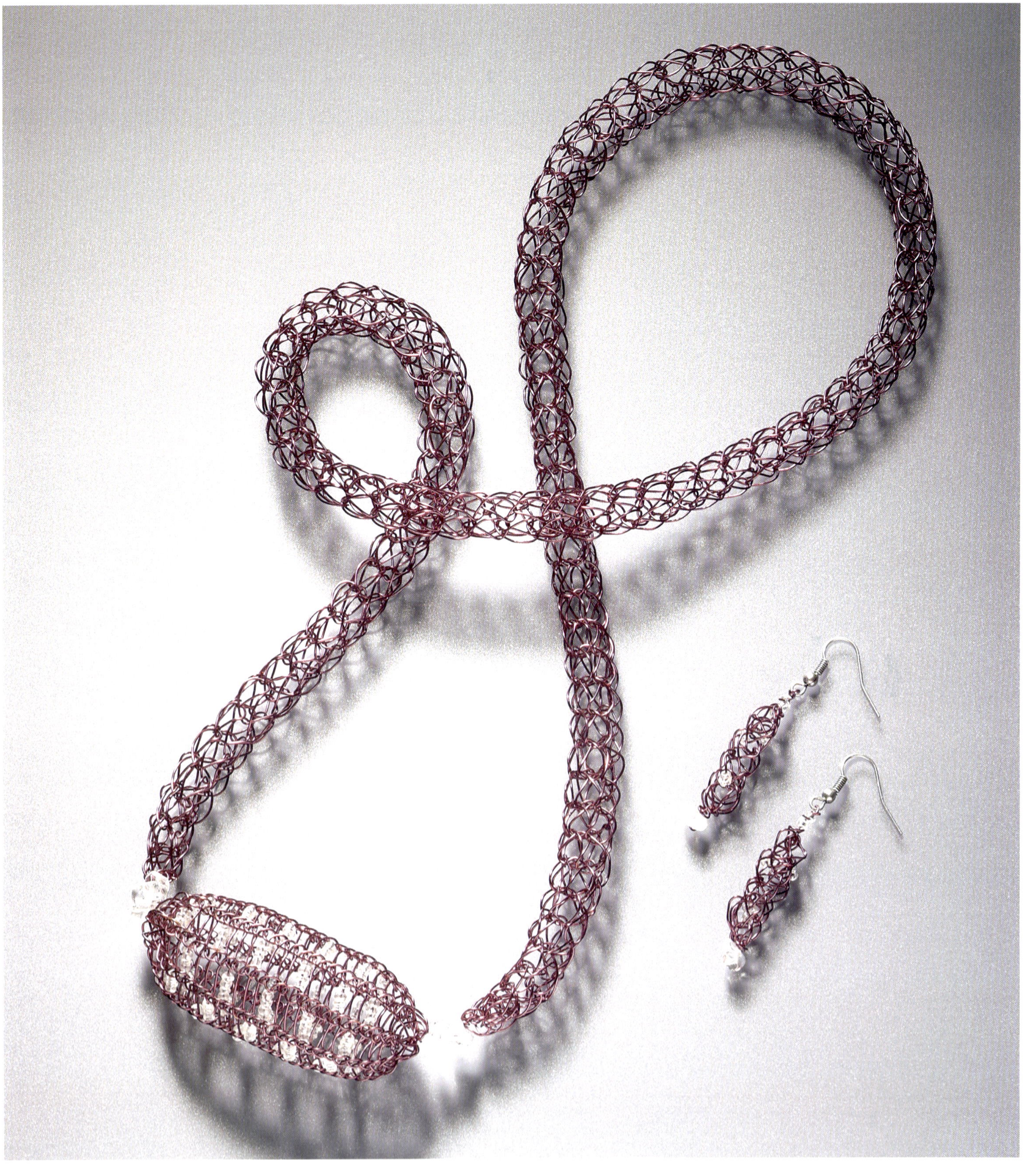

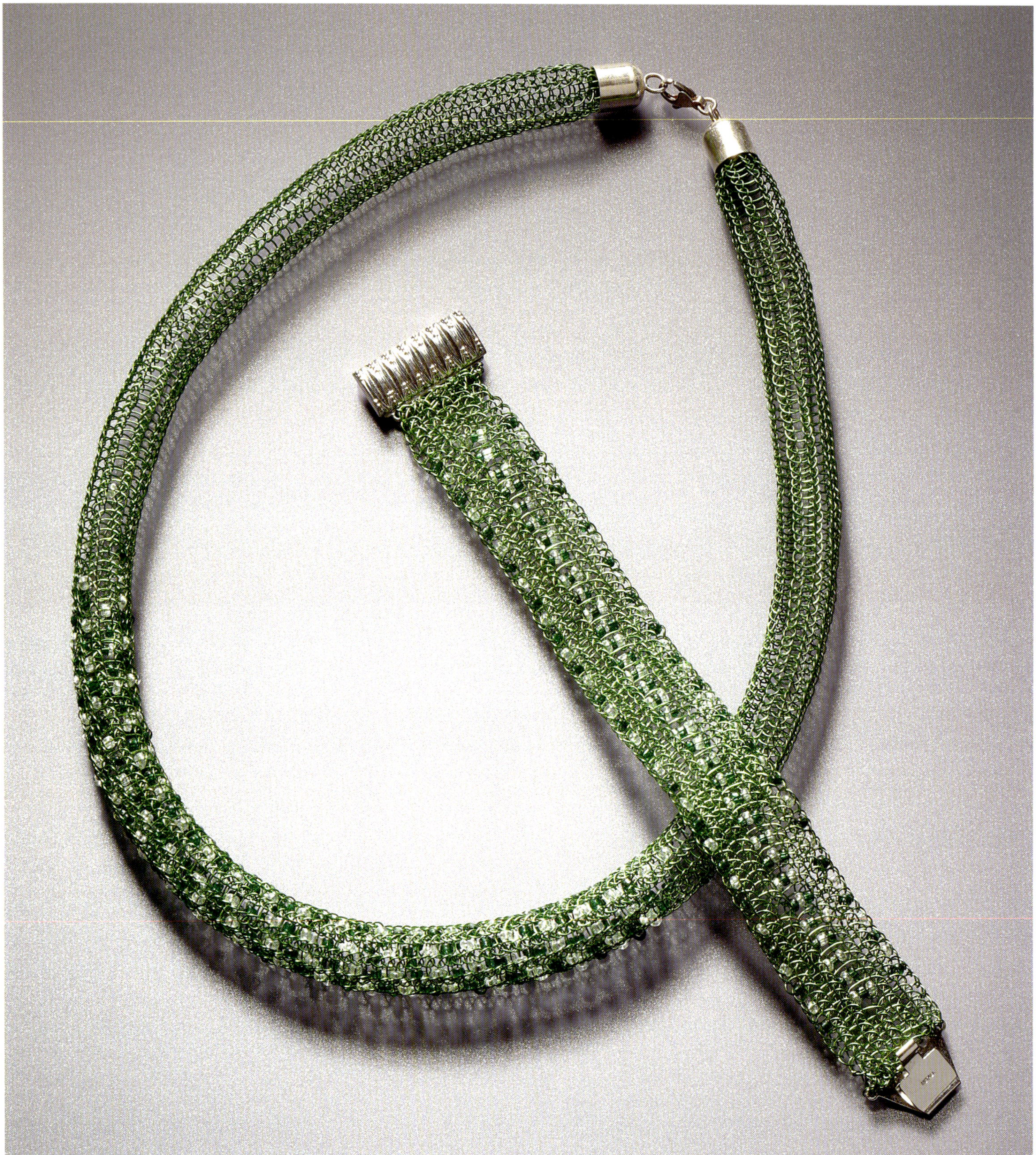

37 MEADOW DEW

NECKLACE

For the necklace and the bracelet, alternatingly thread green and white rocailles onto the wire.

Then knit 6 inches simple (**TECHNIQUE 3**) with the metal knitting loom (dia. $9/16$ inches). This corresponds to about 72 rounds of winding and knitting. During the following ten rounds (about $3/4$ to 1 inch) the beads can "flow in," that is, you insert a bead during the winding rounds as you like.

IMPORTANT: Note that at first the beads are inserted at larger distances, and then these distances become shorter at the last two to three rounds before the decorative section as such. So the part of the necklace decorated with beads does not start at one point but rather the bead pattern is introduced gradually.

For the pattern as such, add a bead after every other peg. Because of the uneven number of pegs (or the gaps in between) the beads form two parallel running spirals.

Once a length of 6 inches has been reached with this bead pattern, allow the beads to "run out" over ten winding and knitting rounds. So you work in continuously less beads during the first two to three rounds and increase the distances in the following rounds.

Now 6 inches are made without beads. The thread is now $19 1/4$ to $19 3/4$ inches long.

Cast off the end stitches and pull the knitted tube together at both sides, then twist and shorten the ends of the wires. Slightly press the ends of the tubes together and glue them with superglue into the caps of the lobster claw clasp.

BRACELET

For the bracelet, a rhomboid metal knitting loom is utilized. It has the advantage of having edges where the finished knitted tube can be easily folded into a flat band. In order to add beads the wire can be run behind a peg which sits on an edge. Start out with eight rounds of winding and knitting without beads.

IMPORTANT: For these eight rounds you need **ALL OF THE PEGS!**

After the eighth round of knitting, a corner peg must be "put out of service." Lift the stitch that lies on the corner peg and put it over the peg to the left of it. Two stitches now lie on it. Lift the lower stitch over the top one and drop it behind the peg. With the next round of winding the wire is not wound over the edge peg anymore but run past it.

Now add the beads to every other round of winding: one bead after the right peg, three beads behind the front one and one bead in front of the left peg. No beads are inserted at the rear side of the band.

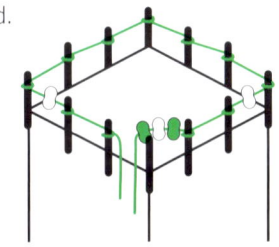

Since the green and white beads were threaded alternatingly a nice color play results, both at the row at the edge where only one bead is located, as well as at the center with three beads.

After about $6 1/4$ inches you close the band with eight rows of winding and knitting. The center peg at the first two winding rounds without beads is wound again and can be knitted along with the second knitting round.

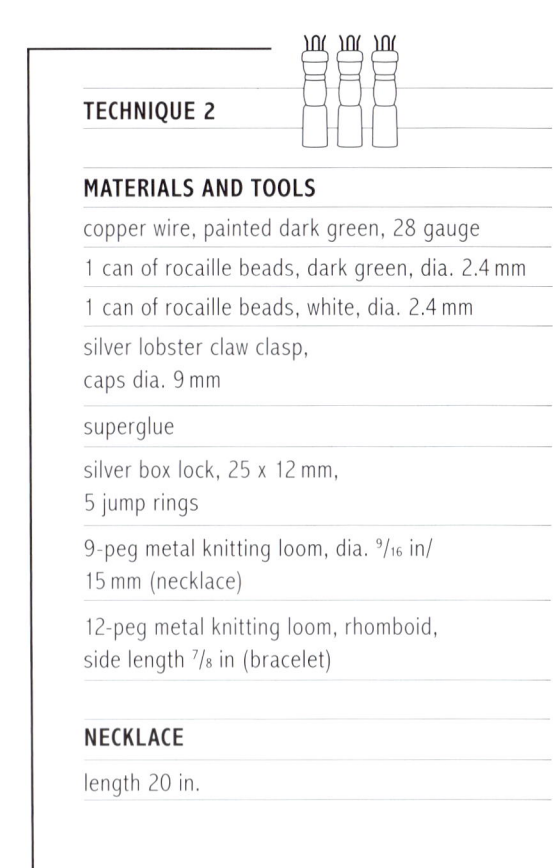

TECHNIQUE 2

MATERIALS AND TOOLS

copper wire, painted dark green, 28 gauge

1 can of rocaille beads, dark green, dia. 2.4 mm

1 can of rocaille beads, white, dia. 2.4 mm

silver lobster claw clasp, caps dia. 9 mm

superglue

silver box lock, 25 x 12 mm, 5 jump rings

9-peg metal knitting loom, dia. $9/16$ in/ 15 mm (necklace)

12-peg metal knitting loom, rhomboid, side length $7/8$ in (bracelet)

NECKLACE

length 20 in.

Cast off the stitches, remove the knitted tube from the loom, and press it flat. The band is sewn to the jump rings of the box lock with both ends of the wire.

IMPORTANT: Leave the beginning and end section of the wire with a length of about 8 inches.

38 ROPE LADDER

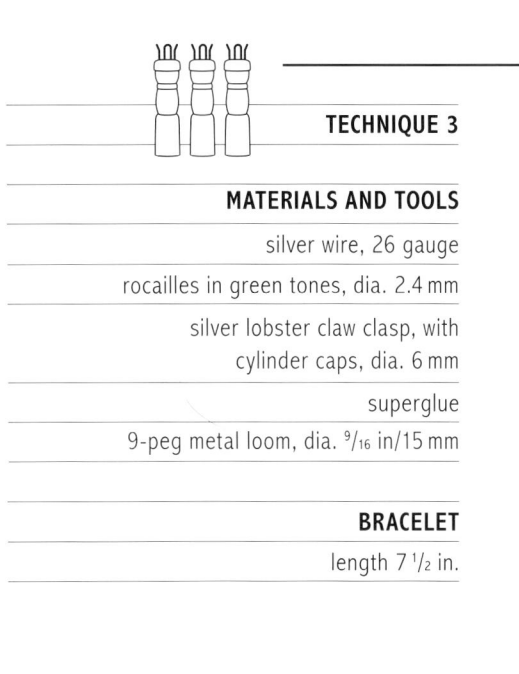

TECHNIQUE 3

MATERIALS AND TOOLS

silver wire, 26 gauge

rocailles in green tones, dia. 2.4 mm

silver lobster claw clasp, with cylinder caps, dia. 6 mm

superglue

9-peg metal loom, dia. 9/16 in/15 mm

BRACELET

length 7 1/2 in.

BRACELET

With this project, only four pegs of the metal knitting loom (dia. 9/16 inches) are utilized. This results in a filigree and trapezoid-shaped band where the rocailles are nicely featured at its narrow side.

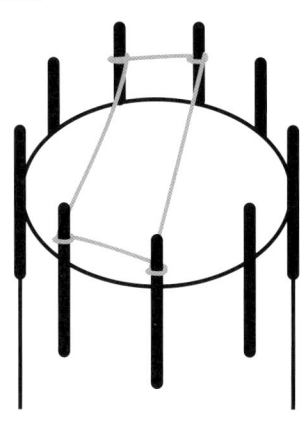

You knit two stitches and then tension a section of the wire. At the opposite end two stitches are knitted as well and the wire is tensioned back to the side where you started from. This is somewhat unusual at first but you will quickly become acccustomed to the sequence, more so as you need less time due to the smaller number of stitches.

Start out with four winding and knitting rounds without beads. Then four beads are inserted during each winding round at the narrow side of the trapezoid and secured during the following knitting round. This results in that one row of wire is always visible between the row of beads.

Work 28 rows of beads as described before and finish with four rounds of winding and knitting without beads.

Then cast off the end stitches and pull together both sides of the band. Wind the ends of the wires two two three times around the ends of the bracelet and press it together so it fits into the cylinder caps of the lobster claw clasp. Glue the ends into them.

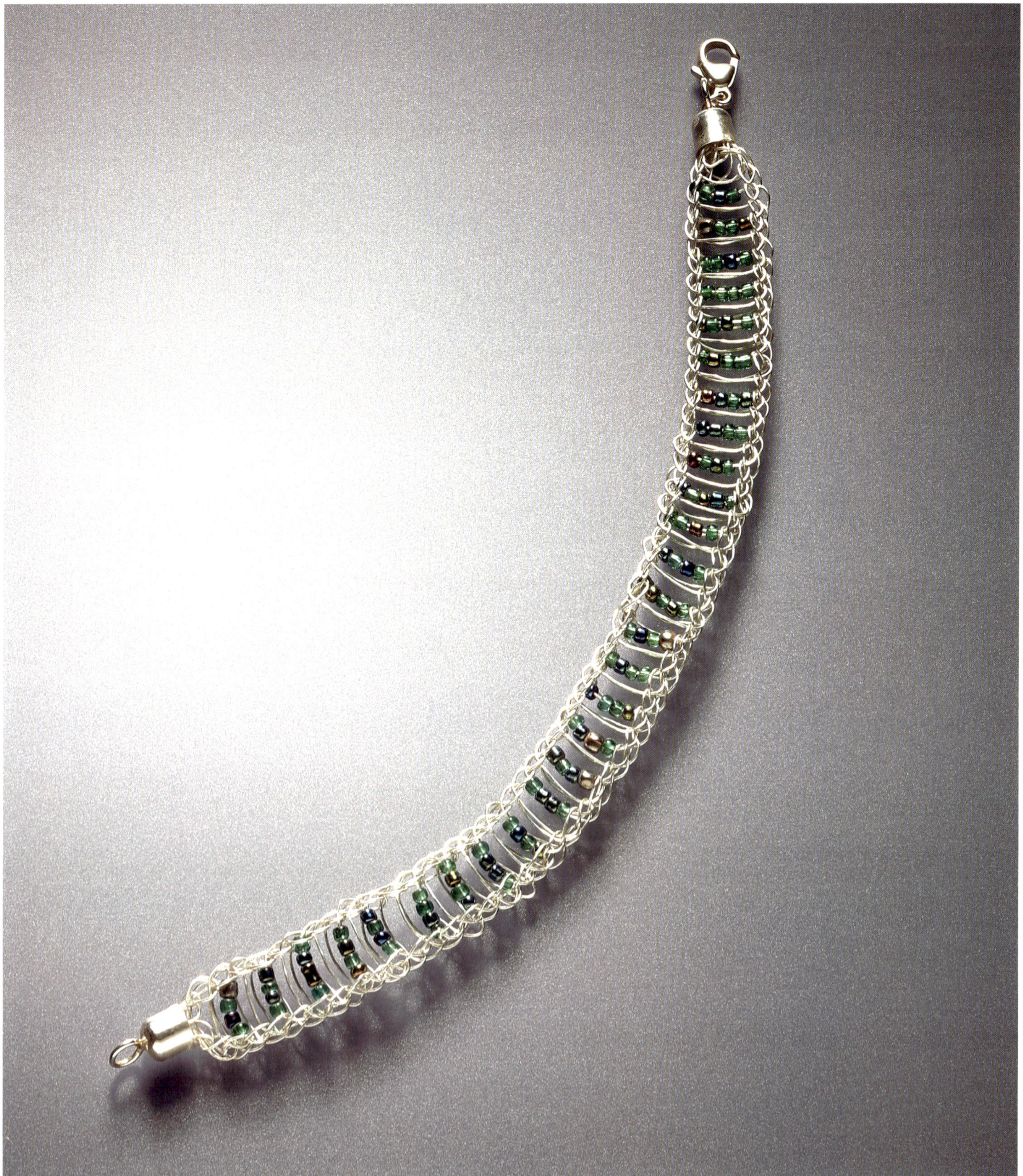

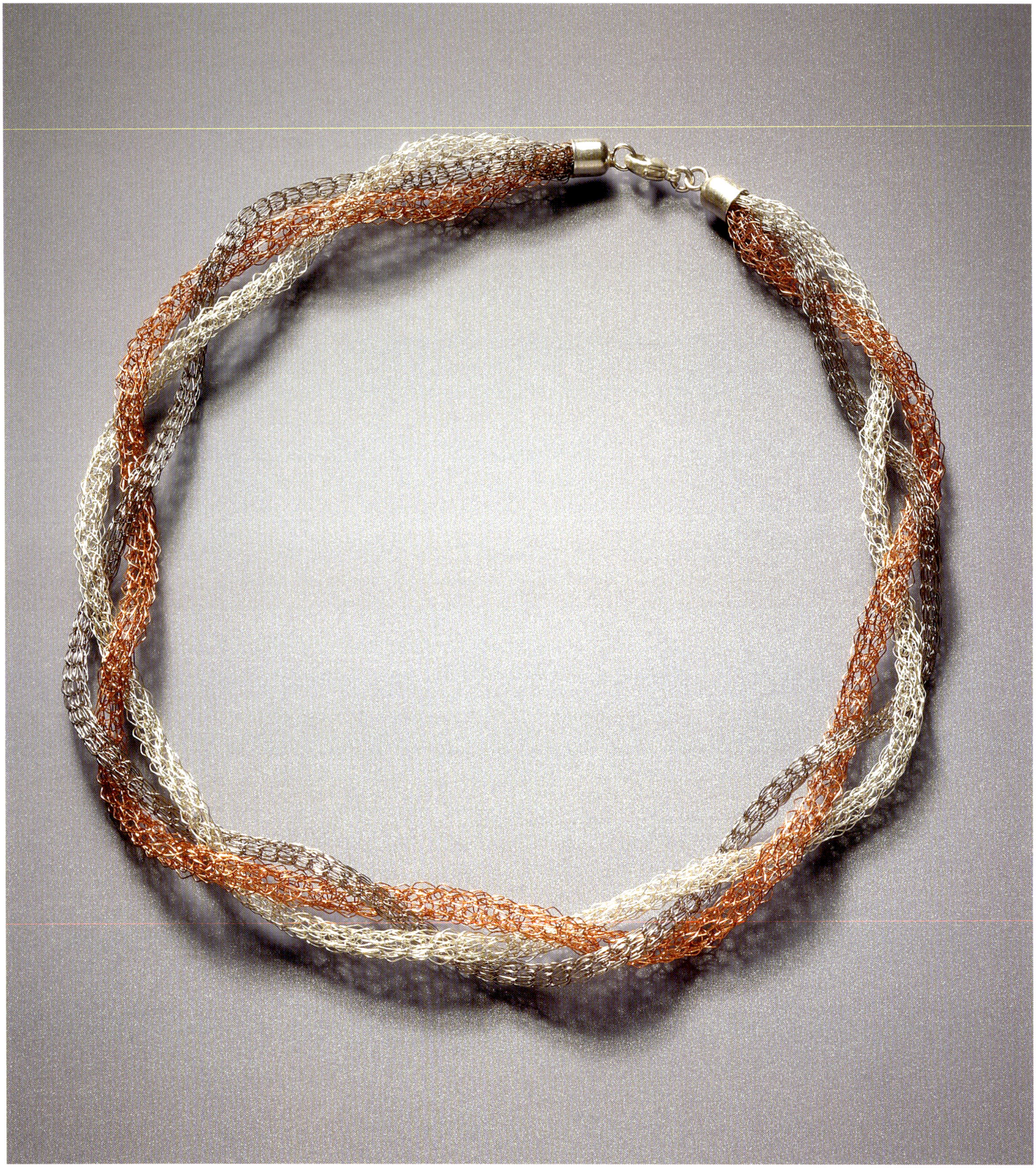

39 BRAID

Three threads of equal length are made with the metal knitting loom (dia. 9/16 inches) for this necklace. The difficulty of this project results mainly from the fine material. While the 28-gauge copper wire is rather robust the 30-gauge silver wire must be treated more gently. And the thin painted copper wire of only 32 gauge is very delicate. So you should have some practice before taking on this project.

Three knitted tubes with a length of 19 3/4 inches are knitted in **OFFSET** technique (**TECHNIQUE 3**) with the 9-peg metal knitting loom (dia. 9/16 inches). When pulling through the loom the tubes become relatively thin so additional pulling after knitting is not necessary anymore. Due to the different gauge of the wires the threads get slightly diverging diameters.

After knitting weave the tubes loosely into a braid and sew the ends together with the ends of the wires. The ends of the tubes are pressed together so they fit into the cylinder caps of the catch. They are secured with superglue.

TECHNIQUE 3

MATERIALS AND TOOLS

silver wire, 30 gauge

copper wire, 28 gauge

copper wire, painted gray, 32 gauge

catch with cylinder caps (dia. 7 mm) and lobster claw clasp

superglue

9-peg metal knitting loom, dia. 9/16 in/15 mm

NECKLACE

21 1/4 in.

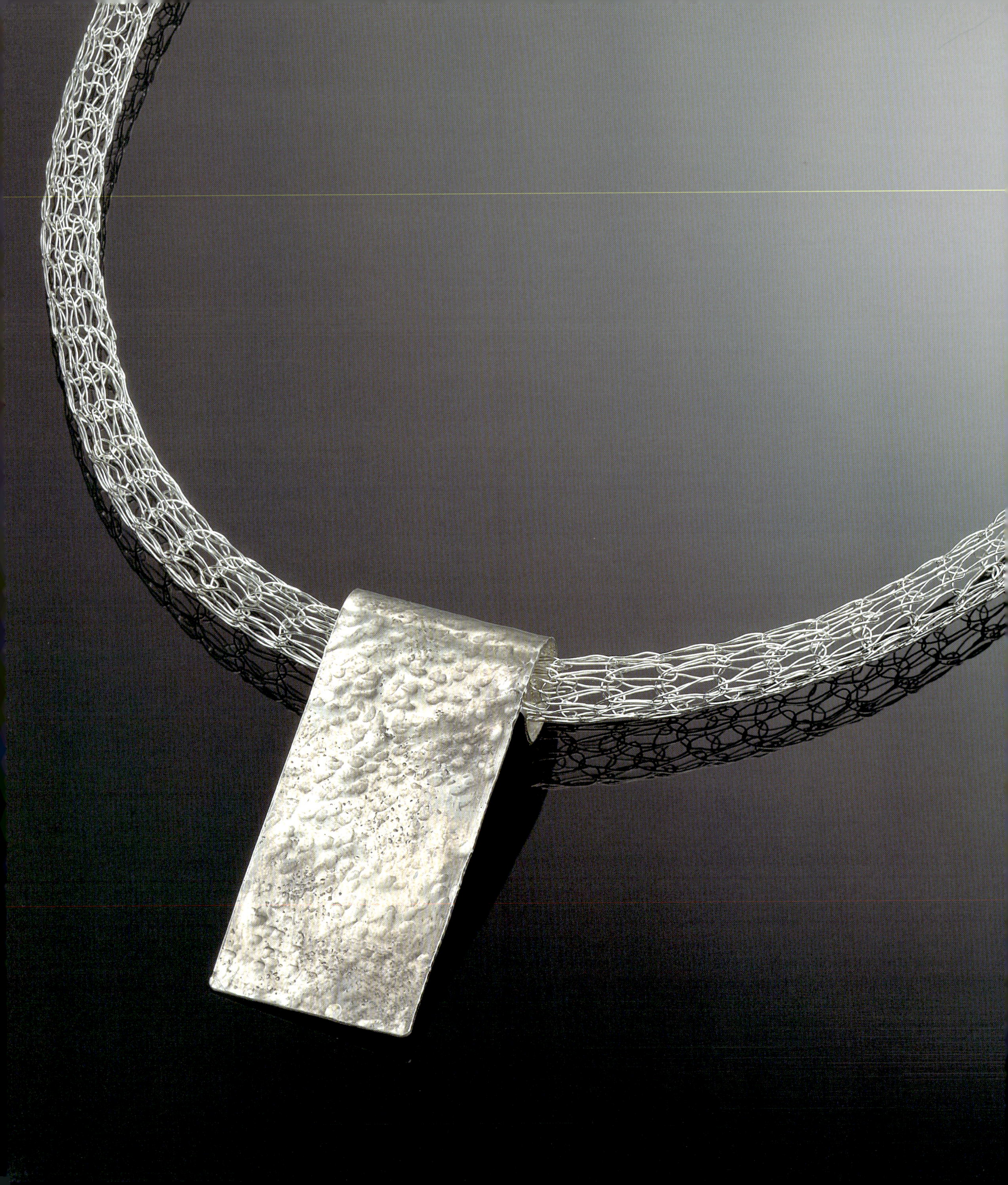

SILVER JEWELRY

"A DECOLLETÉ IS THAT THIN LINE WHERE GOOD TASTE IS BALANCED WITHOUT FALLING OFF."

Coco Chanel

40 HARLEQUIN

TECHNIQUE 3

MATERIALS AND TOOLS

silver wire, 26 gauge

colored metal bells

silver lobster claw clasp, with cylinder caps, dia. $3/8$ in.

superglue

9-peg metal loom, dia. $9/16$ in/15 mm

NECKLACE

length $21 1/2$ in.

I discovered the colored bells by chance. Nine of these small pieces were originally mounted to a children´s ring. I bought three of these rings and removed the bells. Now their metallic look adorns several of my jewelry pieces such as this silver necklace.

Make a thread of a length of $20 7/8$ inches (**TECHNIQUE 3**) with the metal knitting loom (dia. $9/16$ in.) in **SIMPLE** technique.

After knitting the end stitches are cast off and the ends of the wire are twisted and shortened.

Due to the relatively thick wire the necklace is still somewhat stiff after knitting. You can make it more pliable by rolling it back and forth between the hands without pressure. You can also place the necklace on the table and roll it with both hands as if you were making a thin strand of dough.

As the stitches lie close to each other and the pattern of the mesh is not supposed to change the necklace is not stretched any further.

Glue the lobster claw clasp onto the ends of the necklace and finally sew the colored bells to the necklace using a thin transparent nylon thread.

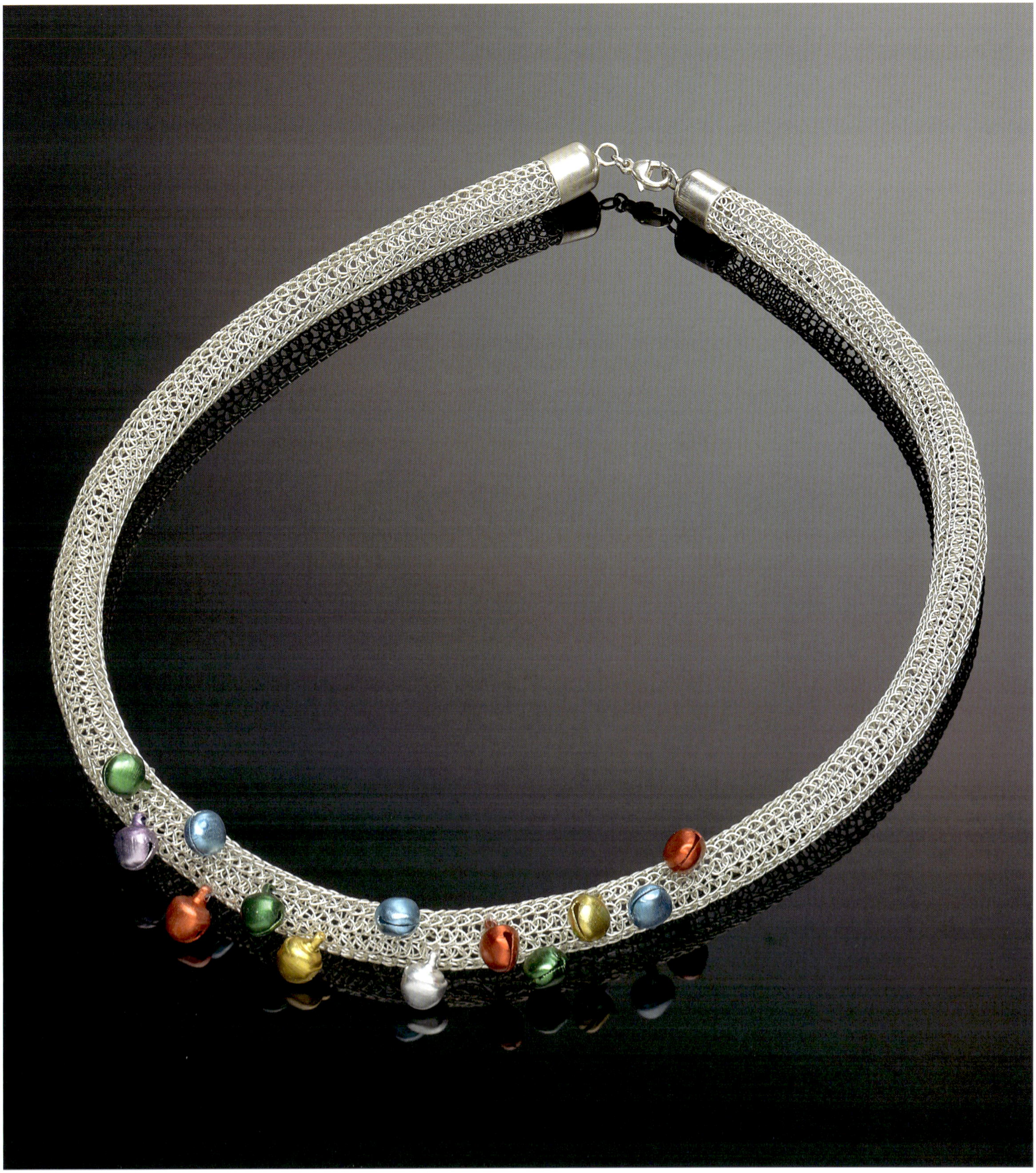

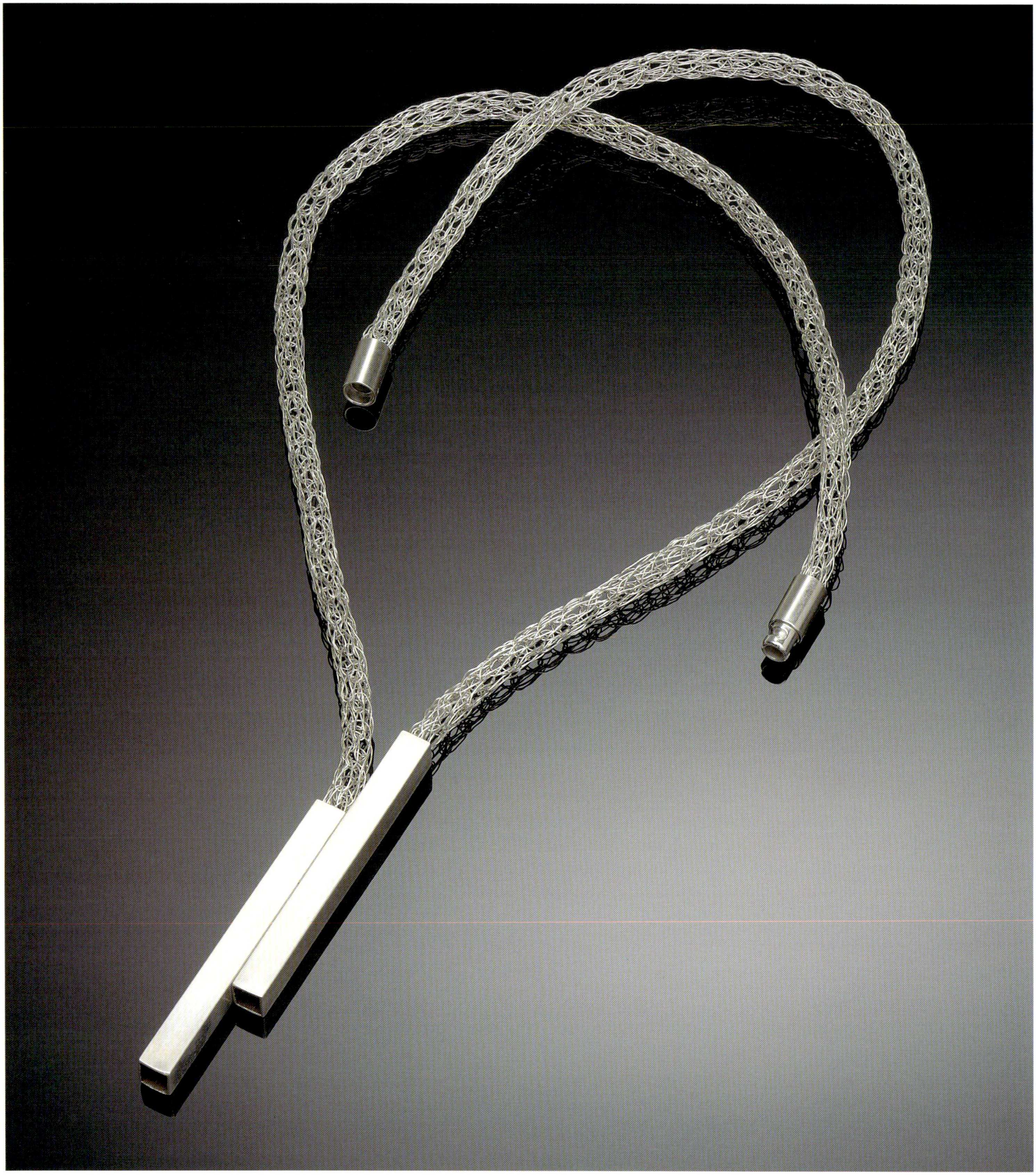

41 TUNNEL

Make two separate threads of 11 1/2 and 11 3/4 inches in length in **OFFSET** technique (**TECHNIQUE 3)** with the metal knitting loom (dia. 9/16 inches). Carefully pull the two necklaces by hand while knitting the two necklaces.

After knitting the end stitches are cast off and the ends of the wires are twisted and shortened.

Using the draw plate the threads are pulled with the metal cores (**TECHNIQUE 4**). Use a 1/16-inch core for the last pulling operation.

IMPORTANT: Reduce the diameter of the metal core in several steps.

Saw the square hinge in half. The sawing edges of the 2-inch-long sections are files with a coarse file and then reworked with the fine file. Slightly bevel the edges.

Using the superglue the two halves of the hinge are glued together. With my project I have offset them about half an inch.

IMPORTANT: Don't use too much glue! It should not be visible where the sections meet.

Now the knitted threads are glued at one side into the bayonet catch. At the other side, glue the necklace into the hinge sections.

IMPORTANT: Make sure you push the ends of the threads far enough into the hinge sections so that the bayonet catch is placed at the rear center of the necklace.

Finally, the hinge sections are polished with fine steel wool.

TECHNIQUE 3

MATERIALS AND TOOLS

silver wire, 30 gauge

square hinge from silver, 3/16 x 3/16 in., length 4 in.

silver bayonet catch, dia. 1/4 in.

superglue

9-peg metal knitting loom, dia. 9/16 in/15 mm

coarse file

fine file

fine steel wool

NECKLACE

length 23 1/2 in.

42 FABLED

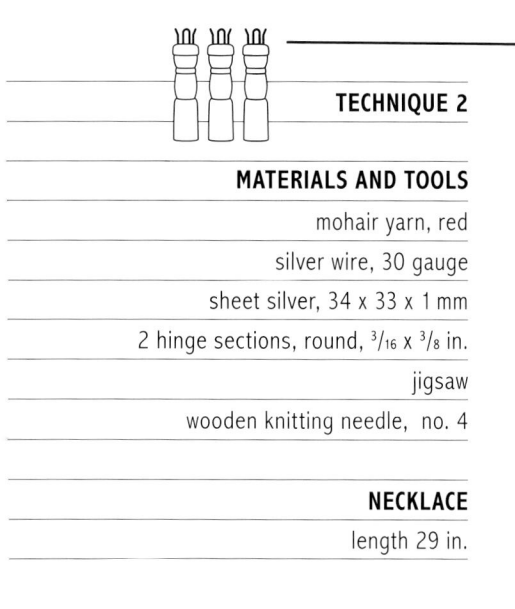

TECHNIQUE 2

MATERIALS AND TOOLS

mohair yarn, red

silver wire, 30 gauge

sheet silver, 34 x 33 x 1 mm

2 hinge sections, round, 3/16 x 3/8 in.

jigsaw

wooden knitting needle, no. 4

NECKLACE

length 29 in.

In the South Tyrol region of Germany, there is a legend of the endless yarn ball. This is based on the desire of the housewife that there always be enough yarn available to dress the entire family and keep it warm. This old legend has inspired me to make this necklace.

First a 41-inch-long knitted thread of mohair yarn is made with the wooden knitting loom. Cast off the end stitches and pull the ends together and sew the ends of the threads.

Now, using the wooden knitting loom again, make a knitted thread from the silver wire with a length of 29 inches. The end stitches are cast off. But both ends of the thread must remain open so the mohair tube can be inserted. To do this, proceed as described in project 26.

TIP:
The two ends of the mohair tube should be of different length where they protrude from the ends of the knitted tube, offset by about 3/4 inch.

In order to attach the mohair tube inside of the silver necklace, run the ends of the wires through the mohair tube several times and sew it. Finally, the ends of the wires are wound three to four times around both of them (mohair tube and silver necklace) and hence diminish the diameter. Then the ends of the wires are twisted and shortened.

Use the jigsaw to saw an irregular slab from the sheet silver (use appropriate metal saw blades!). Five perforations with a diameter of 1 mm mark the edges of a small house and its gables.

Stitch the outline of the house with the mohair yarn and mark the front of the house with an X. The ends of the yarn are knotted at the rear of the plate and shortened.

The two hinge sections are glued at some distance vertically onto the rear of the plate. The two ends of the mohair tube are pulled from the top downward through the hinge sections until the end part of the silver necklace is inside of the hinge. The two sections of the necklace are attached to the hinge sections with superglue.

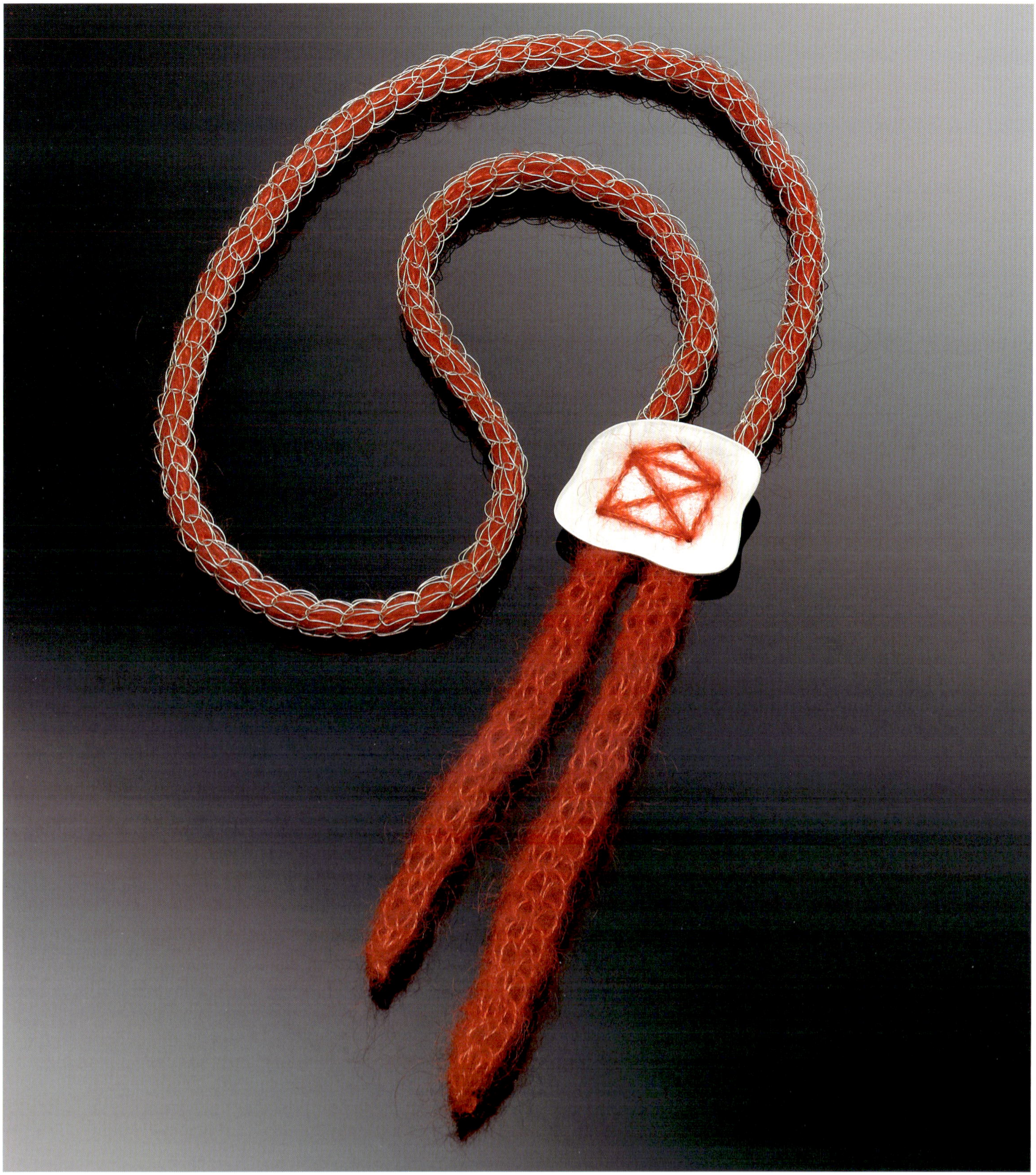

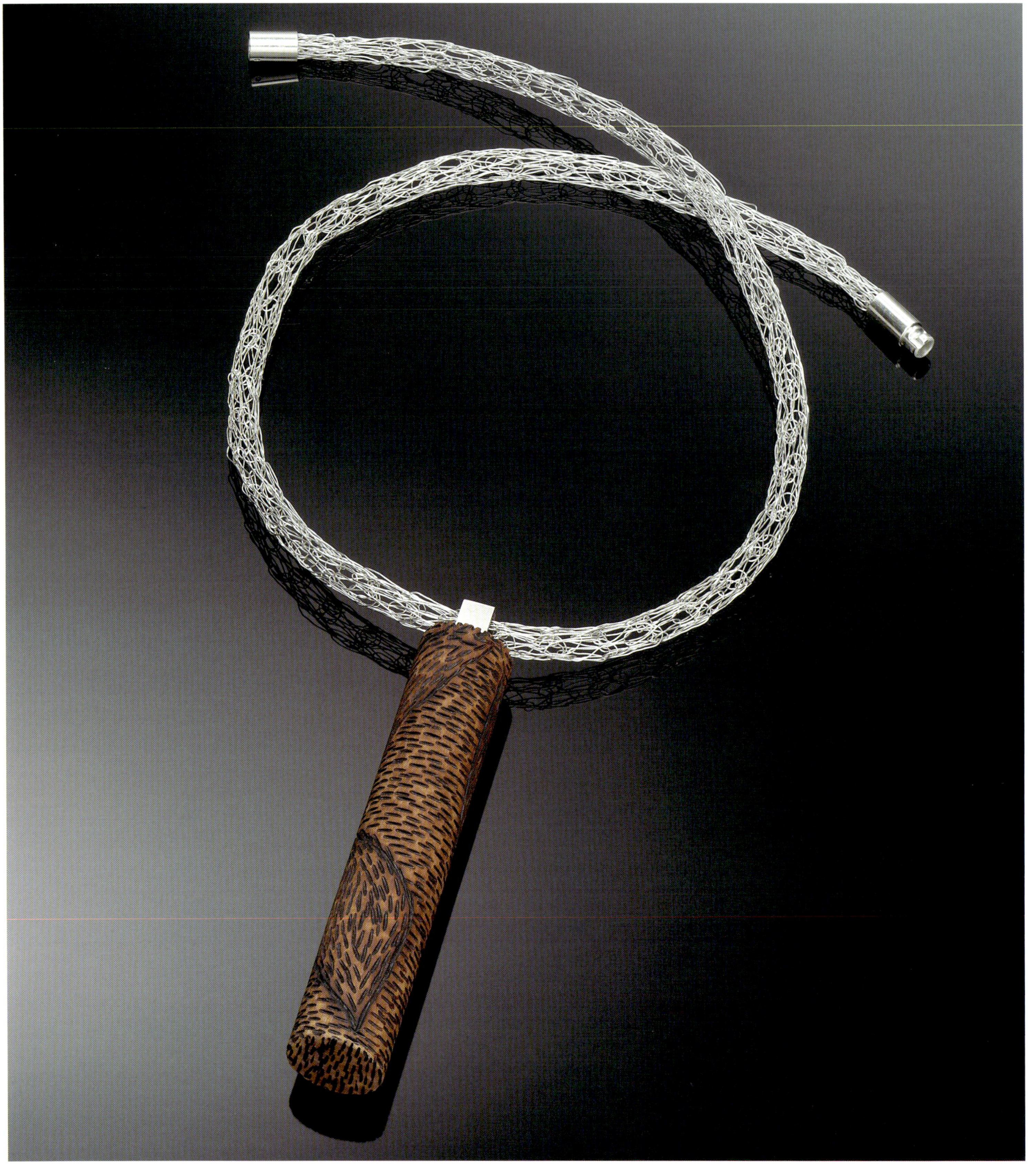

43 BURN WOOD

A necklace with a length of 17¼ inches is knitted in **OFFSET** technique (**TECHNIQUE 3**) with a metal knitting loom (dia. 1³/₁₆ in.).

Because the pattern of the mesh is relatively irregular due to the metal knitting loom's size and the thin wire the necklace thread must be calibrated, that is, the thread is pushed with the draw plate and the metal cores in several steps and the pattern of the mesh is equalized. Work from here on following the indications of **TECHNIQUE 4** and diminish the diameter step by step. Finish the calibration process with a ³/₆-inch metal core when you reach the ¼-inch hole of the draw plate.

Pull together the ends of the necklace with the ends of the wires and twist them two or three times. Twist the ends of the wires and shorten them. Then glue the two halves of the bayonet catch to the ends of the necklace.

For the pendant I have sawed off 3⅛-inch-long piece from a wooden rod with a diameter of ⅝ inches. You can burn the fine marks with a branding pen to make a leaf pattern.

The section of the hinge is glued onto the wooden pendant as the jump ring. After the calibration the silver thread has a diameter of ⅛ inches and fits exactly through the hinge which has an inner diameter of ⅛ x ⅛ inches.

TIP:
Don't leave out the top and bottom sides. As a variation you can use an untreated piece of wood with a nice grain and color or an interesting section of a twig or branch.

TECHNIQUE 3

MATERIALS AND TOOLS

silver wire, 30 gauge

hinge section ¼ x ¼ x ¼ in., interior measure 6 x 6 mm x ¼ in.

wooden rod, dia. ⅝ in., length 3⅛ in.

silver bayonet catch, dia. ¼ in.

superglue

9-peg metal knitting loom, dia. 1³/₁₆ in/30 mm

branding pen

NECKLACE

length 19¾ in.

44 EMBOSS

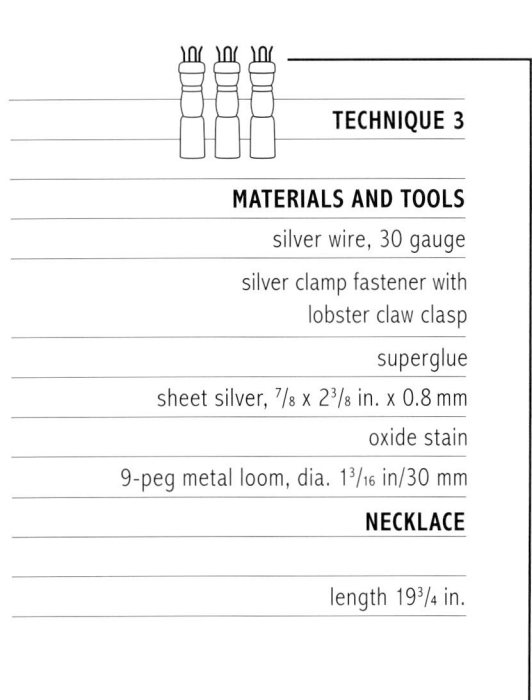

TECHNIQUE 3

MATERIALS AND TOOLS

silver wire, 30 gauge

silver clamp fastener with lobster claw clasp

superglue

sheet silver, 7/8 x 2 3/8 in. x 0.8 mm

oxide stain

9-peg metal loom, dia. 1 3/16 in/30 mm

NECKLACE

length 19 3/4 in.

Make a thread in **SIMPLE** technique (**TECHNIQUE 3**) with a length of 18 1/2 inches with a metal knitting loom (dia. 1 3/16 in.).

Here as well the thread is calibrated. Follow the instructions for **TECHNIQUE 4** and gradually diminish the diameter. Finish the calibration process with a 1/4-inch metal core when you have reached the 0.2 inch / 7 mm hole of the draw plate.

Pull the ends of the thread together with the ends of the wires and wrap them around two to three times. Twist the ends of the wires and shorten them. Then place the ends of the thread into the clamping fastener and glue them.

For the pendant, cut out a rectangle of 7/8 x 23 1/2 inches from the 0.8-mm thin sheet silver with a saw. You can easily achieve the pattern of the surface by placing the strip of silver onto a fine-grained stone and hammering onto the sheet. The coarse surface of the stone is embossed onto the silver. For a particularly fine structure you can put some sand onto a hard surface, place the piece of sheet silver on top of it and work it with the hammer.

In order to achieve an additional patina on the surface of the pendant dip some cotton into oxide stain solution (wear gloves!) and lightly brush over the surface. If you want more emphasis on the oxidation, repeat the process.

After drying the oxide stain is rinsed under running water and the silver sheet is dried.

One end of the pendant is bent into a wave to make a suspension. As the sheet is very thin this is easily done. Look for the appropriate item with a diameter of at least 1/4 to 5/16 inches (pencil, wooden rod, etc.). Place the narrow side of the sheet onto the item and press firmly with your thumbs toward the edge and bend the sheet with the other hand until the metal almost touches the edge again.

Check the diameter so that the silver thread slides nicely through the suspension of the pendant.

TIP:
Make sure you don't hit the edge of the silver sheet with the hammer.

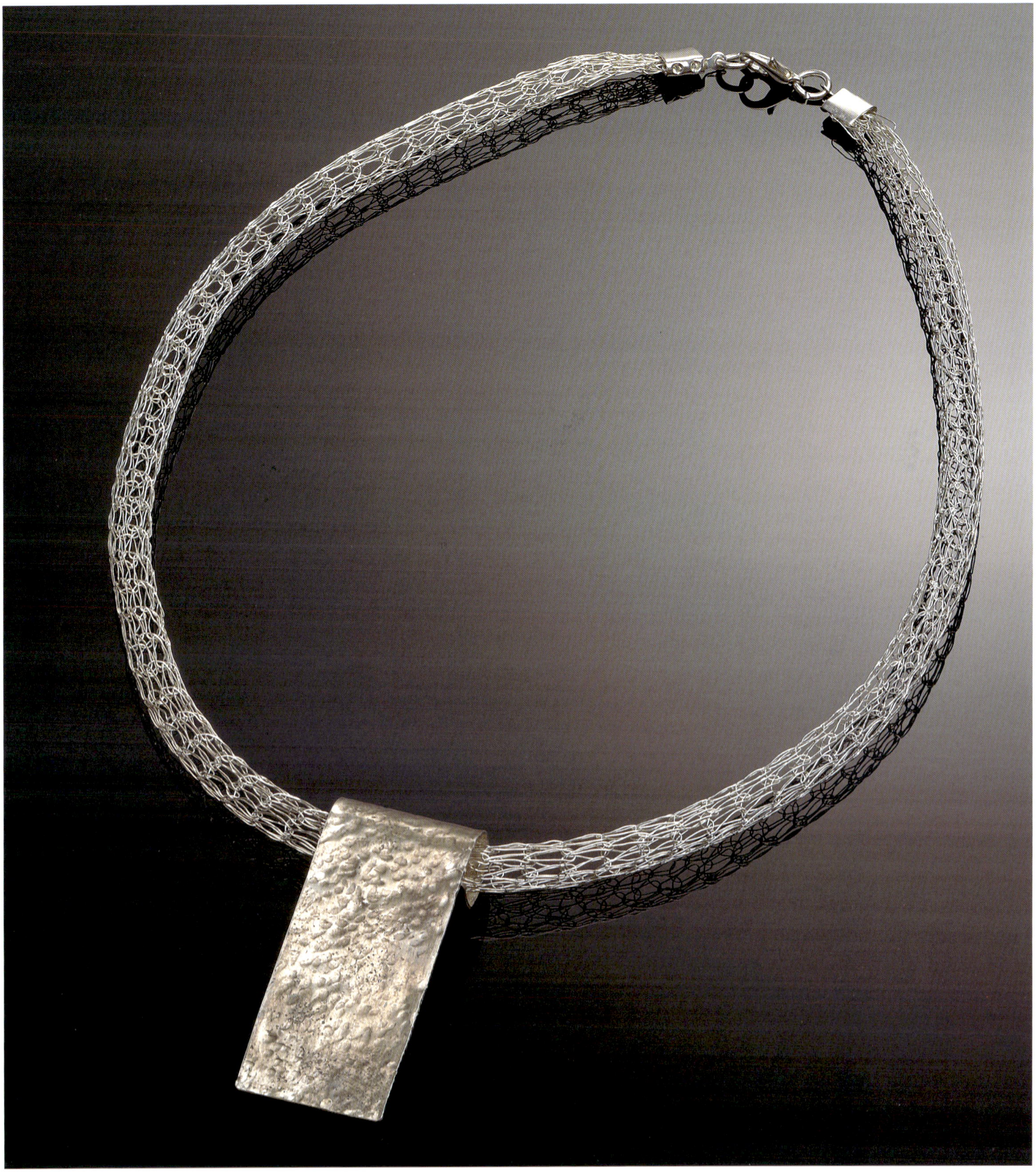

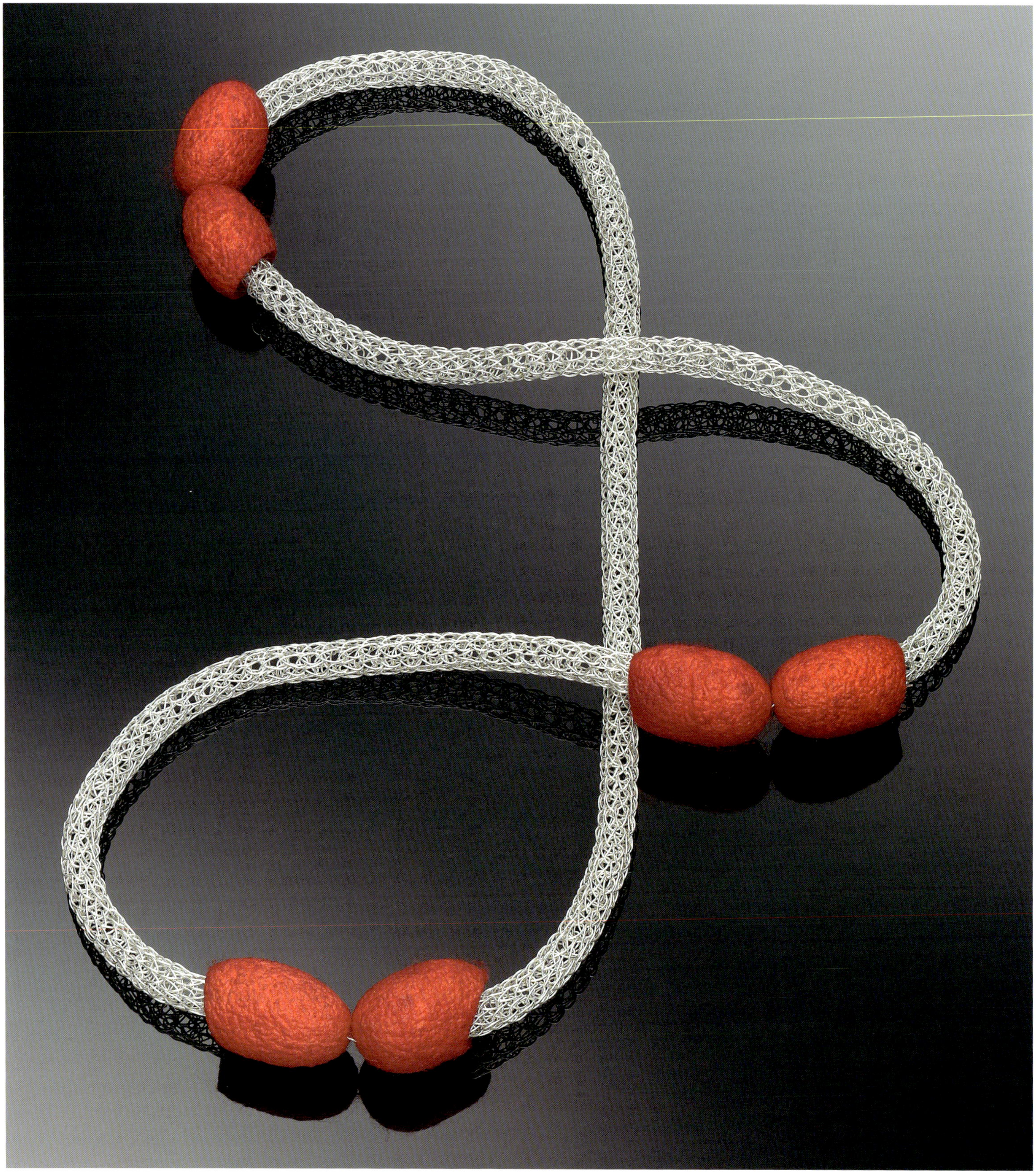

45 COCOON

Three thread sections in **SIMPLE** technique (**TECHNIQUE 3**) are made for this necklace with a metal knitting loom (dia. 9/16 in.).

IMPORTANT: Leave at least 8 inches of knitting wire at both ends.

The sections of thread are 7, 8, and 11 3/4 inches long and are pulled and calibrated. Follow the instructions for **TECHNIQUE 4** and gradually diminish the diameter. Finish the calibration process with a 6 mm metal core once you have reached the 7 mm hole of the draw plate.

After pulling them the threads are about 9, 9 3/4, and 13 3/4 inches long with a diameter of 5/16 inches.

Use a needle to punch a hole at the center of the tops of the silk cocoons. Place the cocoons onto the ends of the threads and pull the end of the wire through the hole.

In order to connect the individual sections of thread with each other take one end of thread each from two threads and run it through the cocoon of the other thread.

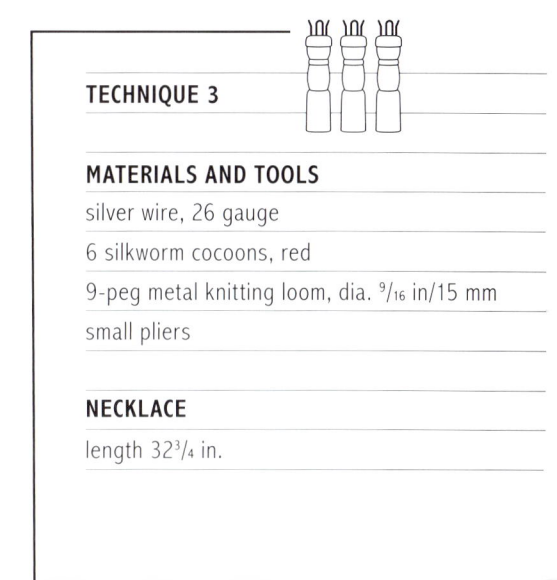

TECHNIQUE 3

MATERIALS AND TOOLS
silver wire, 26 gauge
6 silkworm cocoons, red
9-peg metal knitting loom, dia. 9/16 in/15 mm
small pliers

NECKLACE
length 32 3/4 in.

Pull together the threads from the ends of the wires until the cocoons meet. Inside of the cocoon the ends of the wire are wrapped a few times around some stitches, twisted and shortened. You might want to use a pair of small pliers here.

CONNECTING THREADS

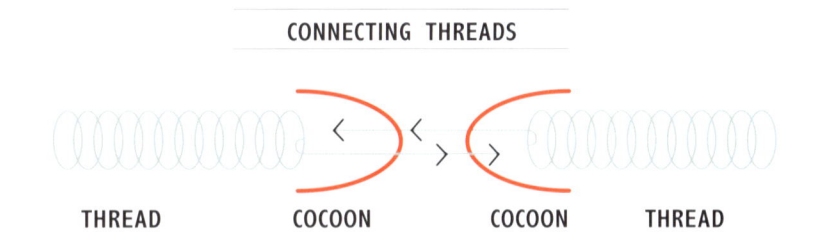

THREAD COCOON COCOON THREAD

46 BEAD STRINGS

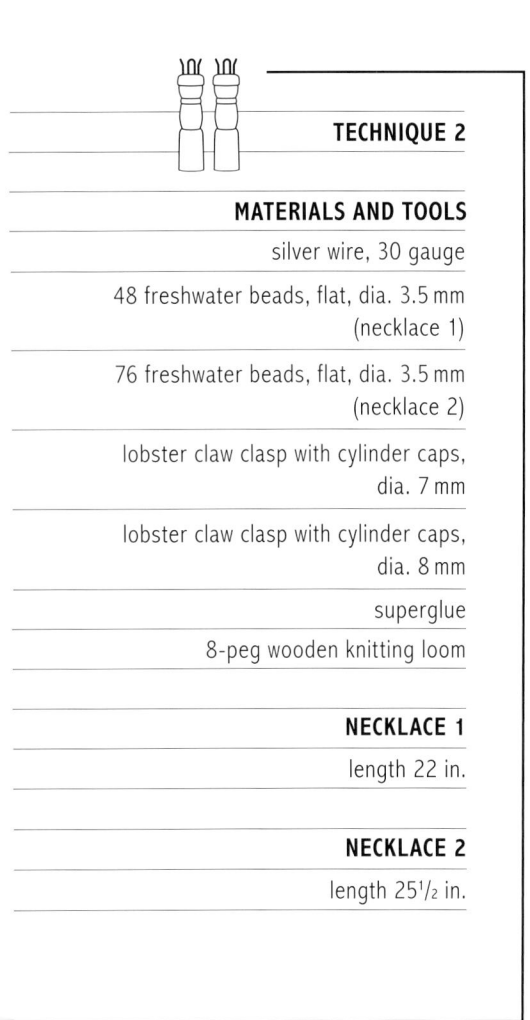

TECHNIQUE 2

MATERIALS AND TOOLS

silver wire, 30 gauge

48 freshwater beads, flat, dia. 3.5 mm (necklace 1)

76 freshwater beads, flat, dia. 3.5 mm (necklace 2)

lobster claw clasp with cylinder caps, dia. 7 mm

lobster claw clasp with cylinder caps, dia. 8 mm

superglue

8-peg wooden knitting loom

NECKLACE 1

length 22 in.

NECKLACE 2

length 25 1/2 in.

NECKLACE 1

First, thread the 48 beads onto the silver wire. Then some 6 1/4 inches are made in **SIMPLE** technique (**TECHNIQUE 2**), which corresponds to about 19 rows.

Now work four beads into every other winding row. Proceed as follows: start with one winding row up to where the beads are inserted after pegs one, three, five and seven. The next knitted row secures the beads.

Now follow with one winding and one knitting row without beads.

With the next winding row the beads are inserted after pegs two, four, six and eight and secured with the knitted row.

This sequence is continued until all of the 48 beads are worked in. This should be at a length of about 8 3/4 inches.

Then you make another 6 1/4 inches (or, 19 rows of winding and knitting) without beads.

Cast off the end stitches and pull both of the ends of the threads together with the ends of the wires, then twist and shorten the wires.

The ends of the thread are then glued into the cylinder caps (dia. 1/4 in.) of the lobster claw clasp.

NECKLACE 2

Thread 76 freshwater beads onto the silver wire and knit 25 rows without beads.

Now four beads are inserted offset **INTO EACH** row, that is, in each uneven row behind pegs one, three, five and seven as well as each even winding row behind pegs two, four, six and eight.

This sequence is maintained until all of the 76 beads have been worked in. This will be when it is about 6 1/4 inches long.

Now another 25 rows without beads are knitted.

Finish the necklace as described earlier and glue on the lobster claw clasp with the cylinder caps (dia. 5/16 in.).

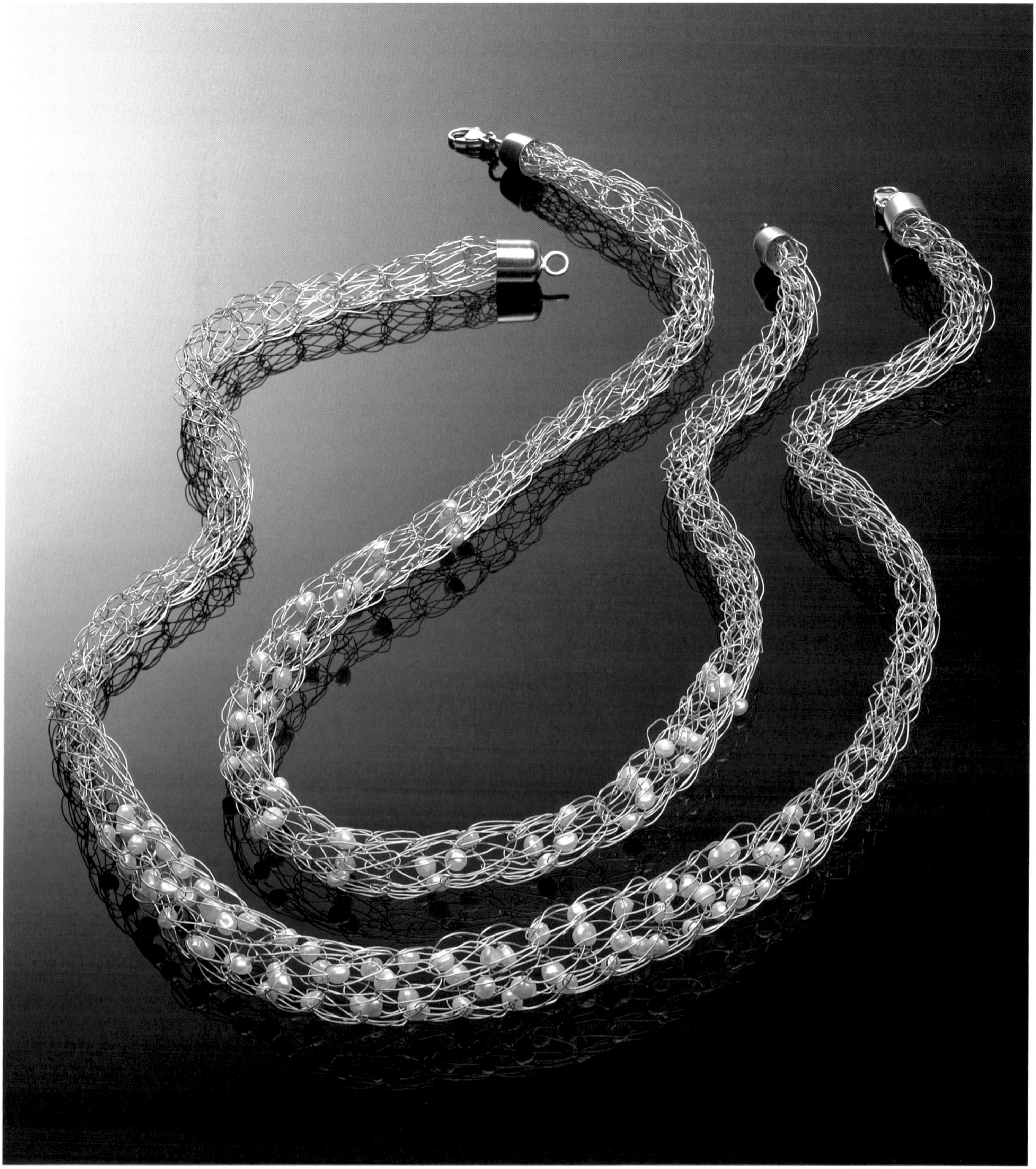

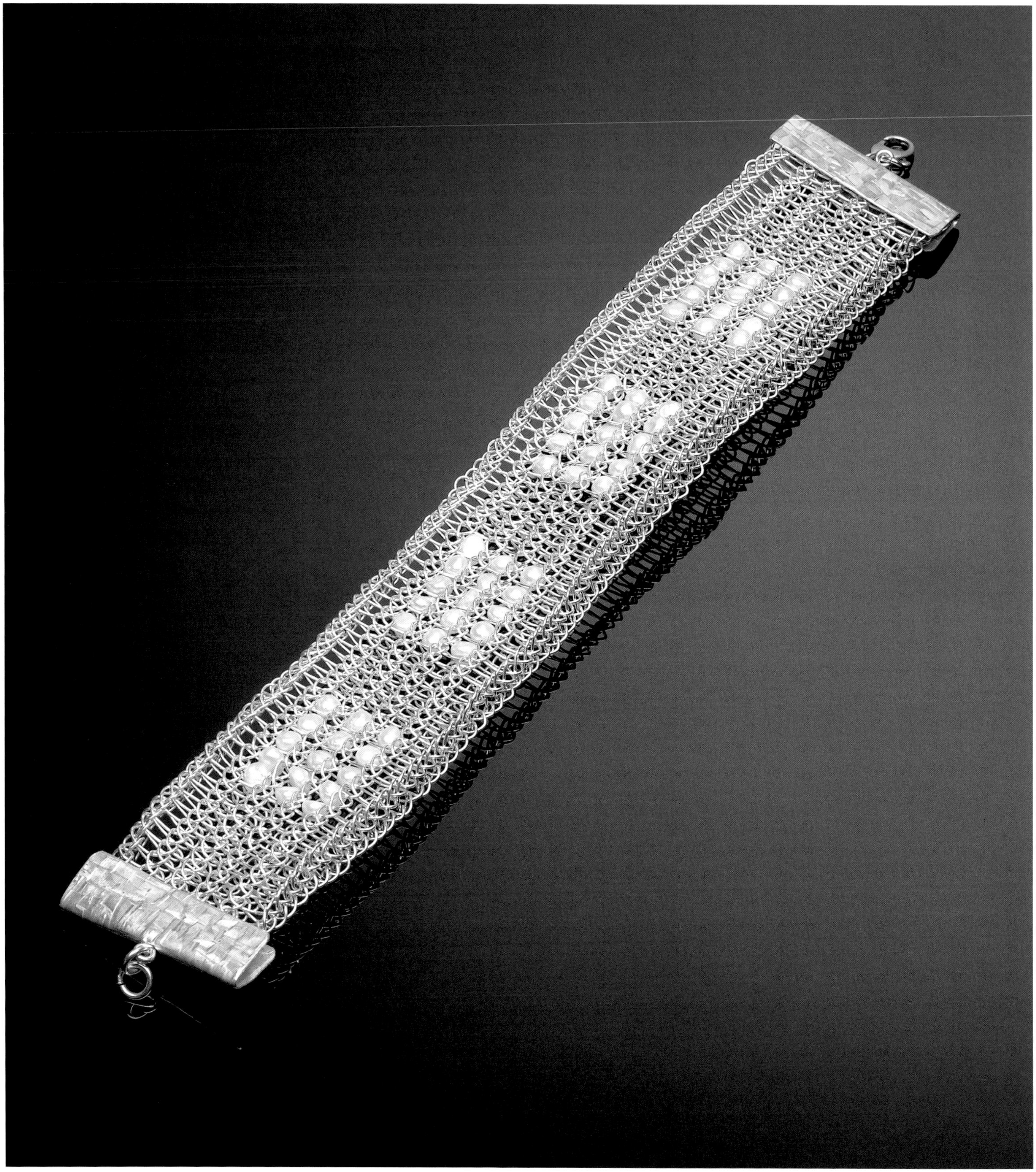

47 FIVE BY THREE

IMPORTANT: Generally you need knitting looms with an even number of pegs for flat bracelets, rings or necklaces so that the top and bottom areas are of the same width.

The noble look of this bracelet results from the harmonious interplay of the shiny materials: freshwater beads, silver wire and forged sheet silver. Due to the fact that the pegs of the metal knitting loom (dia. 7/8 inches) are fairly far apart the result is a loose mesh pattern into which the beads fit perfectly.

Thread the beads and knit in **SIMPLE** technique (**TECHNIQUE 3**) a tube with a total length of 6 1/2 inches. Start with 15 winding and knitting rows without beads. Then follow ten winding and knitting rows where three beads are inserted after adjacent pegs into every other winding row. You insert a total of 15 beads, in other words.

Now eight winding and knitting rows without beads are knitted, then follows another "block of beads" as described before.

You knit a total of four blocks with 15 beads each. After the last block of beads another 15 winding and knitting rounds are made without beads.

IMPORTANT: Carefully continue to pull the tube while knitting. It should not pull tight at the lower end.

Loosely cast off the end stitches and remove the tube from the loom. Press the tube flat so that the rows of beads lie at the center of the bracelet. You might have to pull apart the beginning of the tube so that the bracelet is equally wide along its entire length. Twist the ends of the wire and shorten.

For the clasp or catch use a jigsaw to cut two identical rectangles, 1 1/16 x 5/8 inches, from the sheet silver.

Use the narrow side of the hammer to forge the silver. This results in a fine structure on the surface which reflects the light nicely.

IMPORTANT: Make sure not to damage the edges of the sheet silver.

Use a file to break the edges and round them off. Then bend the rectangle with the pliers at the center so that a U-shaped lateral section is created.

TIP: As the silver sheet is rather thin at only 0.8 mm, you can use a thin wooden rod (such as a toothpick) placed at the center of the rectangle to bend the two "wings" by hand.

At the center of the bent area a hole with a diameter of 1 mm is drilled.

Shorten the pin of eye pin to 3/16 inches and bend it just after the eye at a right angle. Run the pin from the outside into the drilled hole and glue it from below into the bent sheet silver with superglue. Repeat on the other forged section.

Both ends of the bracelet are pushed into the forged lateral sections and glued. You might have to adjust the lateral pieces by bending some more. They should lie flat on the knitted mesh. Two more jump rings are inserted into each eye pin, with a lobster claw clasp on one side.

TECHNIQUE 3

MATERIALS AND TOOLS

silver wire, 26 gauge

60 freshwater beads, flat, dia. 3.5 mm

2 silver sheets, each 27 x 16 x 0.8 mm

lobster claw clasp

4 jump rings, dia. 1/8–3/16 in.

2 eye pins, dia. 1/8 in.

superglue

12-peg metal knitting loom, dia. 7/8 in/22 mm

jigsaw

hammer

fine file

pliers

drill bit, dia. 1 mm

ARMBAND

length 6 3/4 in.

48 FLIRT

TECHNIQUE 3

MATERIALS AND TOOLS

silver wire, 26 gauge

2 silver sheets, each 1 1/16 x 13/16 in. x 0.8 mm

1 silver sheet, each 1 7/8 x 1 in. x 0.8 mm

lobster claw clasp

4 jump rings, each dia. 3/16 in.

oxide stain

12-peg metal knitting loom, rhombic shape, side lengths 7/8 in.

jigsaw

fine file

pliers

drill bit, dia. 1 mm

perhaps soldering material

steel wool

wet sanding paper

ARMBAND

length 6 1/2 in.

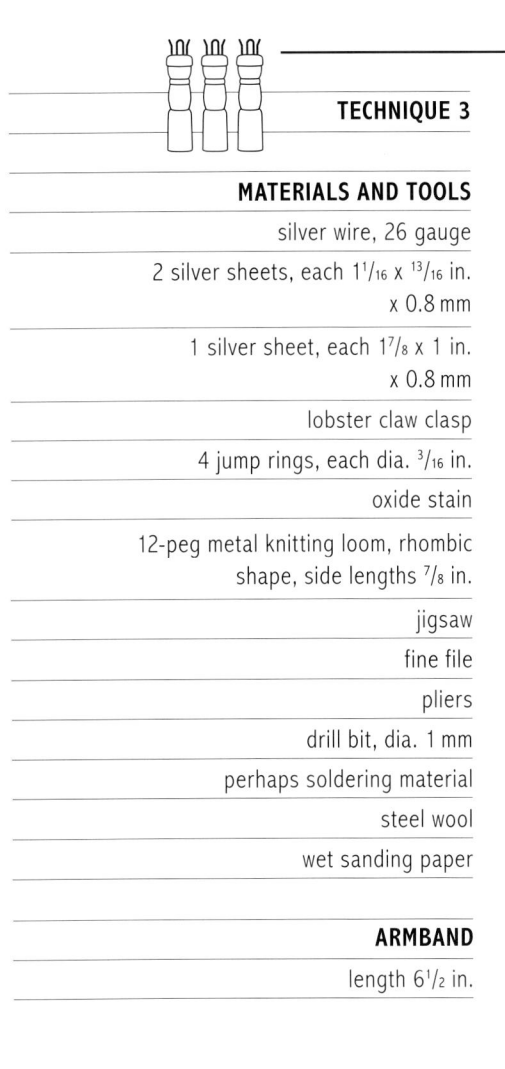

The beautiful black and white contrast of this bracelet results from the black-stained faces of the lateral sections and the decorative element.

Using the rhomboid knitting loom a knitted tube with a length of 6 inches is made in **SIMPLE** technique (**TECHNIQUE 3**). The mesh is somewhat tighter than with the previous project because the pegs of the rhomboid loom are closer together. Pull the tube very carefully while knitting so the beginning will not pull together. Once the desired length has been achieved the end stitches are loosely cast off and the tube is removed from the loom and pressed flat.

IMPORTANT: Make sure the edges feature a stitch and not a peg. This results in a clear edge with a height of about 1/8 inches.

You may have to pull apart the mesh at the beginning of the tube to achieve an even width of the bracelet. Twist the ends of the wires and shorten. Two rectangles of 1 1/16 x 3/16 inches are cut out from sheet silver for the lateral sections and the edges are broken with a fine file. The lateral sections are bent without previously forging the metal (see project 47).

The jump rings for the catch were soldered for this project. You can however attach the jump rings as described with project 47.

For the decorative element a rectangle of 1 7/8 x 1 inch is cut from sheet silver. For this project I cut the rectangle from a larger piece of sheet silver which was previously embossed with a knitting pattern. I cut up lengthwise the extra piece of a knitted tube and placed it flat onto the sheet silver. Using a roller I transferred the knitting pattern onto the sheet silver and then cut out the decorative element. The edges were broken using a fine file and the corners were rounded.

TIP: If you don't have a roller or drum handy you can have the silver embossed by your jeweler or goldsmith. You can alternatively forge a structure with the hammer (see projects 44 and 47) or you may leave the silver as is and only stain it.

Bend the narrow sides of the rectangle backward about 3/8 inch each. This results in a square on the top side of the decorative element of about 1 inch. At the bottom side a gap of about 5/16 inches remains between the two bent pieces which the knitted tube can later be pushed through.

Polish the lateral pieces with the steel wool and then with fine wet sanding paper. Before mounting the lateral pieces and the decorative element they must be stained. There is a commercially available stain solution into which the silver pieces are briefly dipped.

IMPORTANT: In order to get good results when staining the pieces of jewelry need to be degreased first. Follow the instructions and safety precautions of the manufacturer!

After staining the pieces are rinsed well under running water and dried with a soft cloth. The ends of the tubes are inserted into the lateral pieces and glued. To attach the decorative element the tube is inserted through the gap at the bottom side and the two lateral sections are bent a little more so the tube is crimped. If necessary you can use some glue to secure the decorative element in case it is still loose.

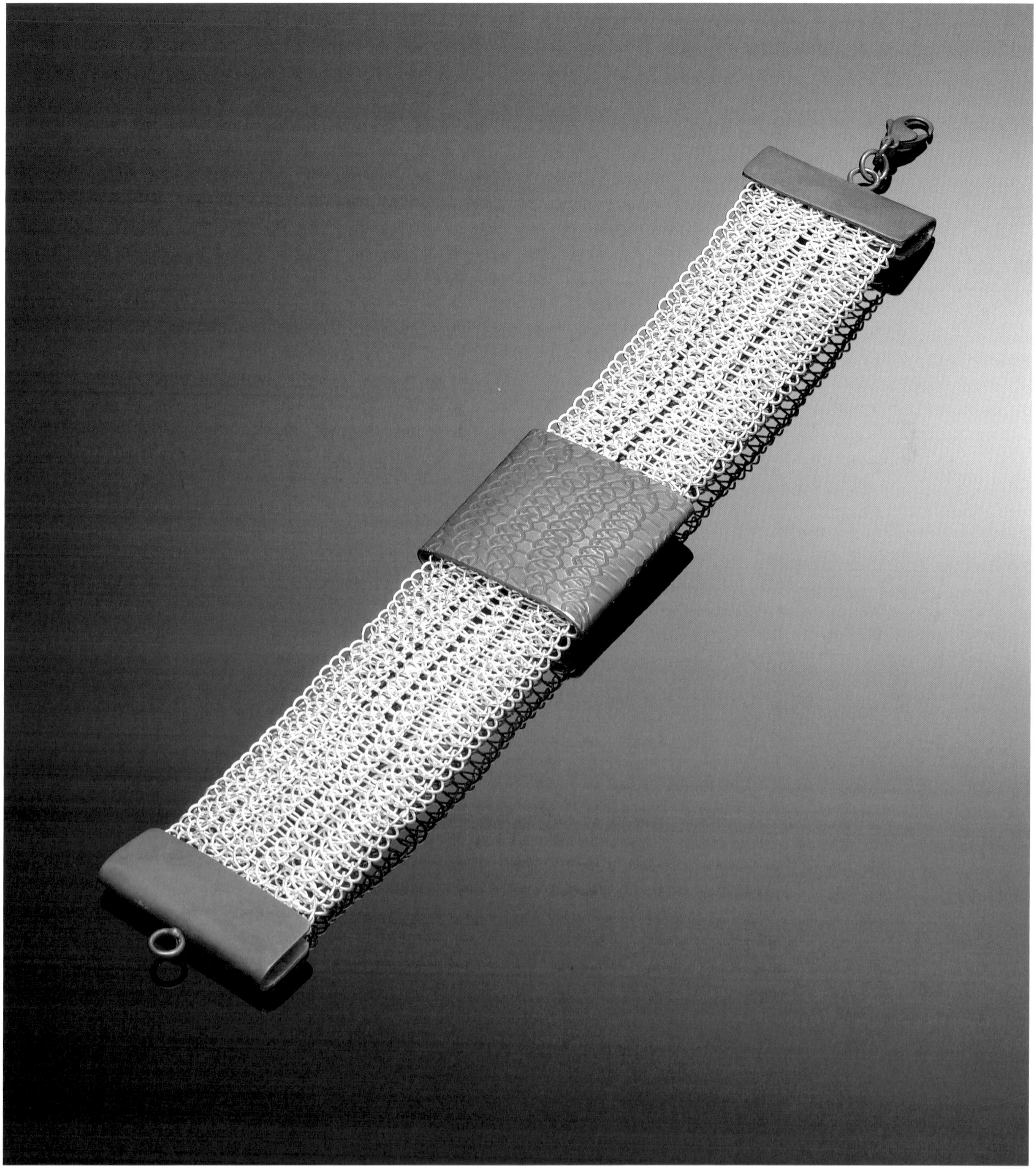

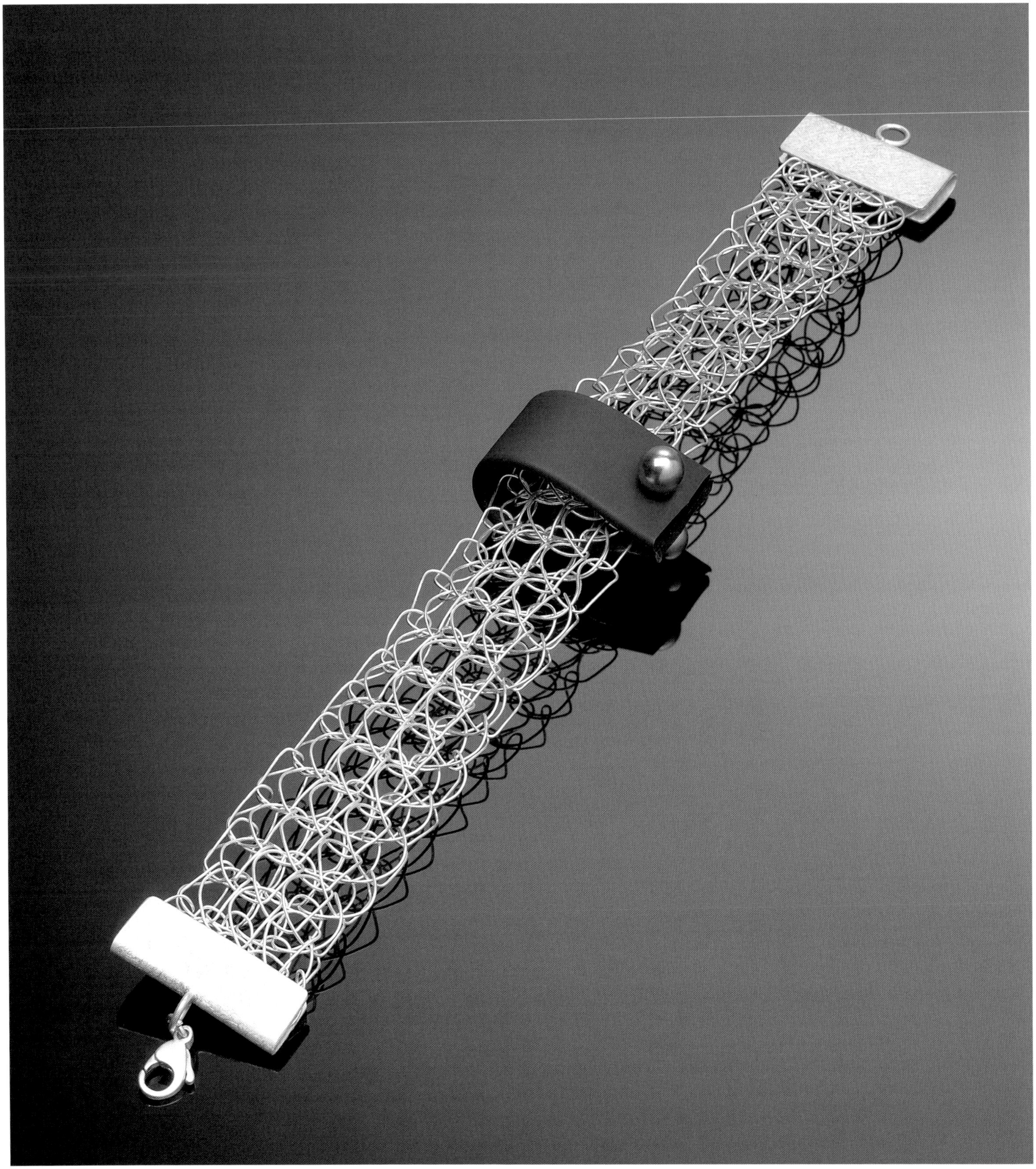

49 AIRY

First make a knitted tube in **SIMPLE** technique until you have reached a length of 6 3/4 inches (**TECHNIQUE 3**). Then cast off the end stitches and twist and shorten the wires.

The tube is pressed flat so that four stitches lie on top and four below to result in an even edge.

Proceed as with project 47 for making the lateral pieces. However, they are not forged but dulled (matted). Use the tip of the file scraping across the surface in circular motions. Change the direction frequently. The circles should be very tight and worked evenly.

The edges are broken with the fine file and the ends of the tubes are glued into the lateral pieces.

The jump rings are attached to the lateral pieces as described with project 47. You can also solder the jump rings. At one side, place the lobster claw clasp with the 1/8-inch diameter jump ring.

Cut a 2 3/4-inch-long strip of the PVC band for the decorative element. Place the cutting edges on top of each other and use the darning needle to punch a hole through both pieces simultaneously.

Place the band around the knitted tube and push the short piece of the 2-mm silver wire through both holes. Glue a silver sphere onto the ends of the wires to secure. The decorative element remains movable on the bracelet.

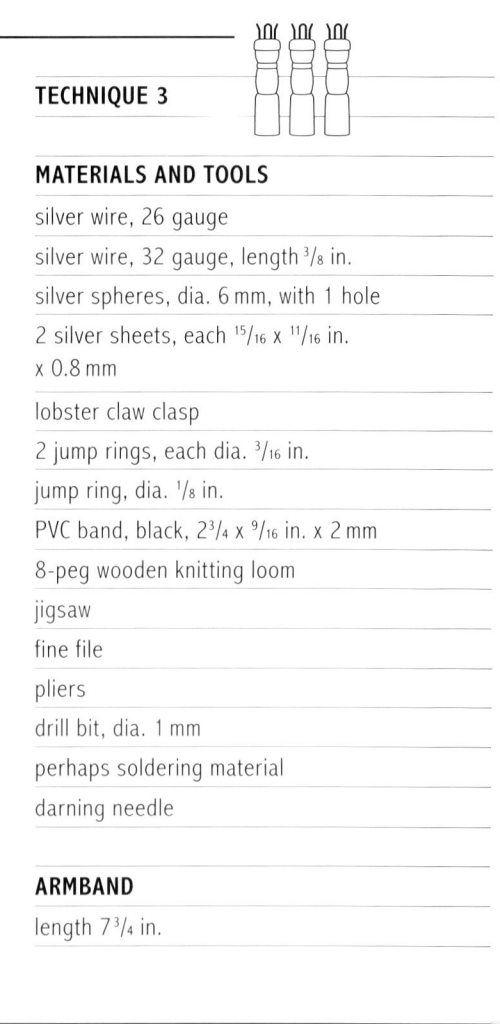

TECHNIQUE 3

MATERIALS AND TOOLS

silver wire, 26 gauge

silver wire, 32 gauge, length 3/8 in.

silver spheres, dia. 6 mm, with 1 hole

2 silver sheets, each 15/16 x 11/16 in. x 0.8 mm

lobster claw clasp

2 jump rings, each dia. 3/16 in.

jump ring, dia. 1/8 in.

PVC band, black, 2 3/4 x 9/16 in. x 2 mm

8-peg wooden knitting loom

jigsaw

fine file

pliers

drill bit, dia. 1 mm

perhaps soldering material

darning needle

ARMBAND

length 7 3/4 in.

50 CHAINED IN

TECHNIQUE 2

MATERIALS AND TOOLS
ARMBAND STRING OF SPHERES

silver wire, 26 gauge

7 lava beads, each dia. 12 mm

4 silver beads, each dia. 4 mm

hook catch, dia. 1/2 in.

6-peg wooden knitting loom

ARMBAND STRING OF SPHERES

length 7 7/8 in.

MATERIALS AND TOOLS
ARMBAND MINI BEADS

silver wire, 26 gauge

rocaille beads, black, dia. 2.4 mm

lobster claw clasp, black, cylinder caps, dia. 3/8 in.

superglue

4-peg wooden knitting loom

ARMBAND MINI BEADS

length 7 3/4 in.

ARMBAND STRING OF SPHERES

Make a 6 1/4-inch-long tube in **SIMPLE** technique (**TECHNIQUE 2**) with the 6-peg wooden knitting loom and cast off the end stitches. Leave at least 6 to 8 inches of both ends of the wires.

The tube is pulled together at one side and five lava beads are inserted at the other open side. Distribute the beads evenly and slightly stretch the sections of the tube between the beads. This reduces the diameter and the beads are secured inside of the tube. The total length of the knitted tube is about 6 3/4 inches.

Now the tube is pulled together at the other end as well.

Thread a silver bead onto both ends of the thread, then a lava bead and again a silver bead. At one side run the wire through the jump ring of the hook catch, and at the other side through the jump ring at the hook.

The wire is then run back through the beads to the ends of the tubes and twisted and shortened.

ARMBAND MINI BEADS

A 6 3/4-inch-long tube is made in **SIMPLE** technique using the 4-peg wooden knitting loom (**TECHNIQUE 2**).

Thread the rocaille beads with bead silk or sewing yarn to form two 6 7/8-inch-long threads.

Slightly twist the two strands around each other and knot the ends of the threads together.

Now the bead threads are inserted into the knitted tube and the ends of the threads are secured with the ends of the wires. Twist and shorten the wires.
The ends of the tubes are glued into the cylinder caps of the lobster claw clasp.

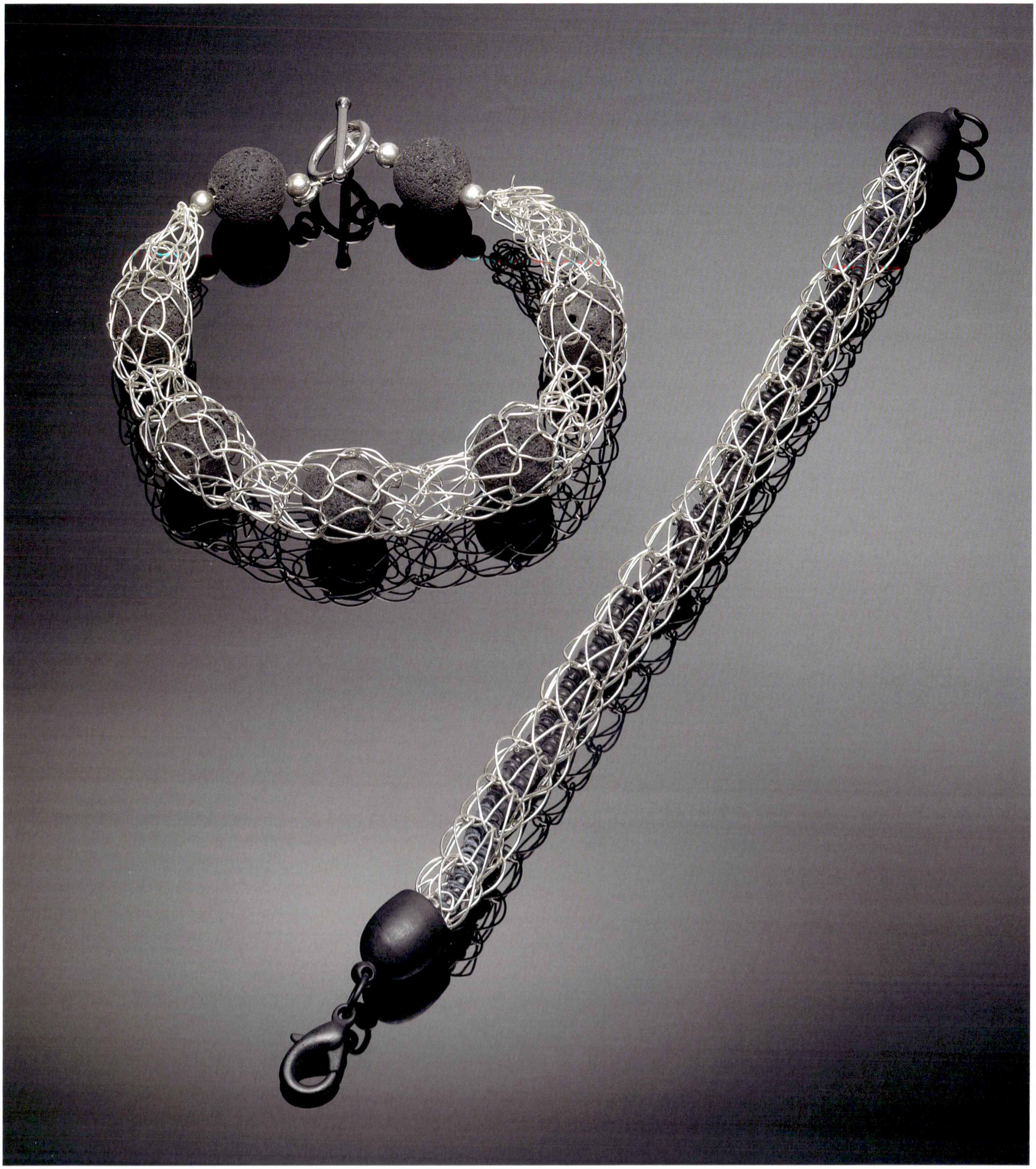

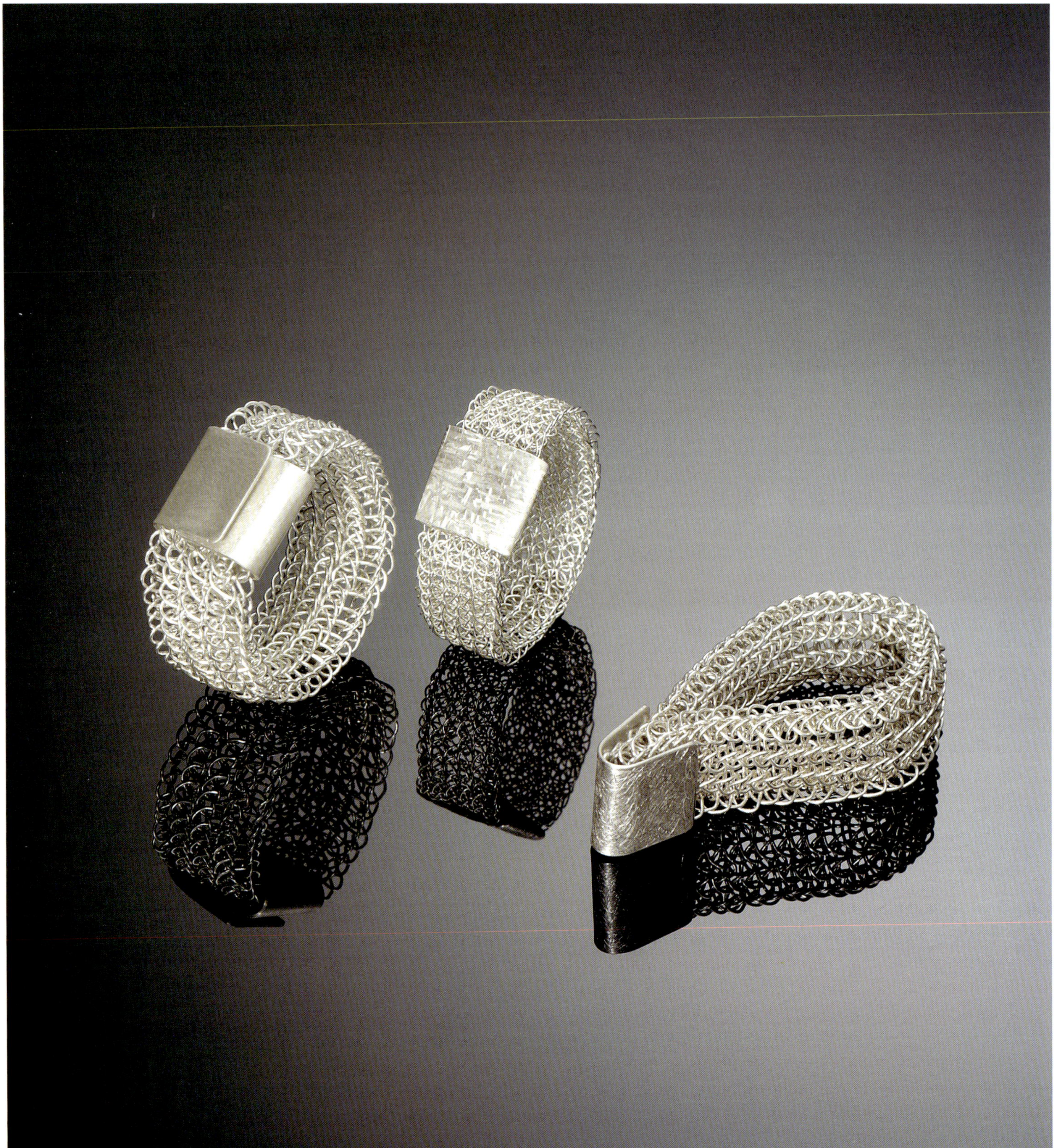

51 RINGED

DELICATE RING

The mesh for this ring (center) is very fine due to the very thin wire and the pegs of the loom being very close together. So this project requires some practice and patience. Corresponding to the size of the ring a tube is knitted in **SIMPLE** technique (**TECHNIQUE 3**), in this case 2³/₄ inches long.

The tube is pressed flat and the ends of the tube are sewn together with the ends of the wires. The ends should not overlap, rather butt against each other.

IMPORTANT: Make sure the tube is pressed flat so that a stitch lies at the edges, not a peg. This way the edge will be more even.

The sheet silver is cut to ³/₈ x ⁷/₈ inches and a delicate surface pattern is made with the narrow side of the hammer. Break the edges with the fine file.

Bend back ³/₁₆ inches of the sheet at both sides of the rectangle. This leaves a gap into which the knitted tube is inserted. The decorative element should lie above the abutting edge of the knitted tube and hence hide the seam.

To secure the decorative element the two flipped "wings" can be pressed together a bit more. You can also use a drop of glue.

WOUND RING

Corresponding to the size of the ring a tube of some 2³/₄ inches in length is knitted in **SIMPLE** technique (**TECHNIQUE 3**).

Press the tube flat and sew together the ends of the tubes with the wires. The ends should not overlap, rather butt against each other. The sheet silver is cut to ¹/₂ x 1¹/₄ inches. Break the edges and round the corners.

Bend a ³/₈-inch area at one side of the rectangle. At the other side, bend another ³/₈-inch area upward at a right angle. Now you can insert the knitted tube into the metal. Then the second bent lateral piece is bent inward until it lies over the first one and overlaps it.

The decorative element hides the seam of the knitted tube. Perhaps use some glue to secure. Use the steel wool and the wet sanding paper to sand and polish the decorative element.

UPWARD RING

Corresponding to the size of the ring make a knitted tube of about 6³/₄ inches, in this case in **SIMPLE** technique (**TECHNIQUE 3**). The tube is pressed flat and the ends of the tube are placed onto each other and sewn together with the wires so that the ends are secured along their entire width (¹/₂ inch) and length of ³/₁₆ inch.

Cut the sheet silver to ¹/₂ x 1 inches, break the edges, and round the corners. The rectangle is bent in a V-shape at the center and the surface is matted (see project 49). The sewn ends of the tubes are inserted into the decorative element and glued.

TECHNIQUE 3

MATERIALS AND TOOLS
DELICATE RING

silver wire, 30 gauge

sheet silver, ³/₈ x ⁷/₈ in. x 0.8 mm

12-peg metal knitting loom, dia. ³/₈ in/10 mm

jigsaw

fine file

hammer

MATERIALS AND TOOLS
WOUND RING

silver wire, 26 gauge

sheet silver, ¹/₂ x 1¹/₄ in. x 0.8 mm

8-peg metal knitting loom, dia. ¹/₂ in/12 mm

fine file

jigsaw

steel wool

wet sanding paper

MATERIALS AND TOOLS
UPWARD RING

silver wire, 26 gauge

sheet silver, ¹/₂ x 1 in. x 0.8 mm

8-peg metal knitting loom, dia. ¹/₂ in/12 mm

fine file

jigsaw

52 ROSE RED

TECHNIQUE 2 AND 3

MATERIALS AND TOOLS
RING DOTS

silver wire, 30 gauge

rocaille beads, dark red, with silver lining, dia. 2.5 mm

9-peg metal loom, dia. 9/16 in/15 mm

crochet hook, no. 2

MATERIALS AND TOOLS
RING BOW

silver wire, 30 gauge

aluminum wire, 32 gauge, length 16 in.

4 rocailles, dark red, with silver lining, dia. 5 mm

3 rock crystal beads

9-peg metal loom, dia. 9/16 in/15 mm

RING DOTS (RIGHT)

Start with **SIMPLE** knitting technique for two winding and knitting rounds without beads (**TECHNIQUE 3**). One peg is always left out.

At every other winding round you add four rocailles behind the unused peg and secure it in the following knitting round.

Winding and knitting rounds without and with beads alternate now until eleven rounds of beads have been knitted. Finish with two winding and knitting rounds without beads.

The knitted tube is pressed flat so that the beads lie nicely centered. Sew together the ends of the tubes abutting with each other.

As described under **TECHNIQUE 1** (image 19 to 25) a small rosette is crocheted. It should have a diameter of about 3/4 inches.

About 20 rocailles are sewn onto the rosette with a piece of silver wire. Don't pull the wire too tightly. The rocailles should move slightly.

The rosette is sewn onto the ring with its wire. The end of the wire is twisted and shortened.

RING BOW (LEFT)

First a thread of about 5 1/2 to 6 inches long is made. Knitting is done on the metal loom (dia. 9/16 in.) in **OFFSET** technique (**TECHNIQUE 3**). The tube is removed from the loom and calibrated with a 1/16-inch core. Then pull the tube together at one side, twist the wire and shorten it.

A ring rail is made from aluminum wire and the rest of the wire is shaped into a bow which runs across the back of the finger. Then pull together the second end of the tube to secure the knitted mesh on the "aluminum scaffold."

Thread the rocailles and rock crystal beads alternatingly and tension the wire over the interior of the decorative bow. The wire is twisted and shortened inconspicuously at the bottom of the bow.

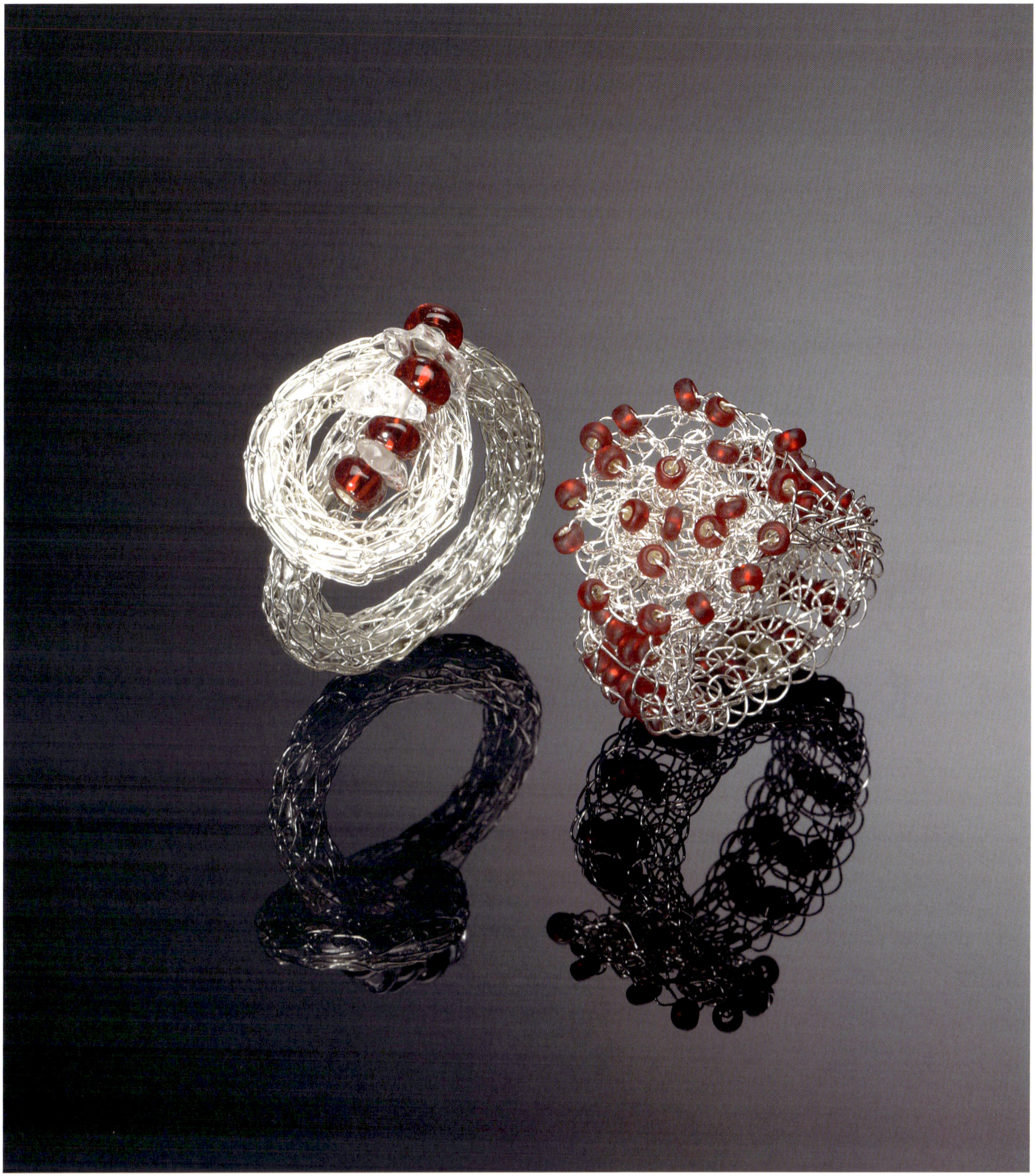

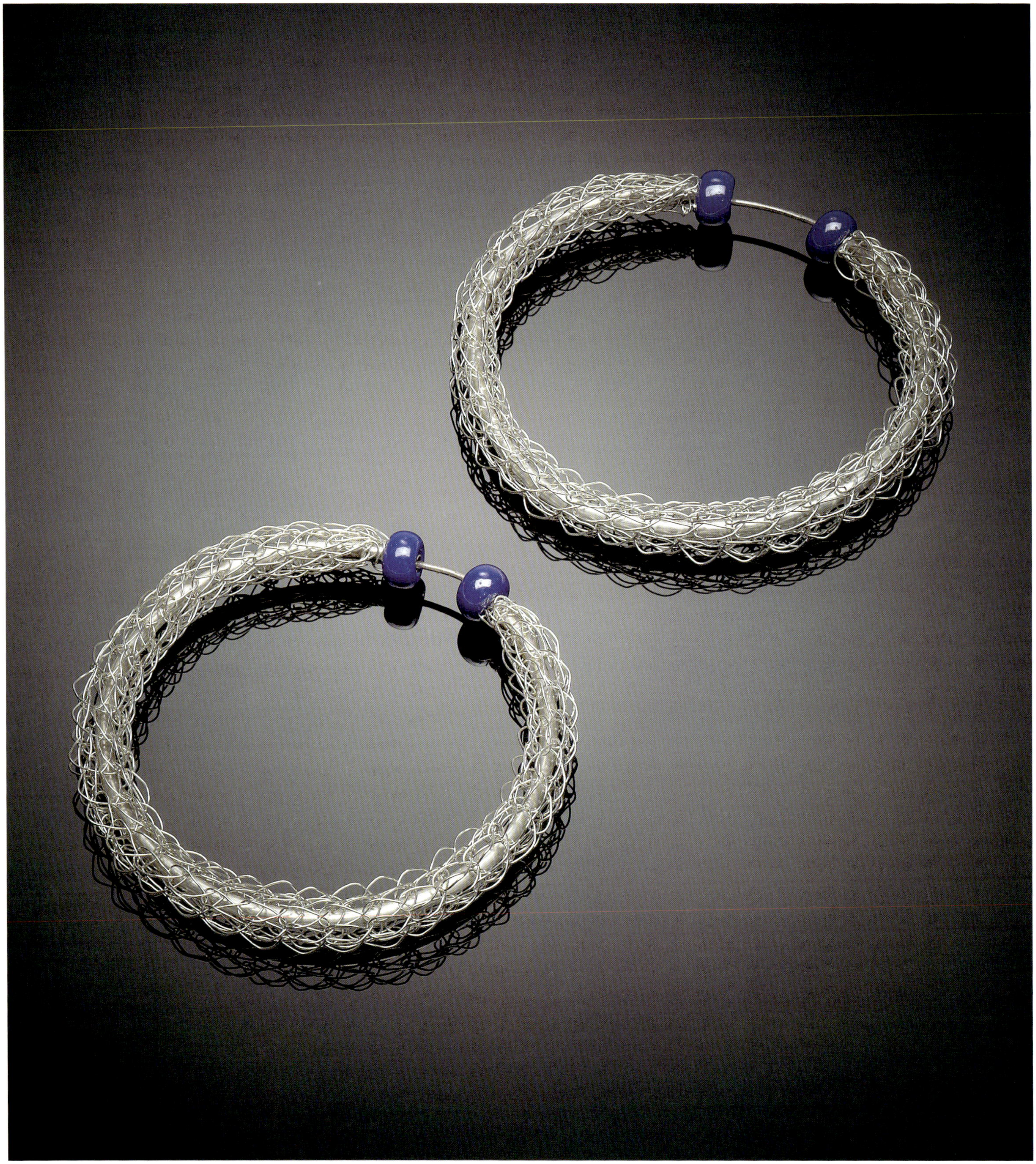

53 CREOLES

Similar to the "bow" ring (see page 156) a kind of scaffold is used to provide the shape. In this case I use silver creoles with a diameter of 2 inches, which can be purchased.

Work in **OFFSET** technique (**TECHNIQUE 3**) with a metal knitting loom (dia. $^9/_{16}$ in.). The tubes with a length of 16 inches are not calibrated. Hence the knitted mesh has a different and slightly more coarse surface structure when compared to the bow ring.

TECHNIQUE 3

MATERIALS AND TOOLS
silver wire, 30 gauge
2 creoles, silver, dia. 50 mm
4 glass beads with large holes, royal blue
9-peg metal knitting loom, dia. $^9/_{16}$ in/15 mm

TIP:
You can make two individual tube sections of 16 inches each or a single one of about $12^1/_2$ inches, then divide the long tube and "knit back" to the desired length (thread).

The knitted tube is pushed onto the creole. Then pull the two ends of the tubes together and shorten the two ends of the thread. To prevent the tube from sliding back on the silver ring of the creole, secure the ends of the tubes with a drop of superglue.

Finally, a glass bead is glued onto each end of the tube ends.

54 MOUNTED

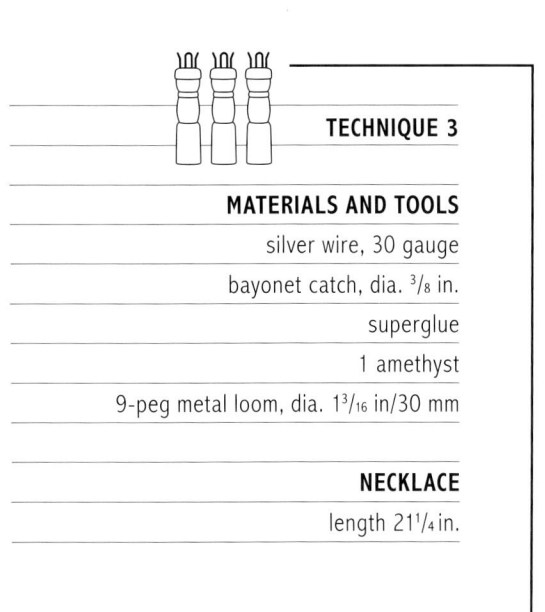

TECHNIQUE 3

MATERIALS AND TOOLS

silver wire, 30 gauge

bayonet catch, dia. 3/8 in.

superglue

1 amethyst

9-peg metal loom, dia. 1 3/16 in/30 mm

NECKLACE

length 21 1/4 in.

The beautiful knitting pattern of this necklace is due to the **DOUBLE** technique (**TECHNIQUE 3**). First make sure that the stone fits into the knitting loom and keep in mind that the interior diameter of the loom is still further diminished because of the inserted knitted tube.

First knit 9 3/4 to 10 1/4 inches, and then place the amethyst into the loom. **GENTLY** push it into the knitted mesh so it doesn´t fall out while you continue knitting.

After the stone another 9 3/4 inches are knitted and the end stitches are cast off. The ends of the thread however remain still open.

IMPORTANT: Both sections of the thread to the left and right of the stone must be of equal length so the stone lies at the center.

For the mesh pattern to be even the thread must be calibrated at both sides. As the amethyst lies in the center the draw plate can´t be used.

Instead, push the metal core at one end into the knitted tube and brush it by hand. Close your fingers around the thread and the metal core and slide your hand from the inside of the thread (next to the amethyst) toward the outside. Carefully stretch the thread. Repeat the process with a smaller metal rod core. The final size is reached with a 3/8-inch core.

Repeat this process at the other side of the thread.

Now shape a nice transition by hand, from the large diameter with the amethyst to the calibrated lateral pieces.

Finally, the ends of the threads are pulled together, the ends of the wires are twisted and shortened and the bayonet clasp is glued to it.

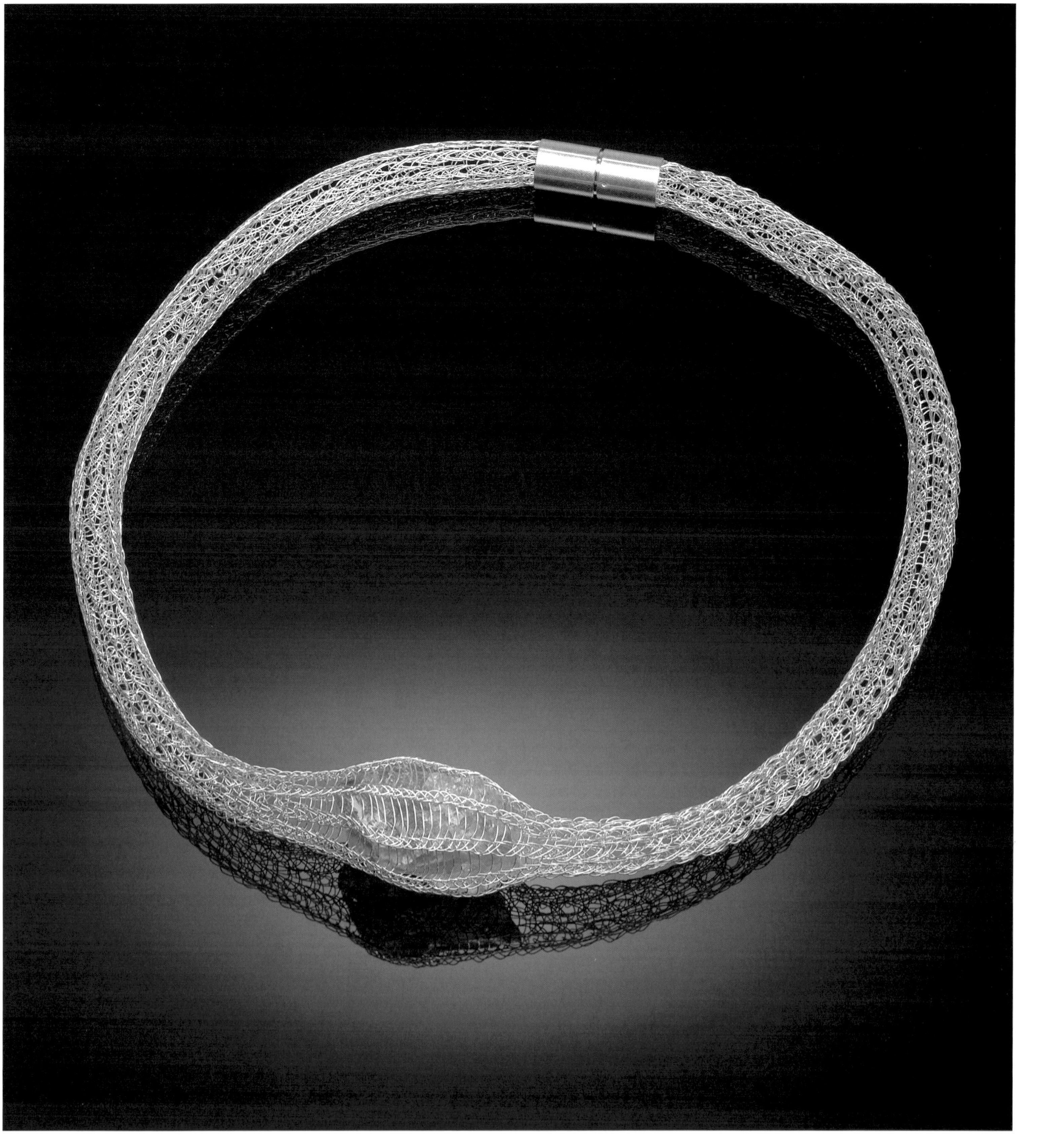

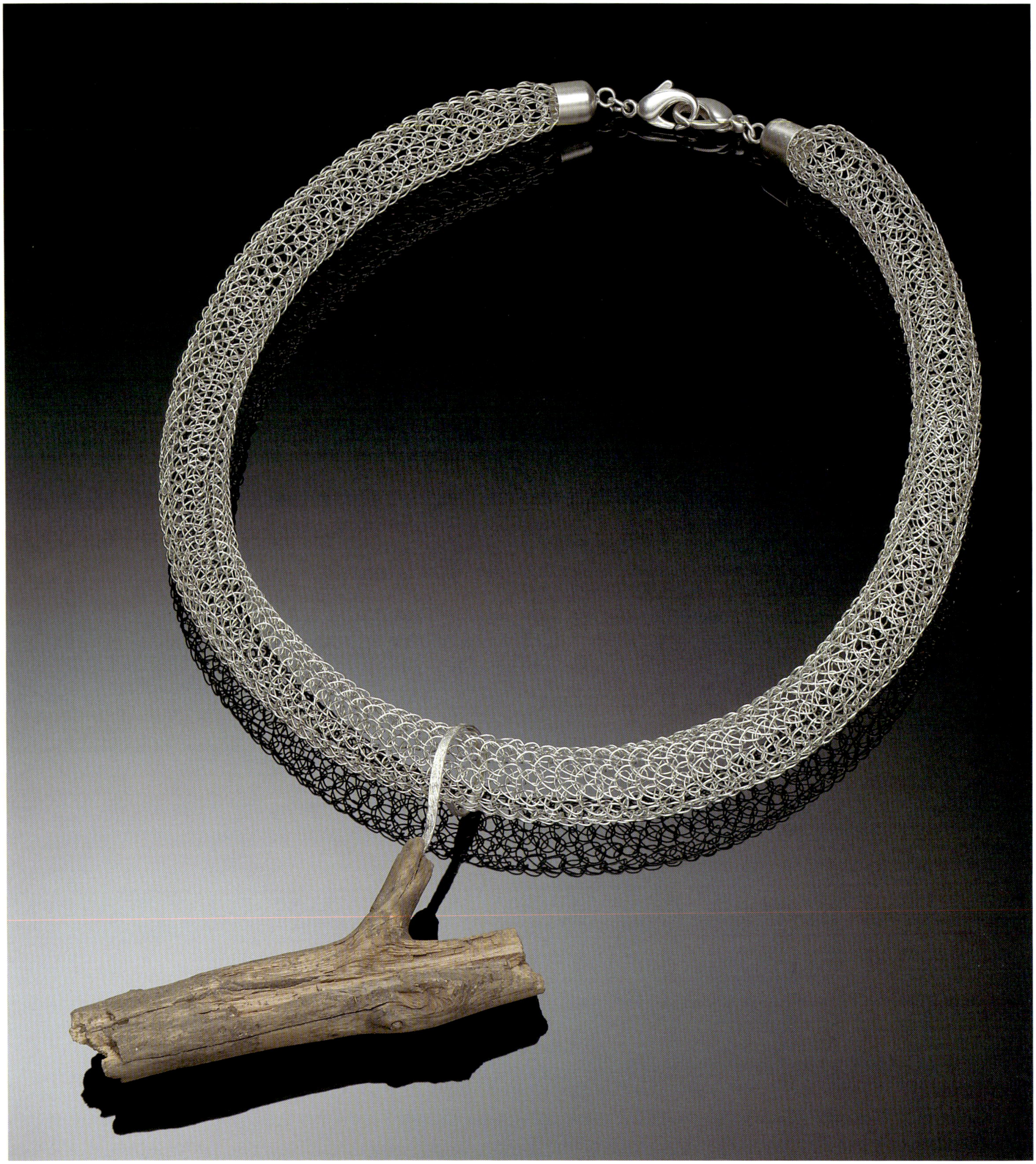

55 TWIG PENDANT

This silver necklace with a tube diameter of 9/16 inches is not easily overlooked! It is knitted in **SIMPLE** technique with a 26-gauge silver wire (**TECHNIQUE 3**). Due to the large diameter of the metal knitting loom the result is a coarse and very loose but firm web.

Knit a tube with a length of 20½ inches and pull the thread while knitting so the diameter is slightly diminished.

The necklace gets a more dynamic touch if you continually turn the tube slightly around its axis (always in the same direction!). Because of the stitches hanging in the pegs the tube offers some resistance on this side against which the wire mesh can be slightly twisted.

After knitting the tube is pulled **WITHOUT** a metal core through the draw plate.

IMPORTANT: It is advisable to reduce the diameter in several stages here as well. The final size is reached when you get to a diameter of 9/16 inches.

The ends of the thread are pushed together by hand and secured with the ends of the wire. Twist and shorten the remaining wire and glue on the cylinder caps of the catch. For the catch I have used two lobster claw clasps to further emphasize it and to create a visual counterbalance to the wooden pendant.

In order to attach the piece of twig or branch to the necklace you make a suspension by bending. Use a hammer to forge a 32-gauge wire into a flat strip. The surface gets a nice pattern that way. Now bend the flat silver strip with pliers into a kind of "question mark," that is, an arc, with its lower end running straight. The arc has to be sufficiently large so the knitted thread will fit through without problems.

In order to add additional shine to the mounting I have matted it with the tip of a fine file as described with project 49. This fine structure creates a beautiful effect. Finally, the edges of the strip are slightly broken with the file.

In order to attach the piece of branch a small screwdriver is used to press a slit into the wood and the straight end of the pendant is glued into it.

TIP:
If the wood is too hard to make a slit by pressing a screwdriver you can make the opening with a drill by widening the hole into the shape of a slit. Or you can cut the end of the silver strip into a tip with cutting pliers so it fits into the drilled hole.

TECHNIQUE 3

MATERIALS AND TOOLS

silver wire, 26 gauge

piece of twig

lobster claw clasp with two hooks, cylinder caps, dia. 3/8 in.

superglue

11-peg metal loom, dia. 1 3/8 in/35 mm

hammer

pliers

fine file

small screwdriver

NECKLACE

length 23½ in.

56 PEARL MASS

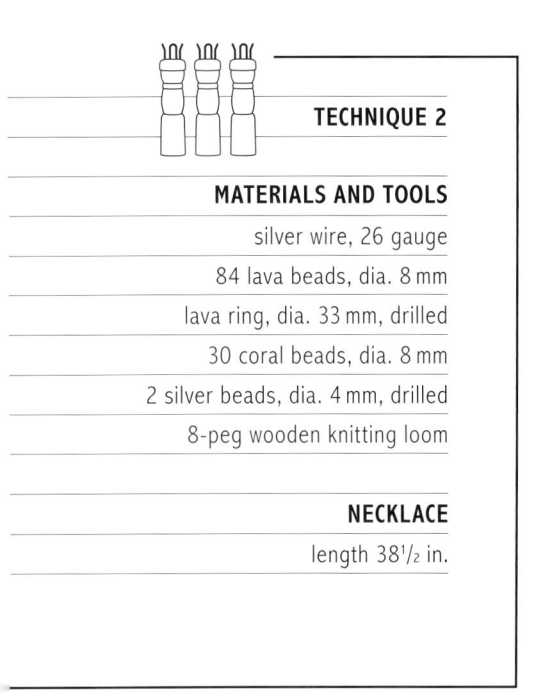

TECHNIQUE 2

MATERIALS AND TOOLS

silver wire, 26 gauge

84 lava beads, dia. 8 mm

lava ring, dia. 33 mm, drilled

30 coral beads, dia. 8 mm

2 silver beads, dia. 4 mm, drilled

8-peg wooden knitting loom

NECKLACE

length 38 1/2 in.

Despite its length this necklace can be made relatively quickly because it is made with 26-gauge silver wire on the 8-peg wooden knitting loom.

First knit a tube of about 36 1/2 inches in **SIMPLE** technique (**TECHNIQUE 2**). Cast off the end stitches but leave them open. The tube is carefully "brushed" by hand to optimize the mesh pattern. It hardly gains in length while doing so.

Now pull together one end of the tube with the end of the wire and fill the tube in irregular order with the lava and coral beads. The beads should lie close to each other. The second end of the tube is now also pulled close and the beads are secured inside the tube.

A coral bead is threaded onto both ends of the wire and the wire is run through the lava ring and a silver bead. Then run the wire through the lava ring and the coral bead back and inconspicuously twist it behind the lava bead. Finally, shorten the wire.

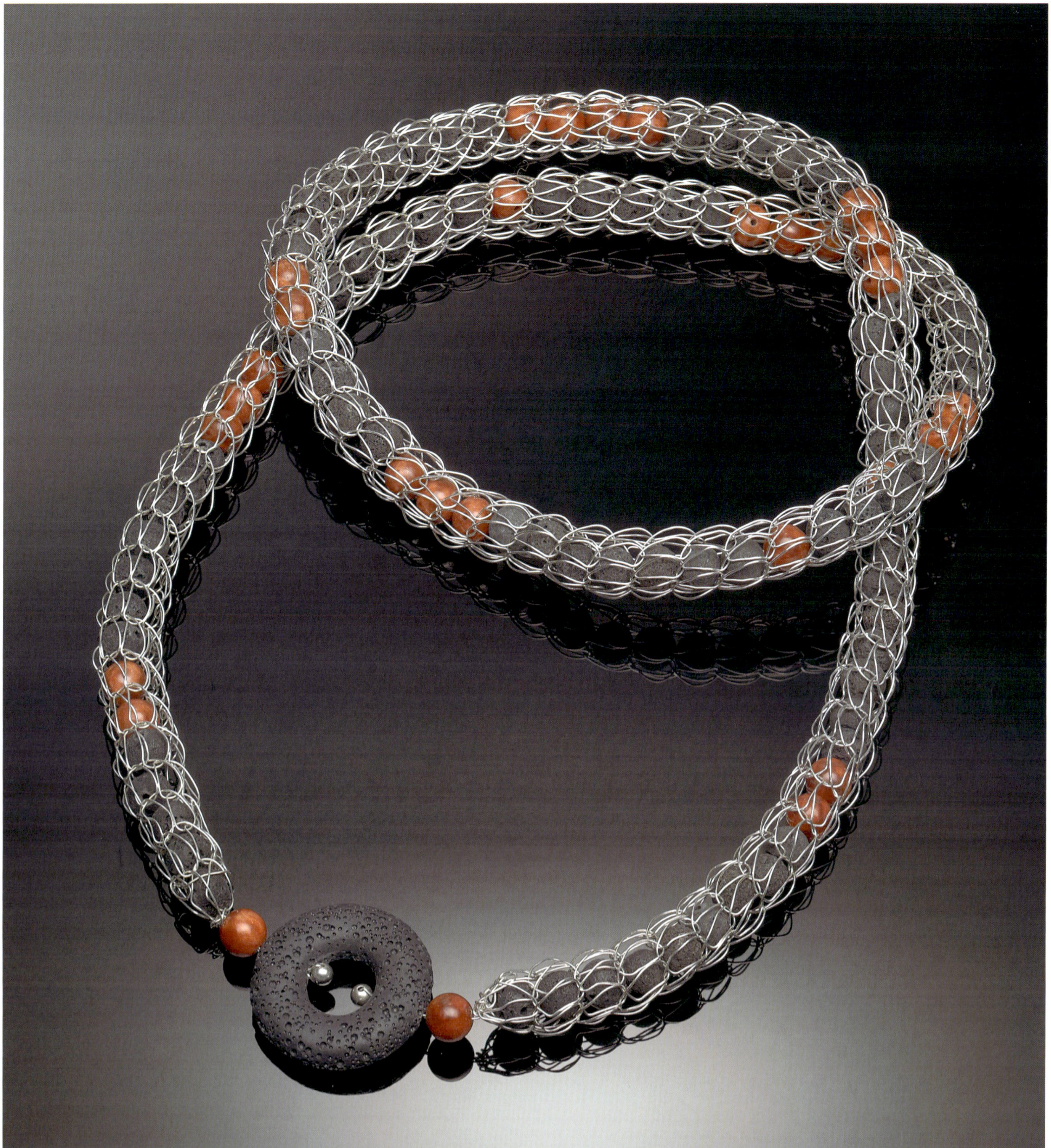

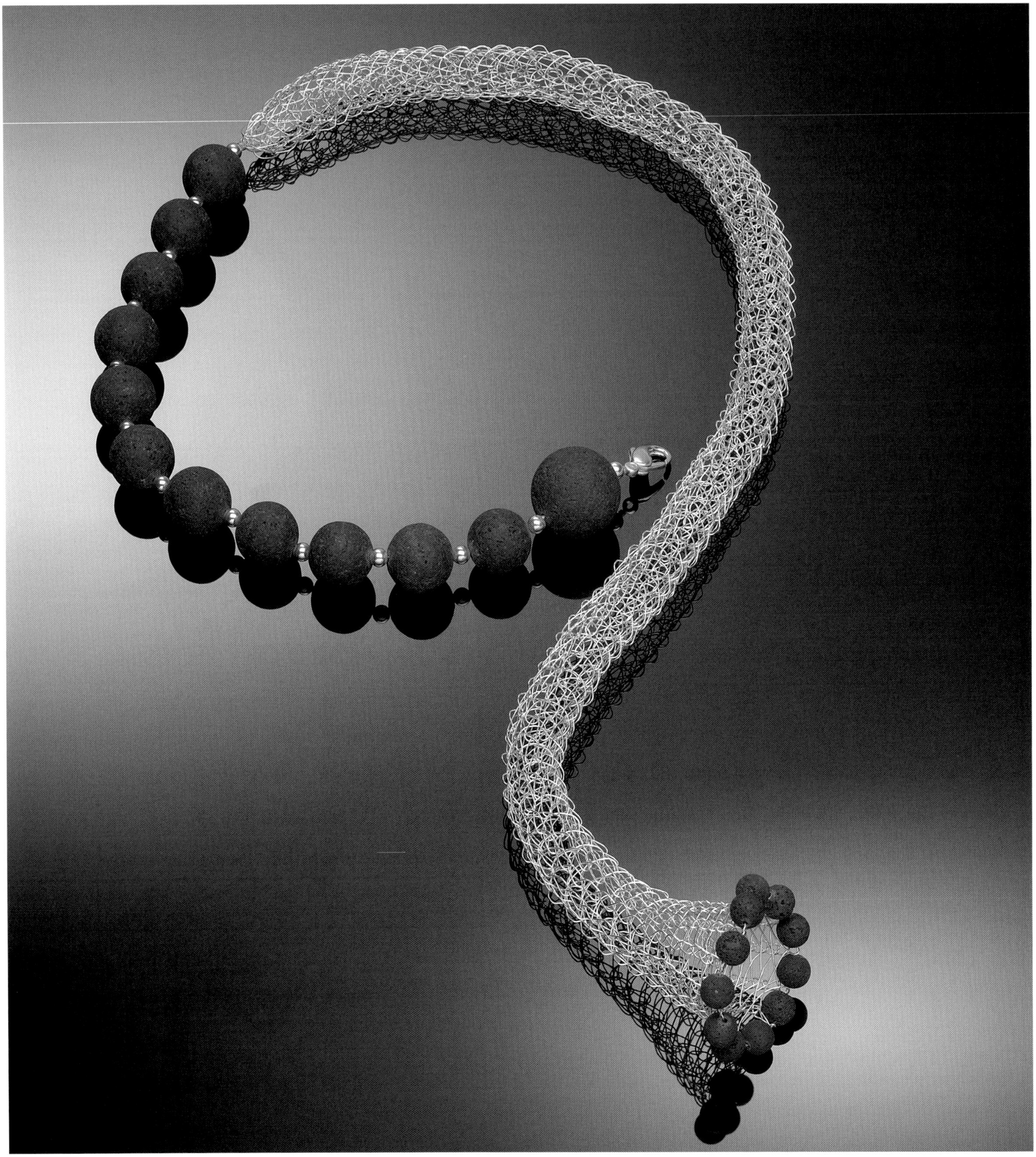

57 BLACK AND WHITE

This necklace is a special project. Its charm results from the contrast between the black and "white" materials as well as from the distinct look of the light and airy silver thread and the solid, heavy spheres from lava rock.

A 22-inch-long tube is knitted in **OFFSET** technique (**TECHNIQUE 3**) with the metal knitting loom (dia. 1 3/8 in.). Carefully pull the thread by hand while knitting.

Remove the thread from the knitting loom **WITHOUT** casting off the end stitches. The end of the tube is shaped like a trumpet. The end of the wire should be at least 7 7/8 inches long.

If the diameter of the thread is somewhat uneven you can use the draw plate to even out the diameter to about 5/8 inches.

IMPORTANT: Only pull the tube through the draw plate to about 2 3/8 inches before the trumpet-shaped end so the shape will not change.

The beginning of the tube is pulled together with the end of the wire. Make a small loop into the wire (about 1/16 inches in diameter) and twist it to the last stitches. Then shorten the wire.

The small lava beads are worked into the trumpet-shaped end. Thread a lava bead and run the wire through the next open stitch. This way it is cast off. Thread another bead and run the wire through the next open stitch. Because of the beads the tube retains its trumpet shape. Twist the wire inconspicuously and shorten.

Now the lava beads are threaded. Since one single wire would be too rigid, bead silk is used here. It is knotted to the small wire loop at the beginning of the tube. Now push the crimp bead over the knot and the wire loop and press it together firmly. This way both the knot as well as the bead silk are hidden and the wire is held together safely.

Now the silver beads and the 18 mm lava beads are alternatingly threaded. The end is made with the 24 mm lava bead and a silver bead.

Thread the second crimp bead and the lobster claw clasp onto the bead silk. Run back the bead silk through the crimp bead, the silver bead and the large lava bead. Now tension the bead silk and press the crimp bead together. Now all of the beads are lined up on the bead silk without gaps. The bead silk is knotted several times behind the large lava bead as additional safety.

Now the lobster claw clasp can be hooked into the silver thread at any location and hence the length of the necklace can be varied.

TECHNIQUE 3

MATERIALS AND TOOLS

silver wire, 26 gauge

11 lava beads, dia. 8 mm

11 lava beads, dia. 18 mm

1 lava bead, dia. 24 mm

13 silver beads, dia. 5 mm

2 silver crimp beads

lobster claw clasp

bead silk

11-peg metal loom, dia. 1 3/8 in/35 mm

NECKLACE

length 34 in.

58 RING AROUND THE ROSIE

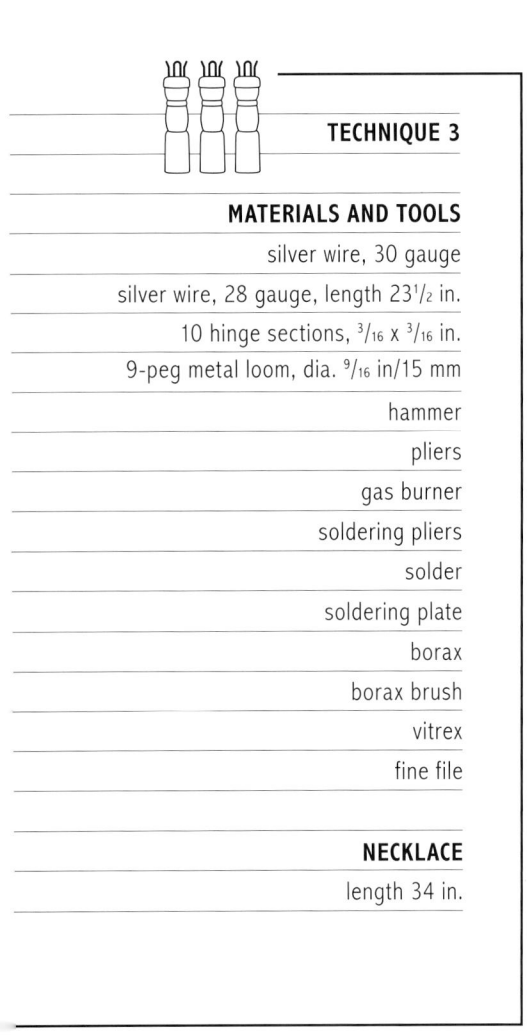

TECHNIQUE 3

MATERIALS AND TOOLS

silver wire, 30 gauge

silver wire, 28 gauge, length 23 1/2 in.

10 hinge sections, 3/16 x 3/16 in.

9-peg metal loom, dia. 9/16 in/15 mm

hammer

pliers

gas burner

soldering pliers

solder

soldering plate

borax

borax brush

vitrex

fine file

NECKLACE

length 34 in.

This necklace requires some patience. But it is well worth it!

First make ten short threads between 5 1/2 and 6 inches long from 30-gauge wire. Use **OFFSET** technique (**TECHNIQUE 3**) on a metal knitting loom (dia. 9/16 in.).

The threads are calibrated on a 16-inch metal core and are hence slightly lengthened to 15 to 16 1/4 inches.

Now make the chain rings from silver wire. First cut the wire into sections of about 16 inches long, and file the cutting edge so it is flat. Then bend the wire into a ring. Since the 28-gauge wire is quite rigid you should use a pair of pliers.

IMPORTANT: The sections can be of varying length (between 5 1/2 and 6 3/4 inches). Bend the thread into slightly irregular rings. This looks more casual on one hand, on the other you don't have to work with total precision...

Bend the wire so that the contact surfaces meet while flat and while under pressure. Now the ends of the wires are soldered together.

To do this, place the wire ring onto the soldering plate and put borax onto the contact surface of the ring. Then put a small piece of solder onto this edge. Now the entire ring is evenly heated with a gas burner until the solder has become liquid and runs into the contact surface. At this moment immediately remove the gas flame so the solder is not further heated.

In order to clean the darkened silver and to remove the borax the ring is placed into a vitrex solution (dissolve vitrex powder in water).

IMPORTANT: Closely follow the manufacturer's indications for handling borax and vitrex.

The soldering points are finished with a file if necessary.

If you have no experience with soldering or you have no opportunity to do so you might give the job to a goldsmith or jeweler.

IMPORTANT: Please note that the technique of soldering silver can't be covered in detail in this book.

After soldering the wire rings are forged flat with a hammer. This provides a beautiful surface finish with the light reflecting in many facets. Finally, the edges of the silver rings are broken with a file.

The knitted and forged chain links are now connected with each other in different sequences.

Hook the knitted threads and the forged silver rings into each other and close the small knitted thread to rings as well by threading one hinge section onto the thread and sewing both ends together with its wires. Twist the wires and shorten them, then push the hinge section over the seam and glue it.

IMPORTANT: Don't forget to place one or two other chain links before closing the knitted chain links.

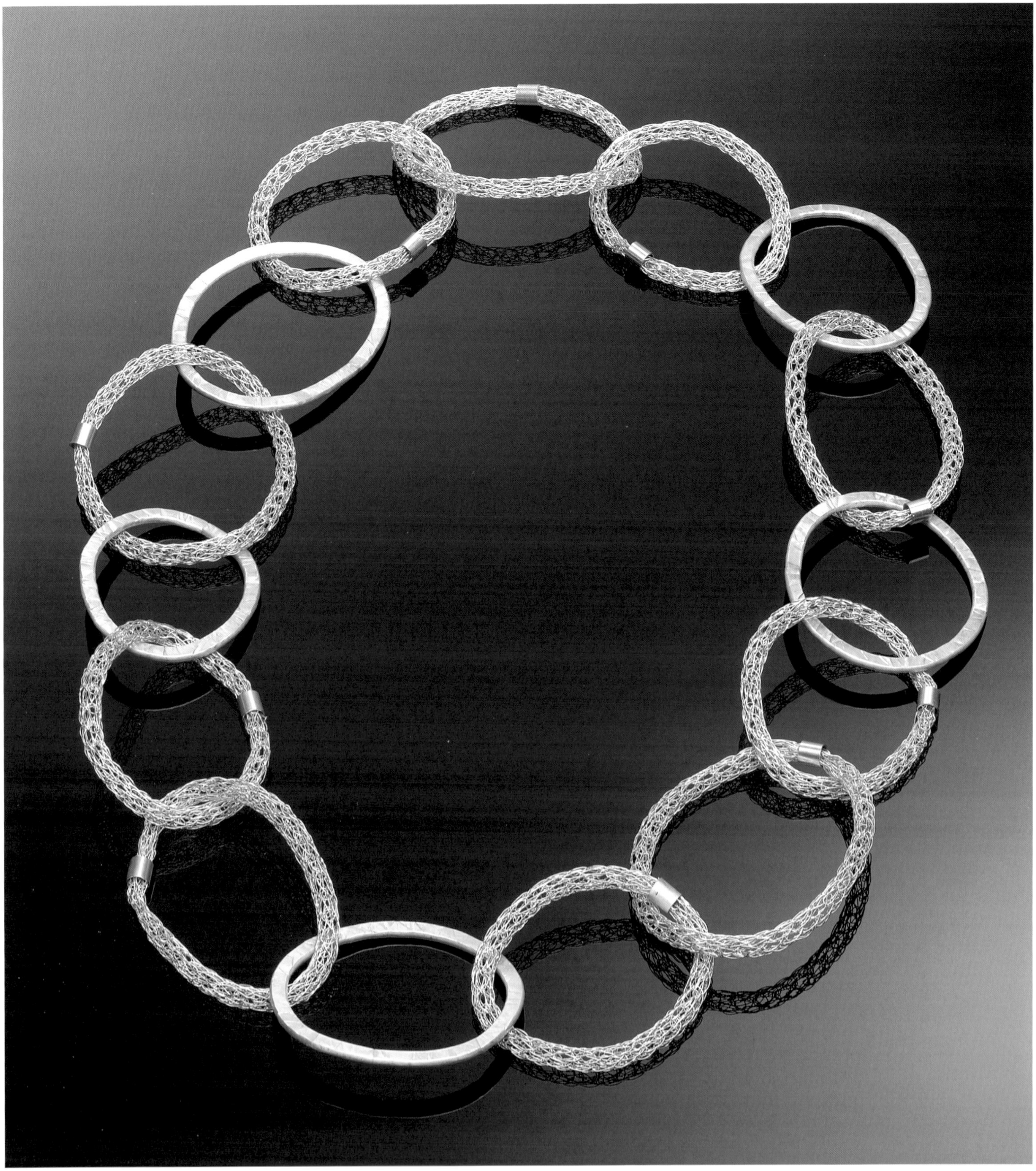

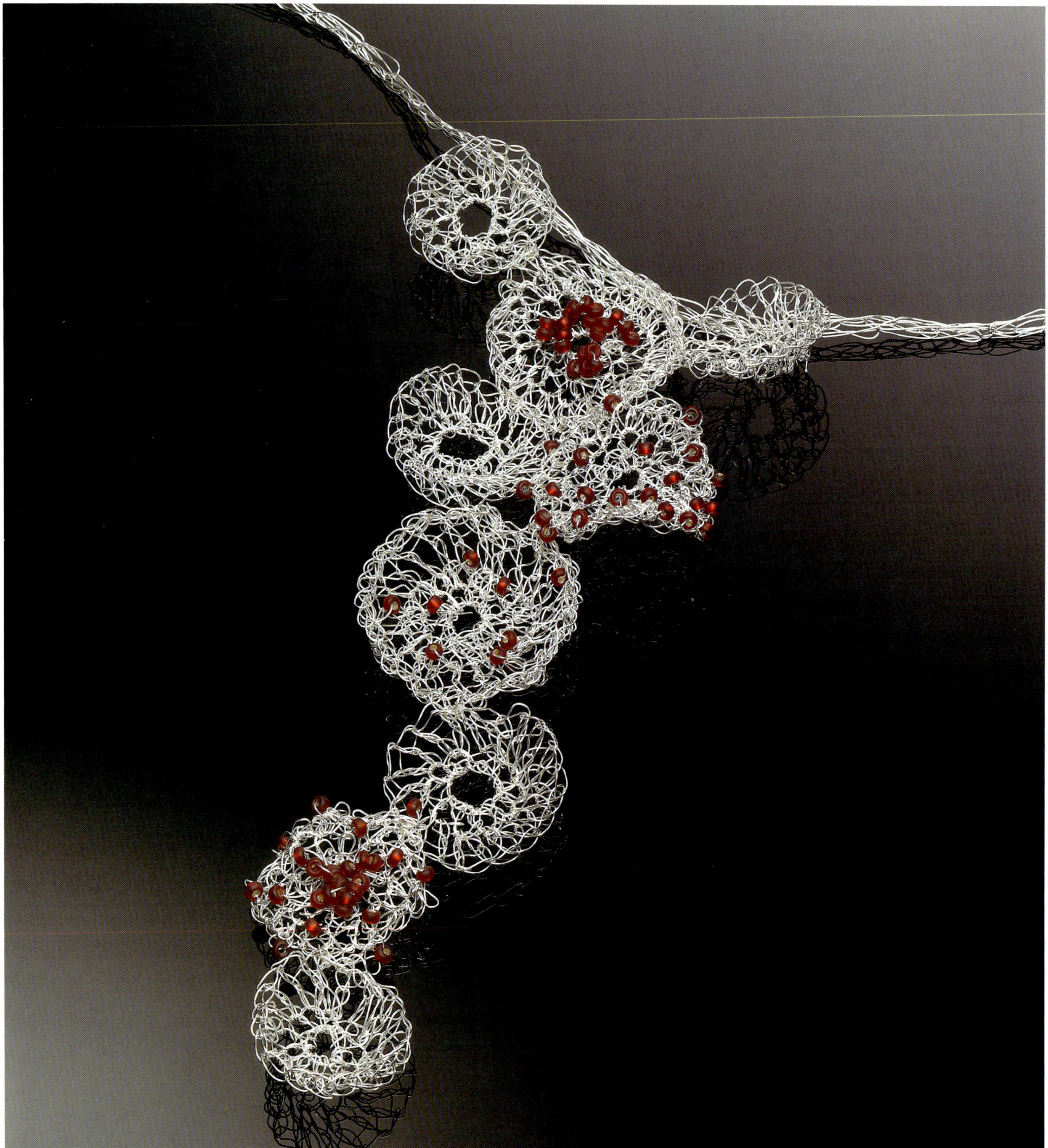

59 FLOWER GEMS

This fine necklace with flower gems is a very romantic project.

For this thin necklace a 21½-inch-long thread is made in **SIMPLE** technique (**TECHNIQUE 2**) and pulled to a length of 23½ inches. This can be done by hand. The ends of the thread are pulled together and glued into the bayonet catch.

Nine individual rosettes of different diameters from 1 to ¹³/₁₆ inches are crocheted. Proceed as described for **TECHNIQUE 1** and work with single stitches and trebles.

Rocailles of varying number and density are sewn onto some of the rosettes.

The end of the wire is twisted at each rosette and shortened. The rosettes are sewn together with the end of the wire. Inconspicuously twist the wires and shorten them.

Finally, the thread is sewn to the flower tendril with some silver wire.

> **TIP:**
> First make all of the rosettes and place them next to each other in all variations before sewing them together.

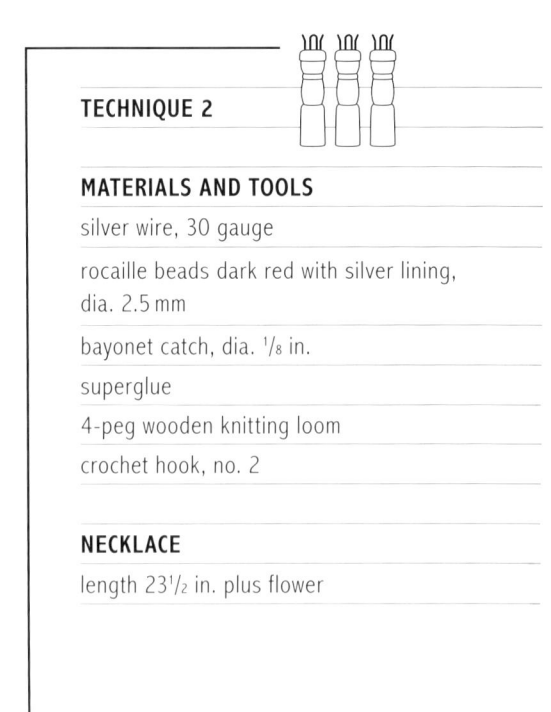

TECHNIQUE 2

MATERIALS AND TOOLS

silver wire, 30 gauge

rocaille beads dark red with silver lining, dia. 2.5 mm

bayonet catch, dia. ⅛ in.

superglue

4-peg wooden knitting loom

crochet hook, no. 2

NECKLACE

length 23½ in. plus flower

60 SILVER GLEAMING

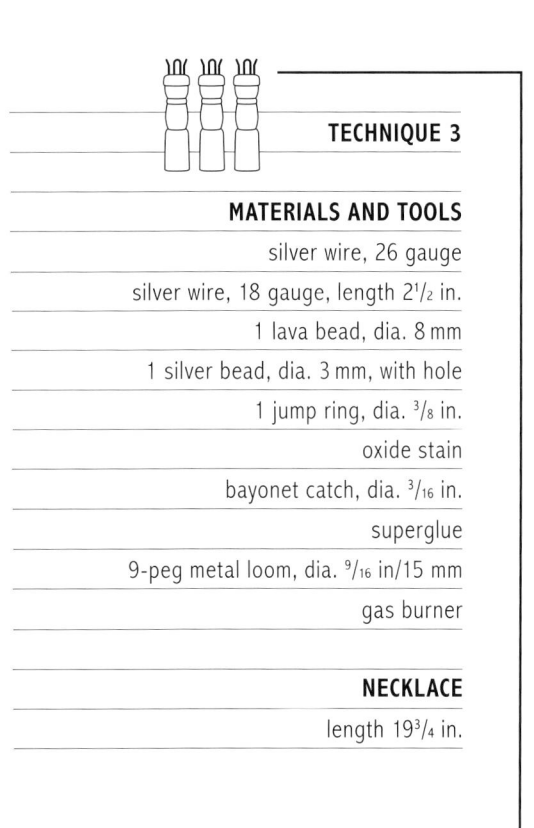

TECHNIQUE 3

MATERIALS AND TOOLS

silver wire, 26 gauge

silver wire, 18 gauge, length 2½ in.

1 lava bead, dia. 8 mm

1 silver bead, dia. 3 mm, with hole

1 jump ring, dia. ⅜ in.

oxide stain

bayonet catch, dia. 3/16 in.

superglue

9-peg metal loom, dia. 9/16 in/15 mm

gas burner

NECKLACE

length 19¾ in.

For this necklace, a tube of 15¾ inches in length is knitted in **OFFSET** technique (**TECHNIQUE 3**) with the 9-peg loom. Stretch the tube by hand while knitting. It now has a diameter of about ⅜ inches.

The tube is removed from the loom and additional auxiliary wires are threaded to the end stitches.

Then clamp the auxiliary wires at one side into a vise while the other auxiliary wires are twisted and held with a pair of flat pliers. Carefully stretch the thread against the resistance of the vise.

In order for the material to become more flexible and to further stretch the thread the knitted mesh is soft-annealed. Use a sufficiently powerful gas burner to do this.

After annealing the thread is once again stretched. You can anneal it once more and stretch it again. This way the thread can be lengthened to 19¼ inches with a diameter of ¼ inch. The mesh pattern becomes very even.

If the thread is too rigid after annealing it can be rolled soft on top of a support surface. Roll the thread back and forth with both hands, as if you were making a roll of dough.

Through annealing the thread becomes very dark. However the coloration is not entirely even. So the thread is briefly placed into a stain solution and then rinsed under running water.

IMPORTANT: When staining, follow the indications and safety precautions of the manufacturer!

The two ends of the thread are pulled together, the wires are twisted, and the two parts of the bayonet catch are glued onto them.

For the pendant, knit a 1¾-inch-long tube in **SIMPLE** technique, also on the 9-peg loom.

TIP:
Here I have used a surplus piece from another project. Particularly when working with silver wire it is worthwhile to keep and reuse such small pieces.

The attachment consists of the 18-gauge silver wire. The 2½-inch-long piece of wire is bent toward the jump ring on one side and pushed through the pendant lengthwise.

The relatively rigid knitted mesh of the pendant is pushed together by hand into a harmonious curve until the tube closely fits the silver wire. The ends of the wires are inconspicuously twisted and shortened.

The lava bead is threaded onto the end of the 18-gauge wire and the silver bead is glued onto it. Before glueing the silver bead, the wire must be shortened so that the pendant and the lava bead are taut without a gap on the wire.

Hook the pendant into the jump ring, and pull the thread through the jump ring as well.

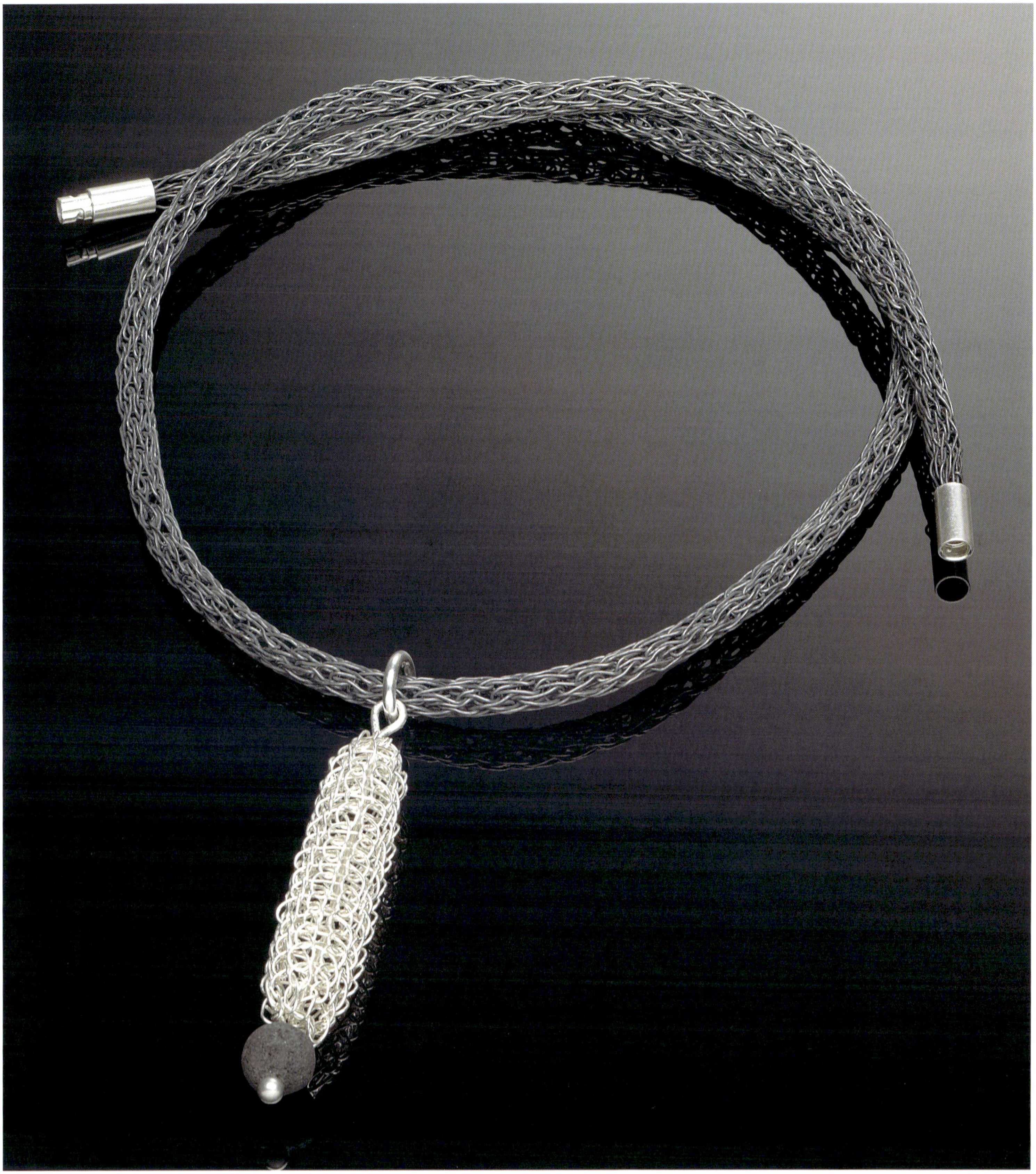

GLOSSARY

AMETHYST
Violet-colored quartz. Its color ranges from a light pink tone to dark violet.

BAYONET CATCH
Mechanical connection of two cylindrical pieces along their longitudinal axis. They are locked and unlocked by inserting them into each other and twisting them in opposite directions.

BEAD SILK
Textile fiber to thread beads.

BORAX
Soldering flux for hard soldering precious and non-ferrous metals. It aids the expansion of the solder when soldering and prevents "swelling."

BORAX BRUSHES
Very fine brushes of varying qualities to apply borax.

BOX LOCK
A catch or clasp that is usually used for bracelets due to its ease of fastening.

BULLION WIRE
(Copper) wire, pure or lacquered.

CRIMP BEAD
Small bead to secure decorative stones and beads, or beads on bead silk or wire.

DRAW PLATE
The draw plate and its metal cores are used to pull the thread in several steps, and to even out the mesh pattern.

EYE PIN OR LOOP
Jump ring with soldered shaft.

FACETED GLASS BEADS
Glass bead with a faceted cut.

FARFALLE BEAD
Small glass bead shaped like a butterfly (farfalle is the Italian word for "butterfly").

FELTED STRING
Loosely felted wool around a core.

FIMO CLAY
Modeling resin that hardens when heated in an oven.

FLUORITE BEAD
Bead of fluorite, a common mineral.

FRESHWATER PEARL
Pearl from a freshwater mollusc.

JIGSAW
Small saw that allows for sawing straight lines as well as tight curves.

KNITTING LOOM
Turned piece of wood with a drill hole along the center axis. It is used to make knitted threads. The top edge features four to eight pegs where the actual knitting is done.

LAVA BEAD
Bead made from lava rock.

LOBSTER CLAW CLASP
Metal hook with a latch as the fastener or clasp.

METAL KNITTING LOOM
Copper tube with soldered pegs. It is used to make knitted tubes from wire.

MURANO GLASS
Glass made with a special technique on the island of Murano (near Venice, Italy).

NATURAL RUBBER
Flexible polymers made from plant products, particularly latex, a milk-like sap.

ONYX
Translucent to opaque black stone.

OXIDE STAIN (PICKLING SOLUTION)
Chemical patina solution for artificial oxidation of silver, gold, and copper.

PEEN
Narrow end of the forging hammer.

POMPON
A spherical decorative element consisting of wool, cotton, or synthetic yarns, usually used as part of clothing items.

ROCAILLE
Small glass bead, round or tube-shaped.

ROCK CRYSTAL
Belongs to the mineral class of quartzes. Its color is either crystal clear or clear with inclusions. It may also look cloudy, similar to ice crystals.

ROSETTE
Decorative round element; here, a flower-shaped crocheted piece.

SILVER LINING
The drill holes of a bead, for example of rocailles, are stained silver.

SOLDER
Metal alloy used to join pieces of metal.

SOLDERING PLATE
Ceramic plate for soldering, extremely heat-resistant.

SOLDERING TWEEZERS
Special tweezers which open when pressed.

SQUARE HINGE
(Silver) tube with a square cross section. It is used to make hinges for jewelry.

TURQUOISE
A mineral, copper-aluminum phosphate, containing water.

TWISTING
Turning several wires around each other.

VITREX
Staining solution used after soldering or oxidizing to clean the surface.